The Wise Loving Being

The
Wise
Loving
Being

Uncommon Wisdom to Overcome Limitations,
Achieve Your Full Potential & Love Your Life

Kim W. Miller

First Edition

ISBN: 979-8-9912937-0-9 (eBook)
ISBN: 979-8-9912937-1-6 (hardcover)
ISBN: 979-8-9912937-2-3 (paperback, IngramSpark)
ISBN: 979-8-9912937-3-0 (paperback, KDP)

Library of Congress Control Number: 2024917540

Publisher's Cataloging-in-Publication Data
Names: Miller, Kim W., author.
Title: The wise loving being : uncommon wisdom to overcome limitations, achieve your full potential & love your life / Kim W. Miller.
Description: Includes index. | Irvine, CA: Two Aspirins Corporation, 2024.
Identifiers: LCCN: 2024917540 | ISBN: 979-8-9912937-1-6 (hardcover) | 979-8-9912937-2-3 (paperback) | 979-8-9912937-0-9 (eBook)
Subjects: LCSH Self-actualization (Psychology) | Self help. | Success. | Conduct of life. | BISAC SELF-HELP / Personal Growth / Success | SELF-HELP / Motivational & Inspirational | SELF-HELP / Self-Management / General
Classification: LCC BF637.S4 M55 2024 | DDC 158.1--dc23

To my Wise Loving Being, who makes all things possible.

Contents

A Word of Caution

Your well-being is my highest concern. It is my hope that this book helps you overcome life's challenges, achieve your highest potential, and live a life you truly love. The concepts in this book were first used in my own transformation. They have also been proven effective with my clients in my coaching practice. But I realize there are some for whom this book may not be a good fit.

This material is helpful only to the extent that you allow. This book guides you through a process, but you have to be open to new ideas, and you have to do the work. You are the only one who can change yourself and achieve your goals. Please invest in yourself and take ownership of your results. Make the time to do the exercises. Take action and do your best. The more you put into this process, the more you will get out of it.

This book does not provide any diagnosis or treatment for mental health disorders as defined by the American Psychiatric Association, nor is it a substitute for counseling, psychotherapy, psychoanalysis, psychiatric care, mental health care, or substance abuse treatment. This book should not be used in place of any form of diagnosis, treatment, or therapy. You should consult with your mental health care provider regarding applying any of the concepts in this book.

This book does not provide financial, fitness, health, investment, legal, medical, mental health, spiritual, or other professional advice. You should seek independent qualified professionals for these matters. All decisions and actions in these areas are exclusively your sole responsibility. You are the only one who can determine what is right for you. You are responsible for finding answers, making decisions, and achieving your goals. You are also fully responsible for your emotional, financial, mental, physical, and spiritual well-being.

If you are experiencing a psychiatric or medical emergency, please call 911 or go to your nearest hospital. If you are having suicidal thoughts, please call or text the 988 Suicide & Crisis Lifeline toll free at 988.

Preface

Is this really the best I can do? Am I living my highest potential?
Am I making a difference? Is the world better because of me?
Am I living a fulfilling, meaningful life I love and enjoy?

These are the tough questions I asked myself in the early part of 2014. There certainly were times I would have answered *yes* to these questions. But the more you know, the more you know there is to know. There came a day when I realized that not only was my answer a resounding *no* to all of these questions, but I was tapping into only a small fraction of my capabilities. The frustrating part was that I could see something was holding me back and preventing me from reaching my full potential.

And that something was me. I could no longer blame my circumstances or others. There was some mysterious internal force that I needed to uncover and overcome. But what was it, how long had it been there, and how could I get rid of it?

During the first part of my life, I didn't notice it. I was on complete autopilot. I did what my family and society expected of me. I performed well in school. I was an athlete, competing in various sports. I was on my high school varsity wrestling team. I sailed competitively in local and national championship regattas, and I excelled on my collegiate sailing team. When I graduated from college, I found a high-paying job, married my college sweetheart, bought a house and a new car, and enjoyed fabulous vacations. I was all grown up and doing well by society's standards.

Everything was great until my mom died in 1990. We spent a lot of time together when I was a child, but I had distanced myself from her over the years as I became an adult. I came to realize she was much more important to me than I had once thought. She gave me strength, and she knew me better than I knew myself. And, as I was about to discover, she became an even more powerful force in my life after her death.

It took me a few months, but I realized that the person I'd become wasn't who I truly was. I didn't like my life, and I didn't like me. I decided to change my life and discover my authentic self, releasing everything that wasn't aligned with the real me. Unfortunately, my marriage was the first casualty. We had already been having challenges and were in marriage counseling, but the changes I made to myself caused bigger problems for the marriage, which proved to be unreconcilable. We reluctantly divorced and sold our house.

I continued to make more changes. I went from being an introverted computer programmer to an extroverted, straight-commission salesman. I went from being quite shy to being more outgoing and confident. I became a Dale Carnegie Course instructor and taught leadership, personal development, and public speaking classes. I expressed myself by taking singing and acting lessons, and I spent more time in nature. Eventually, I moved from Southern California and lived in Hawaii for three years.

After making a lot of progress, I found rock bottom in 2010. I was laid off, going through my second divorce, and raising two young kids on my own. I was eighty-five pounds heavier than I had been just twelve years earlier. On top of it all, I had to declare bankruptcy. I was out of money, out of options, and came within a week of being homeless. I was physically, emotionally, mentally, spiritually, and financially bankrupt. It was extremely difficult to crawl out of this deep pit just to get back to the surface.

After some small improvements, in 2014 I began a determined quest to improve myself. My first step was joining a company that encouraged its employees to take personal development classes. I started to read self-improvement books again, over thirty books each year, and attended every personal development program I could find. My assigned mentor at work and my manager both spent a lot of time coaching me. Additionally, I hired an external coach to help me, and I was in therapy.

I had some limited success with these mainstream methods, but nothing I tried made my life significantly better. The negative patterns I had engaged in throughout my life were only getting worse. I could tell there were still obstacles in my way, but I didn't know what they were or how I could get around them. These obstacles seemed to be getting bigger, as were my negative emotions. I was becoming more judgmental, frustrated, impatient, irritable, and angry about a lot of things. I didn't have much hope that my life would substantially improve. I felt destined for bigger problems, unclear how to change course.

On Friday, March 8, 2019, I was in the fast lane on Interstate 405 in Seal Beach, California, traveling north about eighty miles an hour in the flow of heavy commuter traffic on my way to work when I unexpectedly lost my vision. I was barely able to exit the freeway and get my car into the nearest parking lot. The little vision I still had only revealed blurry shapes, and I couldn't read my cell phone. Panicked, I asked a stranger to call my daughter and tell her where I was.

I sat in my car alone as I waited for my daughter. I was unable to see, I was unaware of exactly where I was, and I had no idea what the future looked like. I felt completely lost and alone in the dark without hope. How I had chosen to live my life up to that point in time wasn't working and had led to complete disaster. I had now reached a deeper rock bottom. The fear was paralyzing and yet the message was clear: if I wanted to survive, then I would have to change *everything*. I would need to start with a blank piece of paper and completely reinvent myself.

My doctor said that the initial vision loss was caused by blood filling my right eye as my retina tore and then subsequently detached. I had already lost the vision in my left eye in 2013, so it was basically lights out for me now. The way I interpreted it, my anger had become so bad that I was literally seeing red, before things faded to black and completely stopped me.

The following months were distressing and scary, to say the least. I was a single dad with two kids and no family or friends nearby. My savings account was empty, and I wasn't sure how I was going to pay rent or buy food. Without my vision, I didn't know what I would or could do for work. I even had moments where I wondered if my family would be better off with me living, or with the proceeds from my life insurance policy.

The first eye surgery restored my vision ... for about five months. It gradually got worse over that time until my doctor eventually took my driver's license away. I was declared legally blind again for the next six months. After two more eye surgeries, vision was finally restored in my right eye. I was lucky.

One year had passed since the detached retina incident on the road, but it was a critical year of personal awakening. Ironically, being blind helped me to "see" clearly. My mind and body weren't doing well, but somehow my soul was stronger than ever. Without any distractions, I could finally listen to what it had to say. I could now see life from a different perspective and understand what was holding me back. I could clearly see the obstacles in my way, and I was able to chart a new way forward.

Over the next two years, I was able to repair relationships, improve my health, lose a significant amount of weight, double my income, and discover my purpose. But the true miracle was that I was finally able to live with a profound sense of love, peace, joy, freedom, and fulfillment. I had become a different person in so many ways.

There was an undeniable, persistent force pulling me forward to help others, and I couldn't ignore it. Each day it became stronger. I wanted to stay at my secure job as a director of information technology and coach my team, but I realized that I was being called to do much more. I resigned from my position so I could focus on helping others full time.

Five months later I felt an overwhelming desire to write this book. I would often get awakened in the middle of the night to write. The wake-up times varied, but each time was significant and meaningful and definitely not random. I had to write, and the words easily flowed out and onto the page. It wasn't like I was channeling someone else and simply transcribing what I was being told. Everything came from my knowledge and my experiences, but the messages were being communicated with greater clarity and in a much more compelling way than I had been able to do before. At long last, I was able to see the wisdom behind my experiences and understood how this could be valuable to others.

It was a very exciting time. I would write all morning, take a short nap in the afternoon, and then resume writing again until bedtime. I only ate a small breakfast and lunch and got by on very little sleep. Within just five intense weeks, the first draft of this book was complete.

I came to understand this experience as part of an ongoing partnership between myself and my Wise Loving Being, which continues to this day. Looking back on my life, I can see that my Wise Loving Being has always been there, trying to get my attention, sometimes subtly, but much more overtly starting in 2018. It has helped me become the person I am today. I can now see why I went down the path I did, and why, if I had led a "normal" life, I never would be who I am today and this book wouldn't exist. I know with confidence that the path I'm on now is the right way forward for me, and I would never want to go back to how things used to be.

I call March 8 Universal Intervention Day, and I celebrate it every year. It marks my awakening into a better life. March is one of my favorite months of the year because it marks the end of winter and the start of spring. It's the month for new beginnings as plants emerge from the barren landscape, leaves and blossoms appear on empty branches, and animals start to create the next generation. And so it was that I emerged from the bleakness of my winter into the new beginnings and abundance of a transformational spring.

Many of us live difficult lives and keep moving forward on autopilot, doing our best. We hope to lead better lives that are more fulfilling and meaningful, with loving and supportive relationships. We know we're capable of more but can't seem to get past our limitations. We call it fate until something finally intervenes and wakes us up. Only then do we go searching for answers and start to live into our full potential.

The information and guidance contained in this book is what I used to transform myself and create Kim 2.0. It is also what I have used to help my clients get similar results. The Wise Loving Being (WLB) Process isn't based on theory or the statistical interpretation of some scientific dataset. It contains practical wisdom and advice that has worked for many people. And I'm not asking you to do anything that I haven't done and proven to be effective.

My purpose or mission in life is to empower people to overcome their limitations, reach their full potential, and live a life they truly love. I'm excited about the possibility that this book will help a great many more people than I can possibly reach one-on-one, and I hope this book can help you too. I look forward to hearing about your transformational journey.

My vision is to help a million people transform their lives, who will each impact a thousand more. That's a billion people living their best lives and adding an incredible amount of value and impact to this world, which is in such desperate need of our help. I can't wait to see the results!

Introduction

The Wise Loving Being underscores the fact that your life matters. You belong. You are important. You are worthy. You can make a difference. There are those who desperately need your help and are anxiously waiting for you to show up and lead. This includes other people, animals, plants, and the planet.

This book will show you how to significantly improve your life and take it to the next level. Everyone deserves to live a life filled with love, peace, joy, freedom, and fulfillment. You will learn how to transform your life, strengthen your relationships, and achieve your full potential.

Everyone has at least one area of their life they wish was going better. They know they can do a lot more, but they feel stuck and blocked by something. They've tried everything they can think of to improve, but nothing has helped them to make a breakthrough. Although they made a lot of progress when they first started taking self-improvement classes and reading books, the big changes are no longer happening. It's always the same story. They feel motivated in the short term, may implement one new habit, but after a month or two, return to their old ways. This pattern of looking for a better way, making short-term changes, and falling back into familiar patterns makes their old, unhealthy behaviors stronger. They're still stuck and, in some ways, getting worse. Most call it fate and stop trying to make things better. They give up and lose all hope.

As a result, they may become angry, anxious, depressed, or frustrated, and experience other negative emotions and thoughts. They may seek escape activities, develop addictions, and participate in destructive behaviors. This inner pain often boils over and creates problems for others. Evidence of this happening is all too common in today's world: homelessness, substance abuse, addiction, overdose, suicide, political discord, cancel culture, prejudice, hate, high divorce rates, environmental destruction, crime, violence, murder, mass shootings, terrorism, and war.

The purpose of this book is to take you through a unique, holistic, proven process that helps you overcome your limitations and make positive, permanent, and powerful changes. If you have a bad headache, you typically take aspirin. Aspirin, of course, only alleviates the symptoms of a headache. It temporarily stops the pain but it doesn't prevent headaches from reoccurring. And that's not what this book is about. This book will help you identify the root cause of your headache, heal it, and eliminate it, so headaches don't occur in the first place. And as a nice side benefit, you don't need aspirin anymore either.

This Wise Loving Being (WLB) Process was developed from my own experiences and perfected by using it with my clients. It is different from the traditional coaching, counseling, therapy, and other self-improvement methodologies available today, which have five fundamental flaws that limit their effectiveness and keep you from achieving your big dreams. I do incorporate many of the top scientifically proven methods available today. For example, from the therapy domain I use key elements from Acceptance and Commitment Therapy (ACT), Cognitive Behavioral Therapy (CBT), and Dialectical Behavior Therapy (DBT), but they only account for a small percentage of the techniques used.

The WLB Process works on multiple levels and on multiple domains. For example, in life coaching, it works at the conscious level as well as the unconscious level. It works on your mind and your body, and it works on all areas of your life. In couples coaching it works on the relationship domain and on the individual domains of each partner. Working on multiple levels and domains at the same time helps you achieve amazing results quickly.

Root cause can mean different things. Some coaches define it as your thoughts, and they teach you better time management, goal setting, and willpower techniques. Some therapists define it as your childhood experiences, and they help you heal your inner child. I define root cause as the origin of your challenges, which is far beyond your thoughts and experiences.

In a way, the WLB Process reprograms your mind by eliminating the harmful, limiting, and false information and replaces it with useful, empowering, and valid data. There is hope for you. You can get unstuck and make important changes that will improve your life dramatically, while also improving the lives of those around you.

This book contains the stories of real people who have done this work. It can help you accomplish a lot of amazing things, which at first glance may sound downright impossible and just plain crazy. But it is completely sound if you have the following **critically important characteristics:**

1. <u>Action</u>. You are ready to take smart action. You understand that knowledge is only valuable if it is used. You understand that making critical changes is the only way to go down a different path.

2. <u>Belief</u>. You believe you are capable of achieving considerably more and living a substantially better life. You have something big you want to achieve.

3. <u>Commitment</u>. You are completely committed to creating a better life. There is no going back to how things used to be.

4. <u>Courage</u>. You have the courage to face your fears, uncover the truth, and endure the often-painful awareness process that brings up old negative feelings of guilt, shame, and regret.

5. Focus. You are able to focus on doing the most important thing in the present moment, to be persistent, and to work hard to achieve your goals.
6. Honest. You can be totally honest and embrace the truth about yourself and the world.
7. Humble. You are humble. You have encountered challenges, realize you don't have all the answers, and are open to learning new things.
8. Motivation. You are highly motivated to make lasting changes to your life, not just for yourself but for others. You have a limited timeframe, so there is some urgency around achieving your goals.
9. Ownership. You take ownership of your life and take responsibility for the results you get. You don't blame others or circumstances. You know you are the only one who can change yourself.
10. Resourceful. You use your creativity and resourcefulness to find the best way forward. When you run out of ideas, you tap into the creativity and resourcefulness of others. You value education and investing in yourself.

What amazing things can you reasonably accomplish by applying the material in this book? If you really do have all ten of the above-mentioned characteristics, I have seen people accomplish one or more of the following items on the Self-Improvement Checklist.

Self-Improvement Checklist

Select which items you would like to achieve in your life.

Overall Life Health
- ☐ Achieve an important goal with the limited time you have left.
- ☐ Achieve your dreams, especially the lifelong dreams you have been putting off.
- ☐ Achieve your highest potential.
- ☐ Be excited to wake up in the morning.
- ☐ Be the best you can be.
- ☐ Create a life you love.
- ☐ Experience more of life.
- ☐ Find your passion.
- ☐ Gain clarity on your identity, purpose, vision, and values.
- ☐ Get unstuck in one or more areas of your life.
- ☐ Improve an area of your life.
- ☐ Increase your motivation.
- ☐ Live a balanced life.
- ☐ Live a fulfilling, meaningful life you love.
- ☐ Live a life filled with love, peace, joy, freedom, and fulfillment.
- ☐ Live your life on purpose.
- ☐ Make a breakthrough.
- ☐ Make a commitment to a compelling future.
- ☐ Make positive, permanent, and powerful changes.
- ☐ Navigate life transitions: career change, empty nest, midlife crisis, and retirement.
- ☐ Play a bigger game, do something great, have a lasting impact, and make your mark.
- ☐ Take action toward a better future.
- ☐ Take your life to the next level of success.
- ☐ Turn your life around.

☐ Understand if you are running away from something you don't like or running toward something you are passionate about.

Charitable Health

☐ Contribute more time and money to helping others in need.
☐ Make a difference for others who desperately need your help.
☐ Offer meaningful contributions to others.
☐ Teach others in need how to become independent.

Emotional Health

☐ Accept, appreciate, love, respect, and forgive yourself.
☐ Banish suicidal thoughts suggesting the world would be better off without you.
☐ Be in control of what you think, feel, say, and do, regardless of what is happening to you.
☐ Become comfortable being authentic, making your own choices, and expressing yourself.
☐ Become genuinely positive, empowered, and motivated.
☐ Become less agitated or irritable.
☐ Build new, healthy habits.
☐ Change unwanted behaviors.
☐ Create a safe and healthy environment in which to live and work.
☐ Feel like you belong.
☐ Feel loved.
☐ Feel more confident, be more assertive, and take more initiative.
☐ Feel worthy.
☐ Find something you enjoy and that challenges you.
☐ Get excited about getting up and enjoying your day.
☐ Give up on your fantasy that someone is going to save you, and you won't have to do anything or take responsibility for making your life better.

- ☐ Give up your need to control others and the world.
- ☐ Have a balanced view of your life and the world.
- ☐ Have hope for a better and more meaningful life.
- ☐ Heal yourself from trauma.
- ☐ Improve your concentration.
- ☐ Improve your overall emotional health and well-being.
- ☐ Learn how to be less anxious, nervous, and tense.
- ☐ Learn how to focus on the present moment instead of thinking about the past or the future.
- ☐ Learn how to sleep better and relax more.
- ☐ Manage challenging life events like the death of a loved one, the loss of a job, a bad breakup, separation, and divorce.
- ☐ Manage panic attacks.
- ☐ Manage your negative emotions, including anger, depression, and sadness.
- ☐ Manage your perfectionism and analysis paralysis.
- ☐ Overcome embarrassment, regret, guilt, shame, failure, and rejection.
- ☐ Overcome feelings of frustration, irritation, and resentment.
- ☐ Overcome feelings of loneliness, despair, and disappointment.
- ☐ Overcome feelings of low self-esteem, self-confidence, and self-worth.
- ☐ Overcome grief from the loss of a loved one.
- ☐ Overcome the obstacles and limitations that are holding you back.
- ☐ Overcome your anxiety, stress, and worry.
- ☐ Overcome your insecurities, self-doubt, self-criticism, and self-sabotage.
- ☐ Overcome your pain and suffering.
- ☐ See your value and worth.
- ☐ Stop acting out and causing problems for yourself and others.

- ☐ Stop being consumed by fear.
- ☐ Stop comparing yourself to others and feeling depressed.
- ☐ Stop complaining and being negative, critical, and judgmental.
- ☐ Stop destructive behaviors, addictions, and escape activities.
- ☐ Stop eating foods that are bad for you.
- ☐ Stop eating too much or too little.
- ☐ Stop feeling helpless and hopeless.
- ☐ Stop feeling like you aren't good enough or smart enough.
- ☐ Stop feeling like you don't belong.
- ☐ Stop feeling numb and start expressing how you feel.
- ☐ Stop feeling overwhelmed and paralyzed.
- ☐ Stop feeling trapped and live with a sense of complete freedom.
- ☐ Stop focusing on the news, social media, and other external things that are negatively impacting you.
- ☐ Stop focusing on the past or the future.
- ☐ Stop living a small, invisible, and fearful life.
- ☐ Stop living an unbalanced life.
- ☐ Stop negative patterns of behavior.
- ☐ Stop trying to be perfect.
- ☐ Stop trying to survive and learn how to thrive.
- ☐ Stop unhealthy, negative thinking.
- ☐ Take back control of your life.
- ☐ Take ownership of your life, and stop playing the helpless, hopeless victim.
- ☐ Transform a life doomed to fate into one of choice and endless possibilities.
- ☐ Transform yourself from being powerless to being empowered and powerful.
- ☐ Turn self-criticism and self-hatred into acceptance, appreciation, and self-love.
- ☐ Turn your fears into strengths. Learn how fears are just doors to opportunities.

- ☐ Understand that you belong, you are important, and your life matters.
- ☐ Understand why you do what you do, are where you are, and think the way you think.
- ☐ Understand why you feel like you don't belong.

Financial Health
- ☐ Become financially free.
- ☐ Build your savings.
- ☐ Create a viable retirement strategy.
- ☐ Create an emergency fund.
- ☐ Eliminate your debt.
- ☐ Improve your credit score.
- ☐ Increase your income.
- ☐ Increase your net worth.
- ☐ Maximize your retirement savings.

Intellectual Health
- ☐ Be honest with yourself.
- ☐ Be more authentic.
- ☐ Be more competent, effective, and efficient.
- ☐ Be more courageous.
- ☐ Be more humble.
- ☐ Be more open-minded.
- ☐ Be more persistent, creative, and resourceful.
- ☐ Be more trustworthy.
- ☐ Become an expert in something meaningful to you.
- ☐ Improve your skills.
- ☐ Increase your knowledge and experience.
- ☐ Maintain a clean car, desk, home, and workspace.
- ☐ Spend more time reading books, learning new skills, and improving yourself.

- ☐ Stop avoiding doing the important things you should be doing.
- ☐ Stop being irresponsible and lazy.
- ☐ Stop being late, and start showing up on time.
- ☐ Stop being unreliable, and start following through on your commitments.
- ☐ Stop gossiping, and start keeping confidences.
- ☐ Stop overthinking, and be more decisive.
- ☐ Stop procrastinating, and complete the important things that need to be done.
- ☐ Stop trying to win at the expense of others.
- ☐ Take more pride in your appearance.

Physical Health
- ☐ Better manage your health challenges.
- ☐ Easily maintain your weight.
- ☐ Eat more nutritious foods.
- ☐ Have more energy and vitality.
- ☐ Improve your health.
- ☐ Increase your fitness.
- ☐ Look and feel great.
- ☐ Lose weight and keep it off.
- ☐ Sleep well each night, and wake up feeling refreshed.
- ☐ Stop eating unhealthy foods you think you can't live without.
- ☐ Stop feeling rundown and getting sick so often.
- ☐ Stop the constant dieting, weight-loss, weight-gain cycle.

Professional Health
- ☐ Become a better leader.
- ☐ Bring out the best in others.
- ☐ Build stronger teams.
- ☐ Communicate more confidently, clearly, and effectively.

- ☐ Create a better project plan that increases the chances of success.
- ☐ Create a better relationship with your boss so they can better support you.
- ☐ Create a more secure, stable job with your current employer.
- ☐ Create an empowering company culture.
- ☐ Develop your leadership skills.
- ☐ Enjoy public speaking.
- ☐ Find a career you love.
- ☐ Find a fulfilling job at a company aligned with your core values.
- ☐ Get a new, better job you love.
- ☐ Get the raise and promotion you deserve.
- ☐ Improve innovation, value, and impact.
- ☐ Improve teamwork, collaboration, and problem-solving.
- ☐ Improve your company's financial results, customer loyalty, and employee engagement.
- ☐ Inspire others to be their best.
- ☐ Invest in the success of others.
- ☐ Make a career change.
- ☐ Make better decisions.
- ☐ Manage projects more effectively.
- ☐ Manage your time effectively and achieve your dreams sooner.
- ☐ Maximize your influence, effectiveness, value, and impact.
- ☐ Reduce risk.
- ☐ Set better goals that empower you to succeed.
- ☐ Solve problems more creatively.
- ☐ Speak with confidence.
- ☐ Stop hating your boss.
- ☐ Stop the cycle of changing jobs every couple of years.
- ☐ Unlock the full potential of your team.

Relational Health

☐ Accept and forgive others.

☐ Be a friendlier person and improve your people skills.

☐ Become more open-minded and accepting of others.

☐ Become more supportive of others.

☐ Build trust and stronger relationships.

☐ Create a more diverse group of friends.

☐ Create a more loving and supportive family.

☐ Create positive, loving, and supportive relationships.

☐ Develop closer relationships.

☐ Elevate the love in your relationship to a much higher level.

☐ Escape an abusive relationship.

☐ Free yourself from others.

☐ Get the love back in your marriage.

☐ Have more friends.

☐ Improve and repair relationships.

☐ Improve communication and understanding.

☐ Learn how to connect with others.

☐ Learn to love, understand, accept, respect, and appreciate others.

☐ Reinvent yourself and your relationships.

☐ Resolve conflicts.

☐ Save your marriage and other important relationships.

☐ Set better boundaries with others.

☐ Stop arguing and fighting with others.

☐ Stop hating, judging, rejecting, and being prejudiced of others.

☐ Stop letting others control and abuse you.

☐ Stop trying to control others.

Spiritual Health

- ☐ Appreciate your life more.
- ☐ Be more grateful for all the blessings in your life.
- ☐ Better understand how everything is connected and interdependent.
- ☐ Create a vision that continues long after you are gone.
- ☐ Discover who or what is desperately waiting for your help and leadership.
- ☐ Discover your purpose.
- ☐ Express your gratitude to others.
- ☐ Feel more connected to others and to everything around you.
- ☐ See the world from a more empowering and positive perspective.
- ☐ Understand that problems in life are sometimes happening for your benefit.
- ☐ Understand why you are important and needed.
- ☐ Understand why your life matters.

Go to www.WiseLovingBeing.com/handouts
to find a copy of this handout online.

Is This Book for You?

This book is for people of all ages. Everyone can benefit from its teachings. Far more important than age is having the ten critically important characteristics above. My clients range in age from eleven to eighty-five, although the largest percentage are in their thirties and forties. It's not about age, though, it's about a person's desire to get better and to seek help, which more commonly happens during that age range.

The main character in this book is a client named Elin, who is eighty-four years old. Her advanced age is useful for two reasons. First, if she can benefit from applying this material, then it's likely anyone younger will be able to achieve even better results. It's a challenge really. Nobody wants to be outdone by grandma!

Second, Elin's age highlights an important trend of people living longer, who are still able to work and contribute to society in valuable ways. Life expectancy has risen from around thirty years old in 1900 to seventy-three years old today according to Our World in Data. The World Bank Group, states that the current life expectancy for a woman in Japan is eighty-seven. Life expectancy is just an average. Some people die younger, and others live longer. According to the Gerontology Research Group, the oldest person who has been verified by official records, Jeanne Calment, died in 1997 at age 122. Michel Poulain and Dan Buettner have researched Blue Zones, which are places with a large concentration of people who are mentally and physically healthy, and who have attained one hundred or more years of age.

Yes, there are some people who suffer from a loss of their mental and physical abilities as they get older. But there are others who don't. How long people live and the quality of their lives is sometimes attributed to their good genes. But there are other critical factors that can be much more important, such as healthy habits, diet, exercise, social behaviors, intellectual pursuits, and a desire to live and contribute.

Instead of calling them old farts or gummers, I prefer to call them *more experienced adults.* Our society tends to discount older adults, and there is definitely age discrimination present in the workplace, which is unfortunate. More experienced adults are valuable. Some make meaningful contributions later in life and choose to work up to their death. The more famous alumni are Secretary of State Henry Kissinger at age one hundred, Senator Diane Feinstein at age ninety, Supreme Court Justice Ruth Bader Ginsburg at age eighty-seven, and Mother Teresa at age eighty-seven. Colonel Sanders didn't start franchising Kentucky Fried Chicken until he was sixty-two and worked until he died in 1980 at the age of ninety. For many people, there is no such thing as retirement. It's never too late to start transforming your life.

This book is for people with a wide variety of challenges, problems, and experiences. Elin's challenges are big from her perspective, but there are people who have been through much worse and people who have been through much less. We shouldn't be comparing ourselves to others except to be thankful that our lives aren't as bad as they could be. We should be focusing on ourselves, how we can heal, and how we can move forward.

This book is for anyone who can envision a better way and who wants to enroll others in helping them make it a reality. Whether they realize it or not, they are a leader. They understand that the secret to life is to add as much value and impact as possible. The more value they add, the more value they get back in terms of income, influence, market share, and success. They have a vision for their life. They don't just want to make small, incremental improvements; they want to make big changes. They want to get a high **return on investment**

(ROI). This book is for leaders who want to get their investment back, plus ten times their investment. That's 1000 percent ROI and is called **11X Thinking.**

This book is for people who want to elevate themselves and then go on to elevate others. Organizational leaders at all levels have a big impact on the planet. Their thoughts, words, and actions have a direct and lasting effect on their customers, employees, stakeholders, and communities. Making small improvements to a leader and their organization makes a big difference. Unfortunately, many leaders and organizations only contribute a fraction of their full potential.

This book is also for people who need significantly more help than the rest of us. It's for people who can't seem to lose weight no matter what they try, getting heavier every year. It's for people who think their only financial salvation is playing the lottery, even though they rarely buy a ticket. It's for people who want to have friends but don't even like themselves. It's for people who are having challenges eating just one decent meal a day. It's for people who are living on the streets or in their cars, or who feel they are just one or two steps away from being homeless. It's for people living in abusive situations, who desperately need to escape and find a safe and healthy environment.

Life isn't easy. Many of us go through life on autopilot, doing the best we can to meet the expectations of our family, employer, church, and society. When someone asks how we are doing, we say we're doing "good." But deep down we know something isn't right. We know we're stuck, but we don't know why, and we don't know what actions to take to get unstuck.

Yes, there are areas of our life that are going well, but there are also areas we wish were going much better. We think we should be thinner, healthier, and wealthier. We think we should be closer to achieving our dreams. We think we should be happier and more fulfilled. We think we should have better, more loving relationships.

We think we should be less stressed and worried. We know we should be doing better than our friends, especially the ones we grew up with. We feel trapped. We are sometimes so overwhelmed by anxiety, depression, stress, worry, and feelings of fear, regret, guilt, and shame that we can barely function. We have become good at dealing with our pain and ignoring our suffering.

Some people blame others and circumstances for their current negative situation. It is easy to believe a subpar life is their fate, or that their genes are at fault. According to them, life is out of their control. Their mind protects them from thinking they might be part of the problem and sends the message that there is nothing they can do about it. Their mind tends to focus on their triumphs and quickly overlooks their failures. And, of course, they think there is nothing wrong with the external expectations set for them. Denial is a wonderful thing for those who just want to survive.

On the opposite side of the spectrum are those who take a more internal view and blame themselves for their problems. Everything is under their control, they're doing their best, and they aren't able to get any better. As a matter of fact, they only see things getting worse over time. They focus on their failures and overlook their successes. They don't have a balanced view of their life, only seeing what is wrong. They've lost all hope and have given up.

Sometimes it takes a major disaster before we wake up and discover the truth. For others, it takes time off the grid, living in nature, or traveling to sacred places. Unfortunately, the vast majority of humans never become aware of the truth. They behave like robots and never achieve even a small fraction of their full potential. And that's a huge loss, not only for them but for the world.

It's time to take your power back and change this. It's time to live a purposeful, meaningful, fulfilling, impactful life you love.

How to Use This Book

Let's say you have all ten critically important characteristics listed above. You know you are highly motivated, committed, courageous, honest, humble, and resourceful. You believe you are capable of achieving much more. You can tolerate being aware of your painful past and are ready to take action for a better future. You are a focused leader and take responsibility for and ownership of your life. You have checked off several of the above boxes for areas of your life you would like to improve. So, how can this book actually help you achieve your goals?

This book helps you fix the root cause of the obstacles that are limiting your success. Instead of telling you to take two aspirins to get rid of your headache only to have it come back the next day, this book helps you find and eliminate the source of your headaches. It treats the cause, not the symptoms. If you want to get rid of a weed, you must remove the roots. If you don't completely deal with the root of the issue, it leads to the issue returning, and in many cases, getting worse. Replacing the roots with new empowering beliefs and habits is critical for lasting change.

This book takes a holistic approach to your transformation. It addresses all aspects of you: mind, body, and soul. All eight areas of your life: charitable, emotional, financial, intellectual, physical, professional, relational, and spiritual. Both parts of your mind: conscious and unconscious. Both parts of your brain: left brain and right brain. Everything is connected. Improving one part of your life ends up improving other parts. Improving all parts of your life together and aligning them with your vision is called *transformation*.

This book uses the best available mainstream techniques, as well as the impactful wisdom I discovered on my own. It provides concepts that can help you see your life from different, more empowering perspectives. It provides you with traditional and nontraditional teachings that can help you make big changes to your life quicker than you thought possible. It can help you see that mistakes, embarrassment, and failure are okay and are a normal part of life and learning. It helps you create a plan and take action to create your future.

This book provides numerous real-life examples so you can better understand the concepts and how to apply them. The exercises from chapter 4 onward use material based on the actual stories and responses of real people who overcame their limitations and improved their lives. Each story is specific to that individual person, and there are no compilations of people's stories into a person who doesn't exist, including the main character, Elin.

My clients have asked that I keep their identities confidential. Therefore, I have carefully disguised everyone's identities, including age, birth date, city, gender, and background. I am the only one who knows who they really are, and their anonymity is very important to me. Any connection you might make between one of the characters and an actual person is purely coincidental.

I recommend you first read the book from start to finish so you can fully understand the complete teaching. You might want to mark specific exercises that stand out to you. After you finish the book, you can then come back and complete those exercises. For maximum benefit, I do recommend going through the exercises in the order they are presented.

Each time you read the book, you will absorb the information you are ready to receive. On subsequent readings, new information will present itself, and greater clarity of the previous information will result. This is a natural part of the learning process.

There are forty-eight handouts in this book that provide the major concepts. They appear in line with the dialogue throughout this book. If you would like to access them online or print them, then please use the QR Code or the website address shown below.

The book is broken into five parts. Part One: *Foundation* is made up of the first three chapters, which set the foundation for the characters. Part Two: *Awareness* consists of chapters 4 through 10, which focus on bringing greater awareness to your life. It helps you understand why you do what you do, why you are where you are in life, and why you're reading this book. This is difficult work and requires you to look at the truth of who you really are. It requires you to bring the things that are hidden in the dark recesses of your mind out into the light.

The awareness process can be painful and uncomfortable as you face your fears, remember traumatic events, examine your beliefs, and dredge up feelings of guilt, shame, and regret. This is perfectly normal, yet it is incredibly important. This is the first step in the healing process. You can't fix what you can't see; therefore, it is important to get a complete picture of where you are so you can create the best solution moving forward. Awareness sets the foundation for your transformation and for creating your amazing future self.

Part Three: *New Perspectives* consists of chapters 11 and 12, which provide concepts that help you see your life and the world from new perspectives. It helps you imagine bigger possibilities and create a vision for your new, compelling future.

Part Four: *Transformation* consists of chapters 13 and 14, which help you make your personal transformation. It guides you through the process of creating a blueprint of the new person you want to be, aligning all parts of yourself with your new vision for your life.

Part Five: *Taking Action* consists of the final three chapters. Chapter 15 helps you make a plan for achieving your vision. Chapter 16 helps you take action toward achieving the amazing life you want to create. Chapter 17 provides the last piece of wisdom to help you move forward with confidence.

When I coach my clients, I take them through this same process over the course of sixteen sessions. We usually meet for two hours once per week, but some clients choose to meet twice a week for eight weeks. This time-based approach allows them to process what they have learned and then try it out in their lives. This isn't about just learning the information; it is about using it. Action is required. Information is of no value unless it is used to make your life better. In this book, the process happens over consecutive days, which I don't recommend. Rushing the process yields inferior results, as the story shows.

Combining the knowledge from this book with coaching really helps my clients break old patterns, stop the autopilot mode, and follow through on their commitments. A coach who understands the material can provide an objective external view, help you better understand the progress you are making, and see what is left to do. Change is difficult and requires a surprising amount of effort, so don't feel bad if it's difficult to make progress on your own. I do encourage you to find an accountability partner to help you with the change process. You will be much happier with the results.

If you haven't already, make an unconditional commitment to the new you and to achieving your full potential. Everyone deserves to live a life filled with love, peace, joy, freedom, and fulfillment. We all deserve lives filled with health, wealth, and loving relationships.

I hope this book helps you find your own path forward to living your best life. As someone who has experienced life's highs and lows, who has been on this journey of awareness, transformation, and truth, and who has helped others transform, I can tell you with confidence that it is your birthright. And it's never too late to start. All you need is a pulse.

What is even more amazing is that you can't know all that is truly possible for your life from where you are standing today. You have to start down that new path and add the maximum possible value and impact as you go. Only then will you discover your true potential. It is limitless. It will surprise you. And I can't wait to see what you'll do!

Use this QR Code to access the handouts in this book online.
Or simply go to www.WiseLovingBeing.com/handouts.

Part One:

Foundation

Chapter One

Rock Bottom

"Should I buy Alpo or Pedigree?" Elin asked herself. She remembered her mother always bought Alpo, but Elin's dog, Muffin, preferred Pedigree. She grabbed one can of each and put them in her shopping cart, adding to the items she found in the clearance section.

"Being hungry has a way of solving these challenging dilemmas," Elin said with a smile.

Elin's stomach growled, reminding her that she hadn't eaten anything since early Saturday morning. It was now Monday morning, August 22, 2022, the start of a new week's budget for buying food. Unfortunately, she had spent her entire monthly budget by the third week of the month, when her doctor gave her a new prescription to help with some chronic COVID-19 complications. Elin spent hours yesterday rummaging through her apartment looking for money. She had scraped together a whopping $9.83.

"Wow. My entire life's savings is now in my wallet," Elin said incredulously. No more money would come in from her only source of income, Social Security, until next week, and that was already earmarked for housing and prescriptions. Elin was going to turn eighty-four next month. The past couple of years had been really tough on her, especially with her health and finances. She had just accepted that this was how life works.

When she lived in Grand Junction, Colorado, as a teenager, she had lots of friends who lived on farms. She thought that farmers were the hardest working and most resourceful people she knew. Yes, weather was a factor, but what farmers harvested in the fall mostly depended on the decisions they made and the actions they took in the spring and summer. Looking back at her life, Elin could see that her decisions and actions had led her to exactly where she was today. She always regretted that she hadn't done more. Certainly, her life would be better today if she had.

Elin now completely understood what her mother had gone through back in the late 1970s. It was difficult to live on a fixed income with high inflation, health challenges, and not enough money to pay for basic needs. Elin's prescription medicines were very important, so it was easy to justify eating less and even skipping a few meals. She felt lucky that the US inflation rate peaked two months ago at only 9.1 percent. It was much better than the 13.3 percent inflation rate that her mother endured in 1979.

In that year, Elin was living in a different city than her mother. She discovered what her mother was going through when she stopped by her apartment unannounced just before Christmas. Her cupboards were bare except for three packages of ramen and two cans of Alpo. She didn't have any pets. Elin couldn't understand why her mom hadn't asked for help. Going through the same situation today, Elin realized it was a combination of guilt, shame, and a sliver of pride that remained.

Elin's mother moved in with her a month later. It was a great start to the 1980s. They enjoyed living together as adults and surprisingly got along quite well. Elin was glad she had been able to get to know her mother better and help improve her quality of life. Her mother died in 1985, and Elin regretted not being able to help her out sooner.

As Elin went down the pasta aisle, she saw a lady with a cute dog in her cart. The dog wagged its tail and gave Elin that please-pet-me-and-I'll-love-you-forever look. She asked the owner if she could pet her dog. They all spent a few minutes enjoying each other's company, as strangers do.

The dog reminded Elin of Muffin, who she had many years ago. Muffin was a rescue she had adopted. Some kind of poodle mix. Elin thought Muffin was probably the only being that truly loved and accepted her. She really missed that dog. Elin lived alone and would have loved to get a dog to keep her company, but they were just too expensive to take care of. Plus, her landlord didn't allow pets.

Elin approached the self-checkout registers. She always used them now, mainly to avoid the embarrassment she'd feel if she didn't have enough money to pay for everything. It had happened a few times before, and she was eager to avoid the angry looks from the cashier and the impatient customers in line behind her.

Luckily, the store wasn't too busy this morning, so Elin was able to go directly to an available register. As she started to ring up her items, she paid close attention to the total, making sure she didn't go over her budget. She was thrilled when the total came out to $9.71. "My nest egg of twelve cents is still intact!" she said proudly. "I got this!"

As she reached for her purse in her cart behind her, she saw a man rifling through it. They both grabbed the purse, but the man was too strong. After a brief struggle, he knocked her to the concrete floor and ran off with her wallet.

Elin's face was bleeding, and her right arm was badly hurt. But the real panic set in when she realized she didn't have any money to pay for her groceries. She wouldn't be able to eat anything this week. With no family or friends around, she felt utterly hopeless.

Is this how it's going to end? she wondered, unable to hold back her tears.

A kind stranger from the next register came over to Elin and asked if she was okay. He helped her up, opened a box of Kleenex he had just purchased, and handed it to her. "It's okay. You're safe now. Everything's going to be all right," he said, comforting her.

Elin was visibly shaken and continued to cry. She couldn't even speak. Her eyes were locked onto the floor as she discovered a whole new level of embarrassment and, of course, fear. She wasn't completely conscious of what was happening around her, but she did remember other customers and the store manager coming over to check on her. Soon after, a police officer arrived and took her statement. She indicated that she was fine and didn't need to go to the hospital.

"You're all set!" the kind stranger said, jolting her back to reality. "I paid for your groceries. Can I escort you out to your car, please?"

Elin agreed. She unlocked her car as the nice stranger loaded her groceries into the trunk, then thanked him and drove away.

When Elin arrived home, she began to unpack her groceries. "Why are there two bags?" What she had placed in her cart couldn't have filled more than half a grocery bag. In addition to what she had rung up, she discovered several cans of minestrone and chicken noodle soup, some crackers, a box of pasta, and some spaghetti sauce. There was even a box of Pepperidge Farm strawberry cookies, her absolute favorite—ones she hadn't been able to afford for several years. She then noticed something tucked beneath the cookies: a hundred-dollar bill.

Elin began to cry again and collapsed to the floor. This time with an overwhelming combination of joy, gratitude, and relief.

Chapter Two

Hope

The following Monday, Elin was in the same grocery store at the same time she had been there last week. She was clutching her purse this time, but she wasn't scared. She was excited and had a big smile on her face.

Life had significantly improved since she was last here. She had made it through the week without starving, and she didn't even need to eat the dog food she bought. She used the hundred-dollar gift to pay for her prescriptions and a few other badly needed items. Her face was healing, but her arm was still sore. Taking two aspirins helped ease the pain.

Elin was also excited that she might be able to see that kind stranger again. She had been thinking of all the nice things she was going to say to him. Most importantly, she wanted to let him know how much she appreciated his kindness and generosity.

After going through the entire store without seeing him, she resigned herself to simply focusing on her weekly shopping list. Her budget for this week was twelve dollars, and she was optimistic she would find some great food deals. After grabbing a few items on sale, she ended up in the clearance section. Elin loved this section and could easily spend ten minutes going through every item one by one. Bargain hunting consumed all of her attention.

"Hi, Elin!"

She jumped in surprise and turned to the voice behind her. It was the kind stranger.

"You're looking well," he beamed. "How are you feeling?"

Elin smiled and gave him a big hug. She said everything she wanted to say, feeling lucky that she ran into him again. She hadn't gotten a good look at him before, but now she was surprised by how familiar he looked. She just couldn't remember where they had met.

"I'm sorry, but I didn't catch your name," Elin said.

"My apologies. Where are my manners? My name is Wesley L. Bean, but my friends call me Wes. I'm glad to hear you're doing better. And thank you so much for the nice things you said about me. I was happy to help. It looked like you really needed it that day."

"Nice to formally meet you, Wes. And yes, I did need some extra help that day. Thank you again for your generosity and kindness." Elin paused and looked at his face again. "You look familiar, Wes. Have we met before last week?"

"No, I don't believe we have. It must be another handsome man you're thinking of," Wes joked and winked. "But come to think of it, you do feel like a lifelong friend. I also get another feeling about you. I apologize if this sounds bad, but since we're 'old friends,' I get the feeling you could use a lot more help. Yes, last week was awful, but I'm sensing that you'd like to live a much better life than you are right now. Is that true?"

Elin gave him a puzzled yet curious look. Then, in a serious tone, she said, "Yes, I'd like to live a better life, but unfortunately my time has run out. I'm old. In fact, I shouldn't have lived this long. The world gave up on me a long time ago."

"I certainly understand that, and you can obviously continue down the path you're on. But I see something great shining brightly inside you that's just begging to be let out. Don't you feel that too?"

Elin smiled politely, but this time spoke with a firmer tone. "I used to, Wes, but I haven't felt that way in a very long time. I'm afraid it's too late."

"For crying out loud, Elin! It's never too late. If you have a pulse, you can make a difference. People are living and working much longer today—into their hundreds—and this trend will continue. You have a lot of years left ahead of you. You do know what your name means, don't you?" Seeing that Elin didn't know, he continued. "Your name is a variation of Helen, which means *light* in Greek. I don't think that's a coincidence, do you?"

Elin looked at Wes with disbelief and said, "Uh, I'm pretty sure I was just named after my grandma. I don't think there's anything more to it than that."

Wes smiled and said, "I'm serious, Elin. I know I can help you. I have some very valuable information, and if you take action on it, I promise that you can make your life a lot better. It won't cost you anything. All you need is an open mind and a strong desire to improve. I would really love to help you."

"This isn't some get-rich-quick scheme or multilevel marketing scam, is it? Please, don't waste my time, Wes."

Wes laughed. "Of course not, Elin! Nothing crazy like that. I promise that you'll be grateful for our time together. I've been helpful so far, haven't I?"

Elin smiled and reluctantly agreed. "Well, you have certainly earned some trust with all the nice things you've done for me. What do I have to lose? What's the next step then?"

"Excellent! Well, it's your lucky day, Elin. I have some free time the next couple of weeks before I have to go check up on my family in Hawaii. How about we meet tomorrow in front of the Cinnabon at the Desert Sky Mall at 11:00 a.m.? We can talk, avoid this hundred-plus-degree heat, and get some exercise by walking around the mall. What do you say?" Wes offered with a smile.

Elin nodded her agreement with a shy smile.

"Great! All you need to bring is a goal for the area of your life you want to change the most." Wes gave her a handout titled *Eight Areas of Life* and went over it with her.

Eight Areas of Life

There are **eight areas of life** to explore:

1. **Charitable:** how you use your time and money to give back to others, animals, plants, and the planet
2. **Emotional:** your emotional well-being
3. **Financial:** your ability to meet your basic needs and save for your future
4. **Intellectual:** your character, skills, knowledge, and abilities
5. **Physical:** your overall physical health and well-being
6. **Professional:** how you earn money
7. **Relational:** how you are doing in your relationships
8. **Spiritual:** how you view your purpose, others, and the meaning of life

Go to www.WiseLovingBeing.com/handouts
to find a copy of this handout online.

"Just pick an area and set a goal. Any questions?" Wes asked in an encouraging tone.

"Nope. I'm all good."

They both said their goodbyes and hugged once again. Elin felt excited about meeting Wes tomorrow. In fact, she felt better about herself than she had in a long time. Suddenly, life was interesting and fun again. And she felt something she hadn't felt in a very long time: hope.

Elin finished up with the clearance section and headed for the self-checkout registers. She was thrilled when she rang up a total of only $11.58 for this week's groceries. She headed home with forty-two cents more to add to her life savings. She was still worth less than a buck, but at least things were going in the right direction for a change.

"Aha! I know what my goal is. I want more money," Elin said, feeling proud that she had completed her homework for tomorrow.

Chapter Three

Cinnabon

The next day, Elin pulled up to the mall just after 10:30 a.m. She was excited to talk with Wes. It was another hot day in Phoenix, so she quickly walked inside the mall and found her way to the Cinnabon. She wanted to be at least ten minutes early since that was the respectful thing to do.

Elin showed up primarily because she was excited to have some semblance of a social life again. She doubted that Wes could actually help her, but she vowed to be polite and try to learn something anyway.

Elin didn't leave her house much, especially during the super-hot summer months. She lived by herself, no longer having any family or close friends nearby. This made the summer months quite lonely for her, so today was special.

When Elin arrived at the Cinnabon, Wes was already there. He greeted her with a big smile and said, "Good morning, Elin! How are you today?"

"Good morning, Wes. I'm good. I'm so glad you talked me into this. How are you doing?"

"Well, I am doing great. Although, I'm regretting my decision to meet in front of the Cinnabon. It just smells so good."

"Yes, it does smell good. You know, it always reminds me of the cinnamon rolls my mom would make for me and my siblings when we were kids. I loved waking up to that smell, enjoying a warm cinnamon roll with a big glass of milk, and reading the comics in the newspaper. Those were the days."

"Yes, nothing better than a fresh, warm cinnamon roll. Where'd you grow up, Elin?"

"We lived in Florida, in the Jacksonville area, until I was ten. Then we moved to Colorado and lived in Grand Junction," Elin replied.

"Wow, that was a big move. I love both places, but they're totally different. Why'd you move?"

Elin's eyes became a little watery. "My dad died, so we had to move to Grand Junction to be around my mom's family."

"I'm sorry to hear that, Elin. Losing a parent at any age is difficult, especially for kids. Were you close with your dad?"

"Yes. Very close. I was much closer to him than I was with my mom. I was the youngest of five kids, so my dad constantly spoiled me with lots of love and attention. I loved to sneak into his home office and watch him draw and paint. Sometimes he'd let me sit on his lap while he worked."

Elin thought about those wonderful days. She loved her dad's home office because every day was a fun adventure. There was an amazing array of colors from the paintings on the walls and those propped up on the floor. There were cartoon proof sheets, pallets, his apron with paint smears, and the white sheet on the floor underneath the easel with an incredible rainbow of paint all over it, mainly from her finger-painting exploits. She could still smell the paint, her dad's aftershave, and the gardenias, whose perfume gently wafted through the open windows. She could still remember the sound of her dad's voice talking to her about silly things as he tickled her. They lived on the edge of a forest, and the sounds of birds, bugs, and critters created the most peaceful background noise, interrupted only by the voices of her mother and siblings yelling at each other. She loved the feel of the dried oil paint, but nothing was more fun than getting her hands completely covered with finger paint.

"I'm glad you were able to experience that special time and create those great memories with your dad," Wes said, smiling.

Elin smiled as best she could. Talking about her dad still brought up a lot of emotions. It was just too painful to talk about, even after all these years. Wes could sense that too.

"I'm so sorry you had to go through such a traumatic event," Wes said kindly. "Life can be painful and difficult, as you well know. I'm concerned about you though. You've never really recovered from what happened to you when you were ten, have you?"

"No, I haven't. That was over seventy years ago. I'd rather not talk about it right now. It's still too painful. I don't want to get emotional here at the mall," Elin replied.

"I'm so sorry I brought that up, Elin. Can I buy you a cup of coffee and a cinnamon roll?"

"No, thank you. I'm fine, but feel free to get yourself something," Elin said, trying to compose herself.

"No, I'm good. How about we go for a walk around the mall, and you can tell me about the goal you want to work on. That's why we're here, right?" Wes said in an attempt to change the topic to something more positive.

"Okay." Elin nodded. She was still a little bit upset. This was supposed to be a fun, positive social outing. If she wanted to feel bad about herself, she could have easily done that at home. Maybe this was a mistake.

After walking past a few stores in silence, Wes said, "You know I invited you here because I wanted to help you. I hope you're still up for that. So what's the goal you'd like to work on?"

"I want to have more money. That's my goal."

"Sounds good, Elin. Let's work on that."

Part Two:

Awareness

Chapter Four

Goals

"Have you ever heard of SMART goals?" Wes asked.

"Hasn't everyone?" Elin replied with a bit of attitude, questioning whether Wes had anything of value to teach her today.

"Good. So you are aware of the acronym. Are you also aware of the many different versions of it?"

"Well, I thought it was pretty standard. I remember it as Specific, Measurable, Achievable, Relevant, and Timetable. What else is there?" Elin replied.

"The original SMART Goal acronym proposed by George Doran in the November 1981 issue of *Management Review* used the words *Specific, Measurable, Assignable, Realistic,* and *Time-related*. The versions of SMART we see today generally use *Specific* and *Measurable* for the first two words. I've seen the letter *A* represented by *Assignable, Achievable, Attainable,* or *Actionable*. The letter *R* can be *Realistic* or *Relevant*. And the letter *T* is either *Time-related, Timetable, Time-bound, Time-based, Timed,* or *Timely*. It's confusing because we all think we're talking about the same thing, but there are so many different meanings."

"That's interesting. I wasn't aware of all the different variations."

"I'm fine with your definition of SMART." Wes paused and then asked, "So when you told me your goal, why didn't you put it in the SMART format?"

"Well, that's a good question. I don't know," Elin replied, somewhat puzzled and embarrassed.

"Don't worry." Wes smiled. "You're not alone. I think there are a few reasons for this. In general, people don't set specific goals because they've experienced a lot of failure in the past and want to avoid embarrassment. A December 2015 article in *US News* reported that eighty percent of people who set New Year's resolutions give up on them by the second week of February. We all know that setting a vague goal has its advantages. If our goal is vague, then it's easy to say we accomplished it. For example, your goal is to have more money. Here's a penny, Elin. You're all done. Congratulations!"

Elin opened her hand as Wes dropped the penny into her palm. "That's not what I meant, Wes, and you know it! What I really meant was I want to have financial security."

"Of course you did," Wes said with a grin. "But what exactly does financial security look like? A vague goal also gives us an excuse for not reaching it. Since we don't know exactly where we're going, we also don't know where to begin. No one could accomplish this, so it's easy to justify not taking it seriously, not taking much action, and not reaching the goal.

"What's also interesting is that you didn't give me a date by when you want to have financial security. It's really more of a dream for you at this point, isn't it? Dreams make us feel happy and hopeful, while failing at a goal has the exact opposite effect. Unfortunately, dreams rarely come true and are more often just pure fantasy. It's something people talk about on their deathbed along with all their other regrets.

"I also think people don't use SMART goals because deep down they think they're stupid. There doesn't seem to be any correlation between following the SMART format and achieving a goal. There are other problems too. It's incomplete. It doesn't ask you for all the important information you need to set a complete goal. It doesn't invite you to consult with experts who can help ensure your success and save you time. And because the *A* stands for achievable, people subconsciously set smaller goals they are certain they can achieve. That is most unfortunate.

"I think there's a much better way to go about setting goals, and I'd like to teach you that right now." Wes gave Elin a handout titled *5W'S Complete Goal-Setting Framework* and went over it with her.

5W'S Complete Goal-Setting Framework

The 5W'S Complete Goal-Setting Framework is about setting big, meaningful goals that are whole and complete. It dramatically increases your chance of achieving your goal. It is an acronym for seven words. The "5W" stands for the following five words: *Who*, *What*, *When*, *Where*, and *Why*. The letter *S* stands for *Specific*. It also includes the word *Complete*. The questions around *how* you are going to achieve your goal are part of a different exercise. It is important to separate the two. Creating the goal comes first. The goal must be your own, not one set for you by others. And the goal must be aligned with who you are and where you are going.

Here are the definitions of the seven words presented in a somewhat different order that makes thinking about your goal easier.

- **Specific:** When going through this exercise, make sure you use specific numbers, priorities, dates, and times.
- **Complete:** Your goal should complete a major effort; everything is done, and you have received all your desired results.
- **What:** What is the problem, issue, or opportunity you want to work on? This is a short statement, usually twenty words or less, that can be easily understood by others.
- **Where:** Think about a map. Where are you now? Where do you want to be?
- **When:** When do you need to start? By when must you finish?
- **Who:** Who can you model? Who is an expert? Who can help?
- **Why:** Why is this goal important to you? Why is it important for others? Why does it need to be done right now?

Complete Goal

Let us look at an example to better understand the word *complete*. On May 25, 1961, President John F. Kennedy set a goal of landing a man on the moon and returning him safely to Earth by the end of the decade. That was a complete effort that required many things to be done before it could even be attempted. At the time, the United States had not sent anyone into space, and the Russians boasted one man who had just made one orbit of Earth in space.

Definition of Done

When you define where you want to be, it is important to specifically list everything you will need to accomplish in order to complete your goal. This is called the *definition of done*.

Time Frame

A meaningful goal typically takes three to five years to complete; however, the time frame for a goal can be anywhere from six months to ten years. Anything beyond that is probably more of a vision than a goal.

Well Analogy

The Well Analogy will help illustrate why we don't want to focus on the *how* when setting a complete goal. When you are stuck at the bottom of a well, the goal seems simple: get out as soon as you can. But if it is difficult for you to envision it happening, you just plain don't think it can be done, or you get stuck wanting to create the perfect plan, then you will never set the goal and try. If you make the mistake of thinking there is only one way to get out of the well, the *how*, then you have severely limited yourself and greatly reduced your chances of success.

The How Process

The How Process usually takes much longer than the goal-setting process. You need to interview experts who have done this or something similar before; hold multiple brainstorming sessions to come up with as many potential solutions as possible; evaluate each potential solution and choose the ones you think will work best; and create a detailed implementation plan. You can then execute the plan and see if it works. If it doesn't work, you will have to make some adjustments. Worst-case scenario, you will need to start the How Process all over again and keep doing this until you succeed. Note that your goal remains the same.

Goal Conflicts

A Goal Conflict happens when one goal competes with another goal in its requirements for your time, attention, money, or other resources. This happens a lot when people try to balance the eight areas of life. In order to succeed, there should be one goal that is more important than the others, which is called the **primary goal**. Your other goals should help you achieve the primary goal. They are called **supporting goals**. They need to be done, but only in the context of achieving the primary goal.

Go to www.WiseLovingBeing.com/handouts
to find a copy of this handout online.

"Elin, let me demonstrate the framework with a simple example of taking a vacation. The first word is *what*. The answer is, *I want to take a vacation to New York City this year.*

"The next word is *where*. Think about a map. I'll start traveling from my apartment in Phoenix. My destination is New York City, and I'll be staying at a hotel near Times Square. I will need to book a hotel later as part of the planning process. My *definition of done* includes the following prioritized, specific list of touristy things I want to do: see a Broadway show, walk through Central Park, visit Times Square, shop on Fifth Avenue, go to the top of the Empire State Building, see the Statue of Liberty, and visit the World Trade Center Museum. I also want to eat New York-style pizza, bagels, and a pastrami sandwich.

"The next word is *when*. When will I depart, and when will I arrive? I'm going to depart early Saturday morning, October 1, 2022, and return late on Sunday October 9, 2022, depending on what flights are available, which is part of the planning process.

"The next word is *who*. Who can I model? Who is an expert? There are lots of travel sites I can review. I can buy a travel guide. And I can ask my friend Jean, who went there last month.

"The last word is *why*. Why is this important? This vacation is important because I have burned myself out. I need to recharge and reward myself for working so hard. New York City is a place I've always wanted to visit, and it's currently at the top of my list of destinations. This is important to others for three reasons: I will be much more productive, I will be more fun to be around, and I'll be able to add much more value to them after I return.

"And that's it. Pretty simple, right? Do you have any questions, Elin?"

"No questions," Elin quickly replied. "It seems pretty straight-forward. Let me try it for my goal.

"What I need to solve is my problem of not having enough money. So what I need is financial freedom and security.

"Where am I today? Well, this isn't pretty, but here goes. I have a fixed income from Social Security that is being eaten away by this crazy inflation. I'm receiving less real income and have higher expenses. I have enough money to pay for my Section 8 public housing and some of my prescriptions, but I don't have enough to pay for all of my prescriptions and basic food needs. I have over fifty thousand dollars in debt. I stopped paying my creditors about six years ago at the advice of my local pro bono legal and financial advisors. I don't have any credit cards, and I have zero savings. I'm driving a twenty-three-year-old car, hoping every day that it continues to run. It's not worth anything, and I couldn't pay for any major repairs if it needed them. I don't have any money to replace it, and I can't get a car loan.

"Where do I want to be? I'd like to be able to pay my bills, have reliable transportation, and live in a safer neighborhood. I don't know all the specifics yet.

"When do I need this? Some of this is obviously a higher priority than others, but I'd like to achieve all of this by my eighty-seventh birthday in 2025, which is three years from now.

"Let me tackle *who* next. Who can I model? Who is an expert? Who can help? There is the pro-bono legal and financial firm I have used before. You're obviously helping me, too, Wes. I can do some research on the internet and check out some books from the library. I can also check with employers about possibly getting a job.

"Now for the big question: *Why?* Because I need to survive. I'm close to being homeless. I'm tired of eating unhealthy food and missing meals altogether. I don't feel safe driving my car or living in my neighborhood. I'm scared in general about a lot of things. Fear consumes me on a daily basis. I want to be happy. It's important for others because I can't help anyone until I can take care of my basic needs."

Elin paused and took a deep breath. "That's it. How did I do, Wes?"

"Great job, Elin. As you mentioned, your goal needs more work, but it's an excellent start. You can calculate the specifics by first adding up all your bills, including reasonable food costs. Your debt will get written off by your creditors after seven years, and you can talk with your tax advisor about anything you may need to do there. You should also have six months of expenses saved, a credit score of at least 720 on all three credit reporting agencies, the ability to save ten percent of your gross income each month, and a credit card. You'll need to do some research to determine how much you'll need each month for your new rent and how much it will cost you to move. You can also estimate what your monthly payment will be on a newer car. Then you'll be able to calculate how much net income you'll need each month. You will also need to prioritize the above items.

"It'll take you some time to complete this assignment, and it looks like you know exactly what to do. I'll walk you through the How Process in detail later. As I mentioned, it's critical to keep the Goal-Setting Process separate from the How Process. I'd like to tell you a story that I think will help you better understand this.

"My friend Lisa was in a similar situation as you are right now: she spent all her money each month on basics, she paid cash for everything, she didn't have a credit card, and she couldn't get one. She wouldn't use her debit card online for fear that her account would get hacked, and then she wouldn't be able to pay her rent or buy food.

"Not having a credit card kept Lisa from buying things she needed. When she couldn't find an ink cartridge for her old printer at the store, I'd suggest she buy the ink online. When her car didn't work, I'd recommend she use Uber or Lyft. When she couldn't find a book at the library that I'd asked her to read, I'd suggest she buy it online. But she'd always say, 'I can't. I don't have a credit card.' She never set a goal to try to improve her situation because she always included *how* she would buy the item. She didn't just give up; she never even started. She was just sitting at the bottom of the well feeling sorry for herself.

"I helped Lisa see that her belief was false. She didn't need her own credit card. I showed her several ways she could buy things online: open a checking account at a different bank and use its debit card for nonessential purchases, get a secured credit card from her current bank, or buy a preloaded or reloadable credit card from the grocery store.

"I told Lisa how often she used her 'I don't have a credit card' excuse. She was surprised by how often she said it and how automatic it had become. She didn't even think about it. She was finally able to see how this false belief immediately put an end to anything she wanted to do to improve her life.

"I gave Lisa some critical wisdom that helped her to better understand why she did what she did and, more importantly, how she could change her thinking and change her life from one of limitations to one of possibilities. That helped her start to improve her life, which is completely different today.

"My friend Jiten made the mistake of including a *how* in his goal. He was recently laid off from his job. He was married with two small children. He was rapidly running out of money and was afraid he might have to sell his house. The stress was really intense, and it started to affect his health and his relationships. He set a goal to get a new job and spent his time applying for jobs, sending out resumes, networking with friends, and going on interviews. Unfortunately, after nine months he was still unemployed. The job market was terrible. Companies weren't hiring, and they continued to shed workers.

"I helped Jiten see that he had set a bad goal because it included the *how*. I told him about the 5W'S Complete Goal-Setting Framework and helped him create a new empowering goal. The new goal was to bring in enough money to cover his expenses, which he calculated to be $5,000 per month. That opened him up to looking at all the possibilities he could think of to bring in that income instead of only focusing on one method that was unlikely to happen. I also helped him understand why he had focused so intently on getting a job as the only possible solution. He ended up choosing two of the many income-generating ideas from his brainstorming sessions and implemented them quickly. Within five months he had reached his goal and has never looked back.

"Let me tell you a story about conflicting goals. My friend Mitch, who was in his late twenties, set goals for the next three years. He wanted to be the number-one salesperson in his company nationwide, run a marathon in under two and a half hours, be a millionaire, and get married. At the time he was in the bottom quartile of salespeople, was running only a few miles per week, had no savings, wasn't making enough money to pay for his basic needs, and wasn't dating anyone. Achieving any one of these goals on their own would obviously take up all his time and would be very difficult to do, even if he had a plan and a group of stellar advisors, which he didn't. What's worse is that all four goals conflicted with each other. They were all primary goals; he had not established any supporting goals.

"I helped Mitch better understand why he created these goals, why none of them were realistic, and why none of them were aligned with what he really wanted in life. I helped him create a new primary goal that had supporting goals, and he is now much happier.

"Let me tell you a story about creating a complete goal with a clear *definition of done*. My friend Ethan wanted to be a novelist and dreamed of someday writing a great novel. He had made a little bit of progress, but after seven years had nothing much to show for his efforts. After asking a few questions, I discovered that he had some interesting beliefs about writing. For example, he thought his goal was to only write a first draft of his novel. He also thought he needed to write a book in order to establish himself as an author *before* he wrote the novel he actually dreamed of writing. I asked him if he had ever spoken with a published author. Of course, he said no.

"I helped Ethan understand why he hadn't made much progress on his novel over the past seven years and spoke with him about the difference between a goal and a dream. I also introduced him to the 5W'S Complete Goal-Setting Framework. For the word *who*, I introduced him to two published authors so he could learn how the writing process should go. Regarding the word *complete*, I suggested that his goal shouldn't be to just create a draft of his novel, which would probably sit on his desk collecting dust for another seven years, but to publish his novel and sell a thousand copies.

"I then asked Ethan to create his definition of done. It included writing the novel, having it reviewed by others, finding a professional editor, finding an illustrator, finding an interior book designer, hiring a book cover designer, finding a literary agent, finding a publisher, getting an ISBN, getting the book copyrighted, publishing a paperback and an eBook, setting up a website and online forum for his fans, marketing the book, and receiving payments from his royalties. He was then able to come up with a realistic schedule to get all of this done. He felt significantly more motivated, and having a timeline helped him stay on track.

"I took Lisa, Jiten, Mitch, and Ethan through the same process, and it totally changed their lives. It's not an easy process, and it takes some effort, but it does have the power to transform you completely. They did it, and I'd like to help you do it too. Is that something you'd be interested in, Elin?"

"Yes! I think I could really benefit from that, Wes."

"Excellent! And look, we've returned to the Cinnabon. Nice. This is a great place to end our session today.

"Let me summarize the day for you. It's very important to set a big, meaningful, complete, primary goal. The 5W'S Complete

Goal-Setting Framework guides you through the process and sets you up for success. It's critical that you don't include a solution for *how* you will achieve your goal. The time needed for the Goal-Setting Process is usually a fraction of the time required to complete an effective How Process. Setting a goal happens once, while determining how to achieve that goal can happen multiple times. When you set multiple goals, make sure there are no conflicts: there is one primary goal and multiple supporting goals. Make sure the goals are yours and are aligned with who you are and where you want to go.

"If you don't mind, Elin, I'd like to give you some homework. We can meet here again tomorrow at the same time. Okay?"

"Absolutely. What's my homework?" Elin asked.

"There are two parts. Please examine your beliefs around money. Make a list of everything you can think of that you were told about money. Add any lessons you learned about money through your own experiences. Then go back through the combined list and write down where each belief came from. Second, make a list of your general beliefs about yourself, your different roles, and the world. Again, write down where these beliefs came from. Any questions?"

"No questions. See you tomorrow, Wes!" Elin said with a smile.

As Elin walked back to her car, she reflected on her time with Wes. It hadn't been all bad. In fact, it was quite productive. She actually learned something. She really enjoyed his company and felt comfortable sharing; it was easy talking with him. They were almost like good childhood friends who knew everything about each other, could talk for hours, and were able to just be themselves. She was glad she showed up today.

Chapter Five

Beliefs

When Elin arrived at the Cinnabon the next day, Wes was already there. He greeted her with a big smile and said, "Good morning, Elin! How are you today?"

"Good morning, Wes. I'm good. How are you doing?"

"I'm awesome!" Wes replied enthusiastically. "Let's get started, shall we?"

They began their morning walk around the mall as Wes began speaking. "The first part of our journey together is focused on awareness, and the first topic is around beliefs. In these exercises it's important to be honest and embrace the truth. This can be an uncomfortable exercise, but it is a critical first step in the important awareness process." Wes gave Elin a handout titled *Beliefs* and went over it with her.

Beliefs

Definition

A belief is a statement we accept to be true today. Our beliefs are based on our experiences, what people tell us, and what we tell ourselves. Our beliefs come from our culture, traditions, family, friends, coworkers, teachers, community, government, companies, scientists, religion, the news, social media, and movies.

Challenges with Beliefs

Beliefs seem like a simple concept, but there are a few challenges with beliefs:

- **Acceptance:** We rarely question our beliefs. We accept them to be true.
- **Awareness:** We are not consciously aware of all our beliefs.
- **Conflicting Beliefs:** Some of our beliefs conflict with other beliefs and our goals, needs, and behaviors.
- **False Beliefs:** Many of our beliefs are false. Some beliefs used to be true but aren't true anymore. Some are true for others but not true for us. Some are only true under specific circumstances. Some were never true.
- **Immutable:** We think it isn't possible to change our beliefs. We feel obligated to believe what we have always believed.
- **Inherited Beliefs:** A lot of our beliefs were given to us. They are the beliefs of others. We blindly adopted them as our own.
- **Static Beliefs:** We rarely, if ever, review our beliefs to see if they are still true. We don't update them so they remain static.

Types of Beliefs

There are two types of beliefs.

- **Empowering beliefs** help us do better in life.
- **Limiting beliefs** hold us back and generally cause problems.

Belief Questions

It is important to question our beliefs. Ask yourself the following six questions about each of your beliefs:

1. Is this belief really true?
2. When is this belief true, and when is it not true?
3. Where did this belief come from?
4. What does this belief conflict with?
5. How does this belief affect my life?
6. Is this belief empowering me, or do I need to create a new belief?

Empowering Belief Format

It is important to convert limiting beliefs into empowering beliefs. Make sure your new empowering belief meets the following guidelines:

- **Positive:** Don't include the words *no* or *not* in a belief. For example, the belief, *I'm not a bad person* should be changed to, *I'm a good person*. Don't use words with negative connotations. For example, the belief, *Old people can add value too* should be changed to, *People can add value at any age*.
- **Unlimited:** Don't allow beliefs to limit you in any way. For example, the belief, *I can get a minimum wage job* limits you to entry-level jobs that pay minimum wage. It should be changed to, *I can get a great job*.
- **Real:** Beliefs need to be grounded in reality. For example, you can't have the belief, *Dogs can fly*.

Go to www.WiseLovingBeing.com/handouts
to find a copy of this handout online.

"Elin, do you have any questions about beliefs?"

"None. It all makes sense to me."

"Great! Then let's go over your homework. What are your beliefs around money?" Wes asked.

Elin pulled out her homework and said, "My beliefs around money are:

1. I feel guilty having money when others don't.
2. I am destined to be poor and alone. There is nothing I can do about my financial situation.
3. Women can't make a lot of money.
4. Women can only have certain jobs like secretary, teacher, nurse, and caregiver.
5. Women aren't allowed to be in business.
6. I need to marry a man who earns a lot of money.
7. People should be more self-sufficient. For example, they should plant gardens.
8. There are more important things than money, like good friends and good health.
9. I can't get a job because I don't have any recent work experience.
10. I'm not comfortable doing basic things that certain jobs require.
11. Most jobs are beyond my capabilities.
12. I'm lazy.

"What do you think, Wes? Pretty messed up, huh?" Elin said, looking embarrassed.

"First of all, you did a great job. Thank you for working hard on this and being honest. Seeing your beliefs for the first time can be quite shocking. **Awareness** is a critical step in the change process. It identifies why you do what you do, why you are where you are in life, and why you and I are talking about it today. You can't change something you can't see, so it's critical to bring everything into the light and put it on the table. This is difficult work. Most people avoid this because it's just too painful to see that some of their problems are self-inflicted to varying degrees. Don't worry, though, because after awareness comes the fun part of creating a life you'd be thrilled to live," Wes said encouragingly.

"Regarding your specific beliefs, you're no different than most women who grew up in your generation. Life was a lot different in the 1950s when you became an adult. Most women married young, had children, and took care of the home. The few jobs available for women were mostly supporting roles, like a secretary, nurse, or teacher. Men made more money, even for the same job. It was a man's world back then.

"Today, a woman can be anything she wants to be. The only thing that hasn't happened yet, for some strange reason, is a woman being president of the United States. That will happen soon enough. But seriously, everything is fair game. Women are even excelling at traditionally male-only jobs in the military and police.

"Also, there are many new ways to make money today that didn't exist in the 1950s. With the internet, you can now create your own business quickly, work from home, contract out any work you don't want to do, and make as much money as you want. It doesn't cost a lot of money to start a business. In fact, it can be done for less than a hundred dollars. Chris Guillebeau emphasized this shift in his book, *The $100 Startup*. You can also use the drop-shipping or print-on-demand models where you don't pay up front for inventory. You use a supplier who creates the products on demand and ships them to your customers. The options today are truly unlimited. You're only limited by your creativity and your resourcefulness.

"With that being said, Elin, what conflicts do you see between your goal of financial security and your beliefs around money?"

"Well, I have a belief that I need money," Elin replied. "However, I also believe that:

- Having money is bad when others don't have it.
- I am destined to be poor.
- Women can't make a lot of money.
- There are more important things than money.
- I can't get a job."

"What conflicts exist between your beliefs around money and your behaviors?" Wes asked.

"I believe I need to marry a man to provide me with money, but I'm not in a relationship and I don't date. I need to work to make money, but I don't have a job. I believe people can be more self-sufficient, but I don't do anything because I'm lazy."

"How do your beliefs around money affect your life?" Wes asked.

"They keep me from taking any action that will improve my life. I don't see a way to win, so there is no hope. It makes me depressed."

"Agreed. Please go through each of your beliefs and answer the belief questions," Wes instructed. "Note that you can skip questions four and five about conflict and affect since we've already covered them."

"My first belief is, *I feel guilty having money when others don't*. This belief came from an experience I had as a child when I visited a shantytown with my dad. It was very different from the nice part of town where we lived. He told me we were lucky to live where we did. My answer to the first question is yes, this belief is true for me."

"Wait. Let me stop you right there," Wes interrupted. "That isn't a belief; it's a feeling. Furthermore, this feeling statement is actually about your own guilt, which is a separate discussion we will have later. Please try to restate your feeling statement as a belief."

"Interesting. Okay. How about, *I shouldn't have money when others don't?*" Elin asked.

"You're getting closer. Let me try. I think there are a few beliefs packed in there actually. How about the following four belief statements? *People require money. Money is scarce. There is not enough money for everyone. I am a bad person if I have money and others don't.*

"What do you think, Elin? Do these new belief statements reflect what was contained in your feeling statement?" Wes asked.

"Yes, they do. Again, this is very interesting. So let me try to go through the belief questions. For *people require money*, that's not true for everyone, but it is true for me right now. I wouldn't need money if I lived on a farm and had something of value to sell or trade for the things I needed. This is definitely a disempowering belief. I need to create some new empowering beliefs, but I'd like to do that after we go through all of my beliefs first, if that's all right with you?"

"Agreed. Please continue, Elin."

"For *money is scarce*. That's obviously not true. There are, I don't know, how many trillions of dollars just in the United States alone, and the government can print as much money as it wants. I'd like to just delete that belief, thank you very much. The same for the next belief: *There is not enough money for everyone.* Delete. For *I am a bad person if I have money and others don't*, that is clearly not true. What happens to other people has no effect on whether I'm bad or good. As a matter of fact, if I had more money, then I could actually do more to help others. Delete again!" Elin said with a smile.

"If you don't mind, Wes, I think I can address the next five beliefs from my original list together to save us some time. They all came from my experiences growing up and as a young adult. None of them are true today. I'm not destined to be poor and alone. I can make a lot of money. I can have any job I want. I can run my own business. I don't need to marry a man to have money. I'd like to delete all of these beliefs." She paused and let out a relieved breath. "This is fun. I feel better already!" Elin said enthusiastically.

"For belief number seven on my list, *People can be more self-sufficient*, it's true. This came from watching my grandpa, who lived on a farm and was completely self-sufficient. I could definitely be more self-sufficient, but for some reason I just haven't tried," Elin said, looking puzzled.

"That's a good observation, Elin. There is sometimes a difference between what we consciously want to do and what we actually do. We'll talk more about this concept later. What's most important right now is that you're starting to become more aware of yourself."

"Sounds good, Wes. So the eighth belief on my list, *There are more important things than money, like good friends and good health*, is also not true. It came from my experience of being poor as a young adult. Money, friends, and health are all important and necessary. But what's more interesting to me is that I don't even believe my own belief. I don't have good friends or good health, and I haven't for many years. Isn't that weird?" Elin asked.

"Not weird. Actually, it's quite common, and something I'm going to help you with. Hang in there. I promise things will get better. As a matter of fact, I think the only way for you to go is up," Wes said encouragingly.

Elin smiled and continued. "The ninth belief is, *I can't get a job because I don't have any recent work experience*. I think this is partially true. It comes from trying to find a job a few years ago. I do have some marketable skills, and I'm sure someone would hire me today, but it could take a lot of effort to find a job, and it probably won't pay much. The next two beliefs doubt my abilities. They're true. I can't do math, which is required to be an entry-level cashier at McDonald's. I wouldn't be able to ring up the orders or give the correct change. Customers would get angry with me, and so would the store manager."

"Wait, Elin," Wes interrupted again. "You really don't think you could operate a cash register at a fast-food restaurant?"

"Not a chance," Elin replied. "This is a huge fear of mine. I would just freeze."

"Okay, Elin. We'll come back to this again later. Please continue."

"The last belief is, *I'm lazy*. This came from a family member telling me that I was a lazy person. This is kind of strange to me because I did work hard when I was working. Working hard was ingrained in me by my parents, who had just come out of the Great Depression. I think this belief isn't saying that *I don't want to work*, but more like *I don't actually try*. Does that make sense?"

"It does make sense. I think what you're trying to say is that you're a hard worker, but for some reason, something is holding you back from working on financial security. What do you think?"

"Yes. That's it," Elin replied. "That's what I was trying to say. Thank you, Wes. So I'd like to delete this belief, too, please."

"Excellent idea, Elin. Let me ask you another question. You originally gave me a list of twelve beliefs. Is this a complete list, or did you miss any beliefs around money?" Wes asked.

"I think it's complete."

"How about the belief that says, *I have to be self-sufficient and do things on my own*?" Wes asked.

"Good one. Yes, I left that one out. It's definitely not true, and it's disempowering. I'd like to delete that one, too, please."

"Nice work, Elin. What empowering belief would you like to replace it with?"

"How about, *There are lots of people who would like to help me if I ask them*?" Elin said, smiling.

"I like that. I thought of another belief. How about the belief that says, *People over age sixty-five aren't able to work and make money*?" Wes asked.

"Wow. Yes, that's another one that was hidden from my view. It's definitely false and disempowering. Let's replace it with the empowering belief that says, *Old people can make money too*."

"You're getting closer. Please try to use the empowering belief format from the handout: positive, unlimited, and real."

"How about, *People can make money at any age?*" Elin asked.

"I like it! Now, using the proper format, what are all of your new empowering beliefs around money?"

Elin replied, "My new empowering beliefs around money are:

- There is more than enough money for everyone.
- There are lots of people who would like to help me if I ask them.
- People can make money at any age.
- I can get a great job.
- I am a hard worker.
- There are lots of ways I can make money.
- I can create my own business.
- I can make as much money as I choose.
- The more money I make, the more I can help myself and others."

"I'd like to suggest that you add one more, please. *I can always find a way by being more creative and resourceful.* What do you think, Elin?" Wes asked.

"Oh, that's a good one. Thank you for that."

"Now I need to caution you a little bit. Becoming aware of your existing beliefs, questioning them, and creating new empowering beliefs is a good start. But it is one thing to write them down and quite another thing to live them. Change is difficult. Please recite your new beliefs to yourself twice a day, as soon as you wake up in the morning and just before you go to sleep. Also, think about them throughout the day. Look for ways to take action around your new beliefs so you can prove they are true. This is really the first part of the transformation process.

"So far today, we've talked about your beliefs around money. What are some of your general beliefs about yourself and the world?" Wes asked.

Elin replied, "Some of my general beliefs are:
- Life should be fair.
- I'm too old to do anything about this.
- I'm not going to live much longer.
- I'm a very disorganized person.
- It's hard to make new friends who share common interests.
- My mom was depressed, and I inherited that illness from her."

"This is a good start," Wes said. "As you can clearly see, these are all false and limiting beliefs. I think it will be helpful for you to take this exercise one step further. I'd like you to look at the beliefs under these beliefs. I think there are two stronger beliefs that have been in place most of your life. They have been hidden deep down below the surface and are just too painful to acknowledge:
- There is nothing I can do to improve my situation.
- I don't deserve to live a nice life."

"Ouch. Yes, you're right. I definitely don't want to acknowledge that I have those beliefs, yet there's no denying by my actions that I believe them."

"Can you see how a lot of your general beliefs also conflict with your need for money?" Wes asked.

"Yes. It's interesting that I have so many beliefs that are conflicting with such a basic and important need as money."

"Let's talk about our most powerful belief, our **identity**. It defines who we are and how we should think, feel, speak, and act. **Identity statements** start with two words: *I am*. Who are you, Elin? What is your identity?"

"If you had asked me this question three weeks ago, I would have said, *I am a good person who hasn't accomplished much in the material world*," Elin replied. "Unfortunately, I think the honest answer, based on our discussion today and recent events, is that *I'm an old, poor woman who doesn't try to make things better who has given up on life.* I know that's not what I want it to be, and it's certainly not what I've been telling myself all these years. It's quite depressing actually."

"Don't worry, Elin. It's going to get better. Awareness is difficult. Later on, you're going to create a new empowering identity and new empowering beliefs for all areas of your life, but first we have to complete the awareness process. You need to have a complete understanding of yourself before you can know what changes to make. Thank you again for your honesty."

"Thank you, Wes, for accepting me as I am and for acknowledging that how I feel is somewhat normal and okay. It makes a big difference to me, and it's so different from what happens in the real world. It's nice to just be myself."

"You're very welcome," Wes said gratefully.

"Another set of beliefs people have is around their purpose, vision, and values. And by values, I'm not referring to being a good or bad person. I'm asking you to consider what is important or valuable to you. What is your purpose and vision? What are your values?"

"I don't have a purpose or vision," Elin replied a bit shamefully. "I do have a few values. The first is equality. I think everyone should be seen and treated equally. My second value is respect. I try to treat everyone with respect even if they don't deserve it. My third value is the Golden Rule: I try to treat everyone the way I would like to be treated. I don't like it when I see people mistreating others."

"Excellent. And with that, we are done with the topic of beliefs. Great work today, Elin!

"Let me summarize today's lesson. We've inherited and created a lot of beliefs. Some we are aware of and some we aren't. It's important that we challenge our beliefs, determine if they are true for us now, remove the false and limiting beliefs, and create new empowering beliefs. The next step is to review our new beliefs daily and take action around them to prove they are true.

"Are you ready for your homework?"

"Yes, sir. What's my homework?"

"Please make a list of your habits. I'm defining *habits* as what you think, feel, say, and do on a consistent basis. Write down what activities you do in a typical day, accounting for all twenty-four hours. Write down how you feel, what you think about, what you constantly tell yourself, and what you tell others. What positive and negative experiences do you try to have, and which experiences do you try to avoid? What are your rules for what it takes to have each experience? This exercise is much tougher than it looks, so please spend a little more time on it.

"Some of our habits are so automatic that we aren't even aware of them. It will be helpful if you can speak with others about your habits. Think about people you interact with frequently and people who know you well. When speaking with them, first let them know that you need their help. You want them to be brutally honest with you. You'll need to assure them that you won't get angry and that there'll be no negative consequences. You'll be in listening mode. You'll probably ask follow-up questions to get clarification. You might ask for recent examples to help you better understand. Be sure to thank them when you're done.

"Let's meet here again tomorrow at the same time. Any questions?"

"No questions. See you tomorrow, Wes!"

Chapter Six

Habits

When Elin arrived at the Cinnabon the next day, Wes was already there. He greeted her with a big smile and said, "Good morning, Elin! How are you today?"

"Good morning, Wes. I'm good. How are you doing?"

"I'm wonderful!" Wes replied enthusiastically. "Let's get started, shall we?"

As they began their morning walk around the mall, Wes began with the new lesson. "Today we are going to talk about habits." He gave Elin a handout titled *Habits* and went over it with her.

Habits

Our habits are what we think, feel, say, and do on a consistent basis. It is something we do every day or every week, not occasionally. Some of these habits we know about, but some habits have become **automatic habits**, and we don't consciously think about them anymore. Examples of things we do that become automatic are typing on a keyboard, driving a car, and riding a bicycle.

There are two **types of habits**:
- **Limiting Habits:** These are habits we wish we didn't do. They make it more difficult for us to achieve our goals.
- **Empowering Habits:** These are habits that help us and bring us closer to our goals.

Activities
Activities are the things we do in a typical day. We spend a certain amount of time on each one. Adding up the time for our daily activities accounts for all twenty-four hours. If your days are all different, then you can look at your activities for a typical week. **Escape activities** are recurring limiting activities we do to avoid reality on a consistent basis. They provide us with short-term comforts that cause us problems in the long term. **Addictions** are escape activities we can't stop doing. We have to do them in order to survive

Feelings
How we feel both mentally and physically defines our experience of life. We often feel the same way on a consistent basis.

Words

The words we use on a daily basis also define our experience of life. We often think, speak, text, type, and write with the same words consistently. And it is not just the words; it is also how we say them.

Thoughts

We spend a lot of time each day in our head, thinking about all kinds of things. We don't always think in words. We often think using images or mini movies, which are much more powerful than words. Most of our thoughts are about past experiences and future events.

Experiences

Desired experiences are things we want to experience in our life on a daily basis. They can be either positive or negative, based on the results they have on our life. We have a list of rules for what it takes for us to have each desired experience.

Avoided experiences are things we don't want to experience in our life. They can also be positive or negative. We have a list of rules for what it takes for us to have each avoided experience.

Rules

There are two types of rules. A specific desired or avoided experience can have only one type of rule.

- **AND Rules** are rules that must all be met in order to have the experience. These rules make it difficult for us to have that experience.
- **OR Rules** are rules where only one rule needs to occur in order for us to have that experience. These rules make it easy for us to have that experience.

Experience Questions

For each desired and avoided experience, answer the following three experience questions:

1. Do you view this experience as having a positive or negative effect on your life?
2. Are these OR Rules or AND Rules?
3. Do you have this experience on a consistent basis, yes or no?

Default Future

What you do every day determines what path you are on and where you are going. You develop an **autopilot** that automates most of your day. It leads you down a **default pat**h to a default future. Unfortunately, for most people, the default future is not where they dream of going. It is important to change your daily habits so they are aligned with your **desired future**.

Habit Connection

Our habits around what we think, feel, say, and do are all connected, and one of them can affect all others. They can all play off each other and create a **downward spiral**. For example, if we are feeling depressed, then we tend to say and think negative things, which leaves us feeling tired and sluggish. We also stop doing things we enjoy and stop interacting with others. And all of this, in turn, makes us feel even more depressed and so on. The good news is that the opposite is also true. If we can inject a positive habit, then it can affect all others and start an **upward spiral**. It is more difficult to change what we think and feel, but it is much easier to change what we say and do.

Limiting Habits: Costs, Benefits, and Payoffs

Limiting habits have both short-term and long-term **costs**, but they provide us with only short-term or temporary **benefits**. Furthermore, they provide us with a **payoff**, which gives us something we value or helps us prove something important to ourselves and others. It is critical that we understand all the costs, benefits, and payoffs for each limiting habit.

Go to www.WiseLovingBeing.com/handouts
to find a copy of this handout online.

"Elin, let me provide you with an example. My friend Sophia was a perfectionist. She worked long hours. She replied to emails around the clock, took on extra responsibilities, and redid work her team had done that didn't meet her high standards. She would revise her work three or four times to make sure it was perfect. She tried to be the perfect wife at home too, keeping the house immaculate, cooking great meals, and making sure her husband was happy. She didn't get much sleep. She constantly criticized herself. She also thought about her past and all the things for which she felt guilt, regret, or shame. She worried about future events and all the things she needed to do.

"Sophia was having challenges at work with her boss and with some members of her team. She constantly fought with her siblings and parents and often said awful things to them. She wanted to experience respect, love, and financial security, but she hadn't been able to. She held her negative emotions in her neck and upper back and often had headaches. She felt overwhelmed, inadequate, stressed, anxious, angry, embarrassed, and depressed.

"By Friday night every week, Sophia was such an emotional wreck she would start drinking and wouldn't stop until she passed out. The short-term but temporary benefit was that it provided her with three hours to escape her emotional pain and suffering, and she got some much-needed sleep. But she usually did or said something embarrassing, and she sometimes fell down or injured herself. The excessive hangover on Saturday morning with the headache and nausea made her feel terrible. It also kept her from doing personal projects, exercising, and seeing her therapist.

"Of course, the negative thoughts and emotions returned. She then added to that by criticizing herself more, which led to more negative feelings of anger, anxiety, and depression. The long-term costs were starting to appear as health problems. Every Saturday, she swore she wouldn't drink again, yet every Friday she always did.

The downward spiral continued. The payoff was to prove that she was unworthy, irresponsible, and unlovable. She was consumed by limiting habits that were destroying her life. Her default future was nowhere near her desired future.

"I helped Sophia become aware of her habits, understand why she did what she did, and create empowering habits that transformed her life. She learned how to take simple actions to avoid the downward spirals and maintain her emotional well-being. She gave up alcohol, learned how to manage her perfection, created positive relationships, and is much happier at work and at home. Her default future is now aligned with her desired future.

"Elin, let's take a look at your homework, starting with your activities. What do you do in a typical day? Also, let me know approximately how much time you spend on each one. Please account for all twenty-four hours."

Elin pulled out her homework and said, "In a typical day, I do the following:

1. Get ready to go: have coffee and something sweet to eat, clean the kitchen, brush my teeth, make my bed, get dressed, do my hair, put on makeup (2 hours).
2. Play computer games (1 hour).
3. Take care of my cousin Carl's cat and his house (2 hours).
4. Prepare and eat breakfast (1 hour).
5. Run errands (3 hours).
6. Watch TV (6 hours).
7. Eat lunch (1 hour).
8. Eat dinner (1 hour).
9. Sleep (7 hours)."

"Elin, why do you take care of Carl's house and cat? Does he pay you for that?"

"I'm just trying to help Carl out. He's a snowbird and only lives here six months during the winter. I don't do this all year long. I guess I feel some sort of family obligation to him. No, he doesn't pay me. I do buy most of the cat food. The cat needs me. And it's not really his cat. It lives in the neighborhood somewhere and likes to spend time on his patio."

"Well, that's one lucky cat. Which of your nine activities help you with your goal to have financial security?" Wes asked.

"I don't think any of them do."

"Correct! Taking care of Carl's cat actually costs you money. Which of your nine activities are escape activities?" Wes asked.

"Playing computer games and watching TV."

"That's right. Now if you include the escape activities, Carl's house, and running errands, it looks like you have twelve hours available to work on your goal. That's a lot of time, Missy!"

Wes saw that Elin looked a little bit embarrassed. "Don't worry, Elin. This is quite common. We'll talk about this more later. I appreciate you being honest.

"I have one more question about your activities, specifically the first and fourth items. It looks like you have two breakfasts. Can you please explain that?"

"Yes. Several years ago, there was a fire at my neighbor's apartment at four a.m. I had to leave my house quickly as the fire spread to my house. I don't want to be unprepared if a fire happens again, so I get up really early and get ready to go, just in case I need to," Elin explained.

"How many fires have you experienced in your home in your lifetime, and what are your beliefs around this?"

"I've had two fires in my home in my lifetime: this one and one when I was a child," Elin replied. "I believe another one will happen, so I need to be ready for it."

"You have experienced two fires in your life, and they were about seventy years apart. You believe another one will happen, and you want to make sure you are ready for it; therefore you wake up at four a.m. every day. It seems like you also have a belief that fires at home don't happen between the hours of nine p.m. when you go to sleep, and four a.m. when you get up. Can't a fire happen at midnight or two a.m.? And if so, then what?"

Elin thought for a minute. "You're right, Wes. My beliefs around a fire in my apartment aren't really based on reality. It's not logical. I can't explain it. I just have a fear there will be a fire and I won't be ready for it, even though it is unlikely to happen in my future."

"Thank you for thinking about this objectively. Fear is a very powerful force in our lives and causes us to do things that sometimes don't make a lot of sense. In this case, you'd have even more time available to work on your goal if you only ate one breakfast, and you'd probably sleep better, which would help you be more productive," Wes said with a smile. "We'll talk more about fears tomorrow. Now let's look at the next part of your habits. What feelings do you experience on a daily basis?"

"I feel hopeless, scared, frustrated, and depressed," Elin shared. "I also have a lot of regret, guilt, and shame. These aren't positive feelings, but I do try to think about things I'm grateful for before I go to bed. Physically, I get an upset stomach and feel ill when I am stressed, which unfortunately happens often."

"Elin, what words do you think and say on a daily basis?"

Elin looked at Wes and shook her head, realizing the list was long. "The words I think and say on a daily basis are:

- I'm so tired.
- I don't want to get up.
- I'm too old.
- I hope it won't be too hot outside today.

- I hope there isn't too much traffic.
- I hope my car starts.
- I hope the cat didn't die and is safely waiting for me.
- I hope Carl's house alarm doesn't go off accidentally.
- I hope I don't get sick again.
- I hope I can interact with some nice and friendly strangers today.
- I wish I could have a do-over and live my life again.
- Bad things always happen to me."

"What do you consistently think about?" Wes asked.

"I relive events from my past that didn't go well for me, for which I feel guilt, regret, or shame. I think about unpleasant situations and interactions I will probably have in the future," Elin replied.

"Elin, would you consider any of your feelings, thoughts, or the words you use on a consistent basis to be positive?" Wes asked.

"Clearly not, Wes," Elin replied with a bit of a snip.

"Elin, this is more common than you might think. Thank you again for being honest. Can you see how you are creating a downward spiral with your habits feeding off each other to make things worse?"

"Yes. It's crazy. It reminds me of a scene in a movie where someone falls into quicksand and gets pulled under by their panicked actions," Elin replied.

"That's a great analogy. **Quicksand** is the same thing as a downward spiral. Your habits of what you think, feel, say, and do work together to take you lower. This causes great harm to yourself. Luckily, you can also get yourself out of the quicksand by doing something small and positive. It breaks the cycle and helps you start to go in an upward direction. For example, just saying something positive, listening to an uplifting song, calling a friend, or going for a walk are all simple things you can do that will affect how you think and feel. Did you have a chance to talk with anyone about your habits?"

"I only had one person I could call: my niece. It was quite an enlightening conversation. She said I'm quite negative. Whenever we talk on the phone, I eventually talk about depressing and negative things. I change the subject to things I have no control over and have no interest in taking any action to change, like politics, fringe groups, and world events. I was aware that I did this, but I didn't realize how much she disliked it.

"She also said I'm always depressed when we start talking on the phone. I always have an external reason for my negativity. I blame the weather; it's either too hot or too cold, or too sunny or too cloudy. Or I blame other people, events, or how my body is feeling. I tend to focus on what's wrong. However, after we've been talking on the phone for a while, I end up feeling better.

"What I wasn't aware of was that I have a habit of disagreeing with my niece whenever she says something positive about me. She gave me several recent examples. One time, she asked me to review something she wrote and to give her feedback. When I was done giving her feedback, I told her I didn't think I was able to add any value. She told me that I did provide a lot of value and that only she could determine if something was valuable to her. I stuck to my guns and repeated that I was too old and couldn't think as well as the 'young people.' She then told me I had basically called her stupid and a liar, which was definitely not my intention. I know she was exaggerating to make her point, but it still stung.

"She also said that I sometimes use labels when describing groups of people, especially ones I don't agree with. I definitely don't consider myself prejudiced in any way, but I do see how labels might not describe exactly how a specific member of a group thinks and acts.

"I was really surprised by this conversation. I realized that my habits regarding what I think, feel, say, and do are so ingrained, so automatic, that it shapes my life and harms me without me even realizing it."

"Great job, Elin. Awareness is always the first step, and it's not usually much fun. Yes, the words we use have a very powerful influence on our lives. It's important to use more empowering, accurate, and positive words. Obviously, we don't want to say extremely positive things that aren't true, but we do want to be fair and balanced to help ourselves succeed.

"What are your current desired experiences and rules? For each experience, answer the three experience questions."

Elin replied, "My first desired experience is *to be financially secure*. It is positive, it uses AND Rules, and *no*, I don't experience it. In order to experience this, I must do all of the following:

- Get an increase in my income from Social Security.
- Have enough money to pay for food, prescriptions, rent, utilities, and car maintenance.
- Own a new car.
- Have enough money in my savings account to cover my expenses for six months.
- Have a credit card.
- Have a job.
- Have a good credit rating.

"My second desired experience is *to have companionship*. It is positive, it uses AND Rules, and *no*, I don't experience it. In order to experience this, I must do all of the following:

- Own a cat or dog.
- Volunteer and interact with others.
- Have a male companion.
- Have a few close friends I can do things with on a daily basis.

"My third desired experience is *to control my personal life*. I like to think this is positive for me, but it's actually negative, it uses AND Rules, and *yes*, I do experience it. In order to experience this, I must do all of the following:

- Live alone.
- Drive myself and others to places.
- Don't participate in social activities.
- Don't accept anything from anyone; therefore I won't be obligated to them, and they won't be able to control me.

"My fourth desired experience is *to have an unhealthy emotional well-being*. It is negative, it uses AND Rules, and *yes*, I do experience it. In order to experience this, I must do all of the following:

- Isolate myself.
- Be negative.
- Don't let others get too close.
- Limit my contact to only a few people.
- Live a chaotic life.
- Live an unbalanced life.
- Feel bad emotionally.

"My fifth desired experience is *to participate in enrichment activities*. It is positive, it uses AND Rules, and *no*, I don't experience it. In order to experience this, I must do all of the following:

- Read a variety of books and articles.
- Attend lectures on Earth sciences.
- Visit the library often.
- Join a book club.

"My sixth desired experience is *to think negative thoughts*. It is negative, it uses OR Rules, and *yes*, I do experience it. In order to experience this, I can do any of the following:

- I experience things that I view as negative.
- I think about negative things that could occur in the future.
- I think about past negative life events for which I feel regret, guilt, shame, or embarrassment.

"My seventh desired experience is *to be a good person*. It is positive, it uses AND Rules, and *yes*, I do experience it. In order to experience this, I must do all of the following:

- Help my cousin Carl with his house while he is gone.
- Take care of Carl's cat.
- Take my neighbors to the hospital and pick up their mail when they need my help.
- Don't break any laws.
- Be kind, friendly, and courteous.
- Follow the Golden Rule.
- Give people money if they need it.
- Tolerate unpleasant people.
- Be courteous and tolerate smells to which I have a negative physical reaction.
- Be giving.
- Be a good listener."

"Elin," Wes interrupted. "Regarding the last desired experience, you labeled it as positive. It looks like the rules are about being good to others, but for some reason you don't mention yourself. Doesn't being a good person include being good to yourself too? What's more is that these rules aren't good for you. You're letting Carl take advantage of you, and you're taking care of a cat that doesn't belong to you and can survive on its own. Isn't this actually a negative experience disguised as a positive experience? Wouldn't a better name be *sacrifice*?"

Elin thought about this for a bit. "Yes. You're right. I didn't see that."

Wes continued, "This is a case of **intellectual justification**. You are intellectually justifying doing something that is negative by pretending it is positive. You are justifying something that doesn't make sense with a logical reason that appears to make sense. This is part of the complex tricks our mind plays on us. We will talk more about this later. For now, just take note of it. Again, this is normal. I appreciate your honesty.

"Now this negative desired experience of sacrifice has several costs, but it also provides you with benefits and a payoff. How might you benefit by sacrificing, and what is the payoff?"

Elin had to think about this for a moment before she spoke. "The benefit is that it makes me feel good about myself because I'm doing 'good' things and being useful. It also helps me focus on someone else, which distracts me from looking at my life, which isn't going well. By giving much more than anyone else would, I am trying to prove to others that I am worthy. I'm trying to show them that I'm not like those bad people who are selfish and mean. I think the payoff is proving that I'm the good one."

"Well done, Elin. We'll talk more about this tomorrow. You will discover how our habits are often driven by our fears of not belonging. Now do you see any conflicting desired experiences?"

"Let me look at my list." Elin went over it carefully. "Huh. Yes, I see a conflict between wanting companionship and having an unhealthy emotional well-being where I want to isolate and not get close to others. There's a conflict between sacrificing myself for others and wanting to participate in enrichment activities. There's a conflict between sacrificing for others and being financially secure. I could keep on going. I see nothing but conflicts here."

"Agreed. Lots of conflicts. You are trying to go in multiple directions at the same time. Again, this is a common challenge people have. I'm going to help you create a new set of desired experiences that are all aligned and moving in the same direction.

"Elin, please continue with your avoided experiences and rules. For each experience, answer the same three experience questions.

Elin replied, "My first avoided experience is *encountering unpleasant people*. It is negative, it uses OR Rules, and *yes*, I do experience it. I can experience this in any of the following ways:

- Be around a person who is unpleasant, disagreeable, or difficult.
- Meet strangers who become unpleasant because they think I'm weak for being nice to them.
- Think about a person who is unpleasant.

"My second avoided experience is *smelling something environmentally offensive*. Please note that I'm physically sensitive to many smells, and no medicine helps this issue. It is negative, it uses OR Rules, and *yes*, I do experience it. I can experience this in any of the following ways:

- I smell something I am sensitive to.
- I gag from a smell.
- I sneeze, cough, or blow my nose.
- I get a headache from a smell.
- I remember a time when I reacted to a smell.
- I think about an upcoming event where I will have to be around people wearing strong cologne or perfume.

"My third avoided experience is *being socially uncomfortable*. It is negative, it uses OR Rules, and *yes*, I do experience it. I can experience this in any of the following ways:

- I don't know what to do.
- I don't know what to say.
- I'm caught off guard.
- I'm unprepared.
- I don't know how to react to an event or emergency.
- Someone asks me a question I don't want to answer.
- I'm around people I don't know or don't have anything in common with.
- I remember a time when I was socially uncomfortable.
- I think about a future event I have to attend in which I know I'll be uncomfortable.

"My fourth avoided experience is *receiving positive things from others*. Rejecting positive things from others has a negative effect on my life, it uses OR Rules, and *yes*, I do experience it. I can experience this in any of the following ways:

- Someone tries to give me a compliment.
- Someone tries to give me money.
- Someone tries to do something for me.
- Someone tries to help me.
- I remember a time when someone tried to do something for me.
- I think about an upcoming event where people might try to do something nice for me."

"Well done, Elin. I noticed that you didn't mention rejection or failure as avoided experiences. Why is that?"

"That's a good question," Elin replied. "I don't know. I clearly want to avoid rejection and failure. They are definitely negative, have OR rules, and I experience them every day."

"Nothing to worry about. This is quite normal. And it ties in well with what we're going to do tomorrow. I'd like you to notice the patterns in your experiences. Looking at your desired experiences, you achieved all of your negative experiences and none of your positive ones. And you achieved all of your avoided experiences. Said another way, you experienced all of the negative things you wanted and all of the negative things you didn't want, but none of the positive things you wanted. Any idea why this might be happening?"

Elin replied, "I have no idea, but I don't like it, Wes. No wonder I'm so miserable. I sure hope you can help me."

"Absolutely. I will definitely help you with this. Hang in there, Elin. As my mom would tell me when I was a child, 'You're doing great, sweetie!'

"The key takeaway here is that you are creating your own world whether you like it or not. You are consistently achieving all of your negative experiences, which are, in a way, your goals. Again, this is quite common. Your rules make it easy to experience the negative and difficult to experience the positive. We will come back to habits later. You're going to create new empowering habits and a new set of empowering desired and avoided experiences. We'll also revise the rules so you can easily win. Before we can do that, I need you to receive all of the teachings and to become much more aware of yourself. When you have the whole picture, then you'll be able to make more impactful changes.

"There are three new habits I need you to adopt immediately. They are all focused on your body, which is key to helping you make changes in your life. You only get one body, so it's important to be kind to it. Also, everything is connected. By elevating your body, it will help you elevate your mind. By doing something positive for your body, you will help create an upward spiral of habits.

"First, please get enough exercise. A good place to start is exercising for at least twenty minutes, three days per week. You should easily be able to accomplish this with our walks around the mall each morning. When your body is happy and produces endorphins, you will feel better mentally. Second, I know that money is a challenge for you right now, but please do your best to eat healthy, nutritious meals. Your body needs the right fuel in order to perform at its best. Third, please get enough sleep. Your body needs time to repair itself and to allow the brain to process all the new information you are learning. Do you accept my request, Elin?"

"Yes, I do."

"Excellent! That's it for our discussion on habits. Let me tell you, Elin, you did a great job today. Becoming aware of your limiting habits can be very uncomfortable. I appreciate that you continue to be honest and focus on seeing the truth about your life.

"To summarize, what we think, feel, say, and do on a daily basis puts us on a default path that leads us to a default future. We spend most of our day on autopilot. We're hindered by conflicting and limiting habits. We create rules that make it difficult to succeed and easy to fail. We intellectually justify our limiting habits and become stuck. It is crucial that we become aware of our limiting habits and understand that they are keeping us from achieving our desired future. Our habits play off each other; therefore, it is easy to get caught in a downward spiral. Taking some small, positive actions can help us get back on track and eventually create an upward spiral.

"Are you ready for your homework?"

"Yes, sir! What's my homework?"

"Your homework is to make a list of everything you're afraid of and where each fear comes from. Let's meet here again tomorrow at the same time. Any questions?"

"No questions. See you tomorrow, Wes!"

Chapter Seven

Fears

When Elin arrived at the Cinnabon the next day, Wes was already there. He greeted her with a big smile and said, "Good morning, Elin! How are you today?"

Elin replied, "Good morning, Wes. I'm good. How are you doing?"

"I'm feeling absolutely unstoppable!" Wes replied enthusiastically. "There is a lot of information to cover today. Let's get started, shall we?" he said as they began their morning walk around the mall.

"Today we're going to talk about fear. This is the single most important topic we will explore together. It is critical that we understand our specific fears because they drive everything we do. I'm going to simplify this information and present it to you in a different way than you've probably heard it before so that I can make it more impactful for you in the transformation process.

"We have two basic **primal fears:** *death* and *not belonging*. Fear helps us survive each day. It is so important that fear information from our ancestors is automatically passed down to us from generation to generation and stored in our unconscious mind.

"To help you better understand your primal fears, I'm going to use the **Caveman Analogy.** Imagine life fifty thousand years ago. Think of a small group of people, a tribe, consisting of several families, who lived together in a cave. It was incredibly dangerous, and people often didn't live past their twenties.

"As an individual, you had to be smart, alert, and athletic. You spent a lot of your time learning how to survive. Dangers that could inflict instant death included hostile cavemen from other tribes, predators, animal attacks, falling off a cliff, storms, natural disasters, and being swept away in a river. You could die after being compromised due to sickness, injury, infected wounds, loss of mobility, loss of autonomy, or the loss of sight or hearing. A slower death could occur if you were unable to take care of your basic needs like food, water, and shelter.

"As a child, your family was your main source of protection; therefore, it was important to please them and follow their directions. You relied on your parents and older siblings to keep you safe. You didn't want to do anything that would embarrass them or make them look bad. If you weren't part of a family, then you would die. You also didn't want to embarrass your family to the tribe because that could lead to the family getting kicked out. The family needed the tribe for protection and couldn't survive without them.

"As an adult, your partner and children were your responsibility to take care of and protect. Children helped you survive when they became old enough to work. It was also your responsibility to teach them the traditions and proper behavior. What they did reflected upon you and could negatively impact your relationship with your tribe. The tribe protected you and your family from the constant dangers. If you weren't part of a tribe, then you and your family would die.

"This meant that, as an individual, you had to belong to both your family and your tribe, follow their traditions, do what they told you to do, add value, and get along with others. The tribe had to like you, believe you were valuable to them, and trust that you wouldn't cause significant problems. Your recurring question was, 'How do I stay in my family and tribe and avoid being kicked out?'

"Everyone had to protect the tribe from internal and external threats. The tribe affected a lot of people, so saving the tribe was a higher priority than saving an individual. You helped the tribe stay strong physically by having more children, preventing people from leaving, and making sure everyone stayed healthy and safe. You helped the tribe stay strong mentally by educating members on the traditions of the tribe. Everyone needed to respect the hierarchy, follow the chain of command, get along, work hard, follow the rules, and do what they were told. Everyone had to make sure that the tribe could meet its basic needs for food, water, and shelter. Everyone helped the tribe survive external threats by defending it against predators, animal attacks, and other hostile tribes.

"Coming back to modern times, we certainly aren't facing all of the challenges cavemen did, but we inherited their fear information so we can survive today."

Wes gave Elin the following four handouts and went over them with her: *Three Levels of Primal Fear, Belonging Strategies, Tertiary Fears,* and *Fear Factors.*

Three Levels of Primal Fear

We all have **three levels of primal fear:** death of self, not belonging, and death of tribe. All primal fears are **existential fears** because they all lead to our death, whether it is imagined or real. Primal fears are so powerful that we will reorder our life against our nature in order to avoid them, sometimes doing bad things we normally wouldn't do, but which we justify because it is better than dying. Primal fears become powerful beliefs that we unconditionally accept to be true. This handout only covers the first two fear levels.

The first level of primal fear, or **primary fear**, is the fear of dying. We fear death from external things like predators, bad people, and venomous snakes. We fear death if we don't meet our basic needs for food, water, shelter, and money. We fear death caused from getting sick or injured. We also fear death from things we imagine can kill us but actually can't, such as heights, small spaces, clowns, and harmless spiders, mice, snakes, and dogs.

The second level of primal fear, or **secondary fear**, is focused on not belonging to our family, tribe, or group. We can't survive on our own, so not belonging is the same thing as death. Therefore, it is critical that we avoid anything that will cause us to be abandoned or rejected. We avoid failure and anything that could make us feel guilt, shame, or embarrassment. The stronger our fears, the more likely we are to seek out a group where we feel we belong, even if they do bad things.

Secondary Fear Statements

Everyone thinks there is something wrong with them. They think there are reasons why they don't belong, which are called secondary fear statements. For example, if we don't think we are good enough, then our fear is that someone will find out, we will get kicked out of the group, and we will die. The stronger our fears, the more secondary fear statements we usually have.

Examples of secondary fear statements are:
- I'm not good enough.
- I'm not smart enough.
- I'm not attractive enough.
- I'm not strong enough.
- I'm not lovable.
- I'm not worthy.
- I'm worthless.
- I'm useless.
- I don't belong.
- I don't fit in.

Secondary Fear Questions

If you need help identifying which statments apply to you, ask yourself the following questions about the key people in your life today and when you were growing up:
- Whose love did I crave most?
- Who did I have to be for them?
- Who couldn't I be for them?
- What did I have to hide from them?
- What did they criticize me about?

Fear of the Past, Present, and Future

- Guilt and shame are the fear of the past catching up with us *in the present.*
- Panic is the fear that something bad is about to happen *right now.*
- Stress and worry are the fear that something bad will happen *in the future.*

Go to www.WiseLovingBeing.com/handouts
to find a copy of this handout online.

Belonging Strategies

To deal with our secondary fears around not belonging, we employ a combination of four belonging strategies: value, coping, anti-belonging, and independent. This is usually done unconsciously. The stronger our fears, the more belonging strategies we use.

Value Strategies

A value strategy helps prove our value to the group and affirm that we belong. We choose things we are good at and recognized for by others. We say to ourselves, *I'm going to add value to the group by being this kind of person*. We typically have more than one value strategy. Some examples are contained in the following **value strategies list.** Select the ones you use.

Brave	Communicator	Creative
Dependable	Entertainer	Expert
Fit	Follower	Funny
Good	Handsome	Hard Worker
Harmonious	Healer	Helpful
Leader	Loyal	Manager
Nice	Powerful	Pretty
Relationship Builder	Resourceful	Rich
Sexy	Skilled	Smart
Strong	Successful	Supportive
Talented	Teacher	Trusted

Coping Strategies

Coping strategies help us hide our flaws, failures, secrets, and what we think is wrong with us so we won't be rejected by the group. These strategies help us survive, and they sometimes help us deal with our emotional and physical pain. They can also cause us to harm ourselves or do bad things to others, even when we know it is wrong. Sometimes we think it is more important to belong than to do the right thing. We tend to use multiple coping strategies. Some examples of coping strategies and their associated behaviors are contained in the following **coping strategies list**. Select which ones you use.

STRATEGY	BEHAVIOR
Align	Align yourself with someone who is doing well and belongs. They may have wealth, power, or success. You give them whatever they need, even when it is wrong.
Avoid	Avoid failure by never being accountable or responsible for anything. Never commit to anything. Communicate in vague, ambiguous ways. Never do anything directly.
Blame	Blame others and circumstances when things go wrong, even if it is your fault.
Bribe	Give money or something else of value in exchange for their cooperation.
Bully	Control others through physical force, verbal abuse, intimidation, spreading false rumors, sabotage, with-holding something of value, or by threatening to do so.
Collude	Cooperate in a secret, unethical, or unlawful way in order to deceive or take advantage of others.
Conceal	Cover up the faults and mistakes of yourself and others.

STRATEGY	BEHAVIOR
Control	Make all the decisions. Control the members of the group because of your power, position, or through policies, rewards, and punishments.
Criticize	Criticize others and make them look bad while hiding your own flaws.
Escape	Escape your pain and suffering through addiction, bad habits, and other comforting activities that make you feel better temporarily but harm you in the long run.
Fearful	Be consumed by your fears and enroll others in giving you attention and sympathy.
Helpless	Pretend that things are too difficult for you. Get others to do your work for you. Tell them how smart, strong, and talented they are while you act like a cute little puppy dog.
Hopeless	Believe there is something wrong with you. Stay in abusive relationships and bad situations. You believe there is no hope for anything better.
Ideal	Think, look, and act like you are the perfect group member. Keep up with the Joneses.
Invisible	Don't speak up, stand out, or make any decisions. Play small. Only do what you are told. Hope that nobody in authority notices you.
Manipulate	Manipulate others with lies and gaslighting. Tell them that their view of what happened is wrong. They are the problem or are a bad and selfish person who isn't doing the right thing or doing what is normal and acceptable behavior.
Perfectionist	Everything has to be perfect or nothing gets done. Everyone else has to be perfect or they are considered to be bad and should be punished or excluded.

STRATEGY	BEHAVIOR
Pleaser	Make everyone else happy. Always agree, even when you don't. Never say no, even when you should. Do everything that is asked of you, even if you don't have time.
Pretender	Pretend to be beautiful, happy, rich, smart, or successful.
Protectionist	Be the only one who has something, can do something, or knows something. Don't share knowledge, skills, or resources. Only hire people less capable than you.
Punish	Hate, harm, punish, and sabotage yourself. Deprive yourself of food, money, friends, and fun because you don't think you deserve it.
Righteous	You always have to be right and make everyone else look wrong, even when that isn't the case.
Sacrifice	Sacrifice your well-being when it is not for the greater good.
Steal	Take things from others. Take credit for the successes of others.
Submit	Let people walk all over you and abuse you without limitation. Have no boundaries.
Victim	Play the victim card to get others to feel sorry for you. Blame circumstances and others for what happened to you. Tell others that there is no way for you to recover or move forward. You are forever broken.
Wait	Wait for more information. Wait for others: to help, to approve, to give you your next assignment, or to tell you the details needed for a specific task.

Anti-Belonging Strategies

An anti-belonging or rebel strategy helps us avoid being rejected for our faults by rejecting the group first. We rebel to ensure they won't ever ask us to be a member. Sometimes we don't believe we belong or don't feel we deserve to belong; therefore we rebel to force the group to reject us to confirm our belief. You rebel when you do things that aren't aligned with the group's identity; you act, look, speak, and think differently. You have different beliefs. You might purposely get into trouble with the group, such as destroying or vandalizing their property.

Independent Strategies

An independent strategy helps us avoid the negative aspects of group membership without being labeled by the group as an outsider. There is a balance here. You don't openly oppose the group. However, you follow your own rules, have your own beliefs, and walk your own path. You sometimes work with the group when your interests are aligned, but you don't need the group to survive.

Go to www.WiseLovingBeing.com/handouts
to find a copy of this handout online.

Tertiary Fears

The third level of primal fear, or **tertiary fear**, is the fear of the death of your tribe or group.

The **characteristics of a group** are as follows:
- We think alike.
- We act alike.
- We have shared beliefs, known as **tertiary beliefs**.
- We look alike.
- We speak alike.
- We come from the same place.
- We have had similar experiences.
- We participate in similar activities.
- We have common interests.

The following are current examples of groups that are formed by the **commonalities** of their members:
- Company, department, or team
- Family Heritage
- Gang
- Ideology: Democrats vs. Republicans, abortion vs. pro-life, same sex marriage vs. traditional marriage
- Nation
- Race
- Region
- Religion
- School
- Socioeconomic status: white collar vs. blue collar

Limiting Tertiary Beliefs

Limiting tertiary beliefs that are created about the members of our group and the outsiders are always **binary beliefs**, which are polar opposites. Some examples are:

US	THEM
We're good, smart, and right.	They're bad, stupid, and wrong.
We're the chosen ones.	They're rejected and excluded.
We're important.	They don't matter.
We belong.	They don't belong.
We're lovable.	They're unlovable.
We're human.	They're subhuman.

False Tertiary Beliefs

Sometimes a tribe will create false beliefs in order to present a better image, hide its flaws, and retain and control its members. The tribe leadership uses its position and authority to manipulate its members through fear, punishment, and the promise of substantial rewards and penalties. Being a good, loyal member of the tribe means accepting these beliefs without question. In this way, the tribe that is supposed to protect its members actually harms them. Cults are famous for this, but many other groups and organizations do this to varying degrees. It is much more common than people think.

Limiting and false tertiary beliefs have been used to justify the following **tertiary fear actions**: censorship, discrimination, crime, ethnic cleansing, genocide, human trafficking, injustice, invasion, murder, prejudice, racism, segregation, slavery, subjugation, terrorism, torture, and war.

Tertiary Fear Benefits

Tertiary fears benefit the members of the group in two ways. The first is belonging. If the outsiders are labeled as bad, stupid, wrong, not chosen, and subhuman, then the opposite is also true. The group members belong. They are chosen, important, human, lovable, and right. They are good enough and smart enough. If the members of the group are looking outside at a common enemy, then they don't have time to look at themselves and each other. They belong because they are unified in their hate. By exaggerating the negative aspects of the outsiders, they also exaggerate their belonging. The more they hate the outsiders, the more they feel they belong. We often see this kind of messaging in the news when they say there is some sort of huge catastrophe about to happen because of an outside group. This causes the tribe to spiral out of control and focus their anger and fear on the outsiders. It sometimes leads members of the tribe to do bad things to the outsiders that they normally would not do.

The second benefit of tertiary fears is around responsibility. When outsiders are blamed for a group's problems, the group doesn't have to take responsibility for how they contributed to the problem. They also don't need to take ownership for fixing the problem or finding a solution. The bigger the problems, the more motivated the group members are to blame the outsiders and frame them as the sole cause of the group's problems.

Labels

We like to use labels when referring to different outside groups. For example, old people, young people, Republicans, Democrats, millennials, and baby boomers. The label saves us time by becoming a shorthand way to describe its stereotypical members and the common ways they think and act. But very few members of a group fit the stereotype exactly. Unfortunately, labels are a form of prejudice and are also inaccurate. We usually learn these labels and their meanings from others, or we create ones based on our limited interactions with a few members of the group. When labels are used, they often have a negative meaning. What is even worse is that they are often a historical summation of all the negative actions done by a few members of the group, conveniently omitting any positive contributions from the vast majority of the other members. In contrast, the label we use for our own group is positive, highlights our many contributions, and emphasizes how perfect we are.

Tertiary Fear Reality

The reality today, of course, is that we are all much more alike than we are different, somewhere north of ninety-five percent alike. We share the same primary fears and fundamental needs. We share the same secondary fears. We all want to provide for ourselves and our families. We all want to stay safe and protect the people we love. We all want to be treated fairly and equally. We all want to be free to make our own decisions. Tertiary fears are almost always false.

Go to www.WiseLovingBeing.com/handouts
to find a copy of this handout online.

Fear Factors

Human beings have learned to rely on eight **fear factors** in order to improve their chances of survival. These fear factors are inherent in our thinking and influence our behaviors. The higher our level of fear, the more we rely on these fear factors. However, these beneficial fear factors also come with harmful side effects. The fear factors are as follows:

Certainty

We want to be 100 percent certain about what will happen.

- **Pro:** We think about all the possible problems that could occur in the future, and we think about everything we can do to mitigate them.
- **Con:** Instead of being present in the moment, we often spend time thinking about unimportant things that are unlikely to happen and will have a minimal impact if they do.

Consistency

We want to do things the same way we have always done them.

- **Pro:** Being consistent means we will get the same good results we always have.
- **Con:** This doesn't allow us to adapt and evolve, especially for the big changes coming. Think Blockbuster, Kodak, and Toys "R" Us and how their business plans eventually failed them because they refused to change with the times.

Control

We try to control ourselves, others, and our environment.

- **Pro:** When we are in control of what happens to us now and in the future, then we will survive.
- **Con:** We often try to control things we can't. Sometimes when we attempt to control another person it actually has a negative effect on both parties. For example, a parent trying to control a teenager can push them into the very situation they were hoping to prevent.

Familiar Bias

We want to stay around things we are familiar with.

- **Pro:** Being around familiar things makes us feel safe. Things we are not familiar with could be dangerous.
- **Con:** We aren't open to trying something new. We stay in familiar situations that are bad for us. This partially explains why people will stay in bad relationships instead of moving on.

Negativity

We focus on the negative things that have happened to us and that are happening around us.

- **Pro:** Negative things can harm us. We want to know how to protect ourselves from similar events. This is one reason why we watch negative news.
- **Con:** We think good things won't hurt us and therefore don't pay much attention to them. We have a hard time seeing bad things disguised as something good that could potentially harm us. Think about those people who pretended to be good populist leaders who became evil dictators.

Scarcity

We believe there are a limited number of resources or opportunities. We fear that if we don't get them, someone else will take them, resulting in our death.

- **Pro:** We ensure our survival by fighting for whatever resources we find, keeping what we have, and never throwing anything away.
- **Con:** We stop thinking about new ways of doing things that eliminate scarcity. We will destroy the very thing we all need. Think back on the COVID-19 pandemic. There were plenty of supplies for everyone until people started hoarding toilet paper, food, and cleaning products.

Urgency

We focus on things we fear can harm us now instead of those things that might harm us in the future.

- **Pro:** By focusing on urgent things now, we can live to see another day.
- **Con:** Sometimes urgent things are unimportant and distract us from the big, harmful things that are fast approaching.

Variety

We want to have multiple ways of accomplishing something in case one of our other methods fails.

- **Pro:** Variety reduces our risk when our one and only way doesn't work out. This is also known as diversification.
- **Con:** Over-diversification often leads to worse results due to the increased costs of managing so many different things. Instead of reducing risk, it increases the likelihood of us not achieving our goals.

Go to www.WiseLovingBeing.com/handouts
to find a copy of this handout online.

"Elin, I know that was a lot of information to absorb. Let me give you an example so we can start to bring this information to life. My friend Kevin grew up with a single mother who wanted him to do well in school. He was supposed to do his homework when he got home, and his mom would then review it when she came home from work. If he got something wrong that she thought he should have gotten right, she would criticize him. Kevin's older sister did well in school, and his mom compared them often. He stopped doing homework when he got home and watched TV instead. When his mom came home, she would yell at him for not doing his homework, and then she would help him do it. Quite often, she ended up doing most of his homework for him. Kevin tried the same technique at school. He did the bare minimum and received very low grades. His teachers weren't happy with him, but they always helped him and passed him on to the next grade level.

"Kevin had made the following connections in his mind: *If I try to do my homework, then I will make mistakes. If I make mistakes, then I will get yelled at. If I get yelled at, then I'm not worthy. If I'm not worthy, then I'm not lovable. If I'm not lovable, then I will get kicked out of my family. And if I get kicked out of my family, then I will die.* In short, *if I try, I'll die.* His fear was even stronger since he had witnessed his mother kick his father out of the house. To Kevin, the threat of being kicked out of the family was very real.

"This fear of not belonging was focused on his mother. But there was another one that was focused on his sister who was five years older and took care of him when their mother was gone. Kevin made the following connections: *My sister won't protect me if I make her look bad. If I get good grades then my sister won't be special. My sister might get kicked out of the family or she might get upset with me. My sister will stop protecting me.* In short, *if I get good grades, I'll die.*

104

"Kevin used eight coping strategies very effectively: *align, avoid, escape, invisible, helpless, perfectionist, punish*, and *wait*. He aligned himself with his sister and tried to be like her. When she decided she wanted to write books, he aspired to be a novelist too. Unfortunately in the process he lost sight of who he was. Interestingly enough, one of his value strategies with his friends was *expert*. He knew more than any of them did about computer games, Pokémon, anime, and English. He even reviewed all of their papers and helped them get As in school.

"Kevin used anti-belonging strategies with his mom, albeit unconsciously. He didn't do what she asked him to do, purposely got in trouble, acted out, and was open about his hatred for her. This only made things worse for him, but he unconsciously felt better when he got into trouble and lost his privileges. He was in control and things were familiar. He was proving that he was unlovable and unworthy.

"When Kevin graduated from high school, his friends went on to college while he got a job at a fast-food restaurant. He wanted to be a great writer, but he rarely wrote. He wanted to be an English major at a university, but he didn't have the grades to get accepted to a school. He was stuck.

"Kevin had many fears: he wouldn't be able to make a living, get a girlfriend, have a family, or have a writing career. He'd be a failure, homeless, lonely, and endure serious health issues. His secondary fear statements were, *I'm not lovable; I'm worthless; I'm not smart enough; I'm not attractive enough;* and *I'm not good enough*. He used the fear factors of *certainty, consistency, control*, and *familiar bias* to lock himself into a predictable upbringing; unfortunately, they set him up poorly for being an independent, successful adult.

"Kevin is a very smart, kind, and caring person with a great sense of humor and lots of potential. I helped him understand what was happening, and he was able to make several small changes that made a big difference. He now has a good relationship with his mother, is actively working on his book, has a higher-paying corporate job, and has found his own way in life.

"Elin, let's start the process of applying this information to your life. What are your *primary fears* or survival fears?" Wes asked.

"I'm afraid of flying, becoming homeless, and dying without someone knowing," Elin replied.

"Flying and being homeless are quite different levels of fear, but both are important to acknowledge. I do have a question about your last fear. I don't think this can be a survival fear because you would already be dead when this happens. I think this is a secondary fear around not belonging. The people who take care of things after you die are your *loved ones*. This is really a secondary fear that says, *I'm not lovable*. Does that make sense?"

"Yes, that makes sense," Elin agreed.

"What are your *secondary fear statements* around not belonging?"

"I have several secondary fear statements," Elin offered. "They are:

- I'm not lovable.
- I'm not good enough.
- I'm not smart enough.
- I'm not worthy.
- I'm an outsider and don't fit in."

"What are your *value strategies* from the list on the handout?"

Elin perked up at this question. "My value strategies are follower, funny, good, hard worker, harmonious, helpful, nice, smart, and supportive."

"What are your *coping strategies* from the list on the handout?"

"My coping strategies are *conceal, escape, helpless, hopeless, invisible, perfectionist, pleaser, punish,* and *sacrifice.*"

"Besides playing computer games and watching TV, what other escape activities, addictions, negative habits, or comforting activities do you engage in?"

"I sometimes eat potato chips and drink soda to help me feel better," Elin confessed. "I physically escape through isolation. I stay at home and avoid other people because they make me feel bad about myself."

"What do you do to punish yourself?"

Elin sighed. "I live in a city where I hate the extremely hot summer weather that lasts at least four months. I live in a small, rundown apartment in a declining part of town where I don't feel safe. I deny myself fun, food, and friendship. I don't do anything to improve my financial situation, and I don't ask for help. That ensures that I continue to be punished. Up until I met you, I didn't exercise or do things to be healthier."

"Do you have any *anti-belonging or independent strategies?*"

"I don't have any anti-belonging strategies. I'm more of a follower than a rebel. I do feel that I use some independent strategies. I either avoid or withdraw from situations where I don't feel I have much in common with others. I don't regularly interact with any groups."

"Now let's look at your *limiting tertiary beliefs*," Wes said. "Think about the main outside groups you complain about. What do you have in common with them?"

Elin replied, "I have the following things in common with them: we're human beings, we're Americans, we have a right to our opinions, we want to make enough money to take care of ourselves and our loved ones, and we want to protect our fundamental rights, including the ability to make our own decisions."

"Related to fears are stress and worry. What do you *worry* about, Elin? What are you *stressed* out about? What keeps you up at night? Where do you feel *overwhelmed?*"

Elin sighed again. "I am worried and stressed out about the following: facing adversity alone, dealing with difficult people that I must interact with every day, having enough food to eat, and being homeless."

"What fear factors do you use on a consistent basis, and how do they affect your goal of financial security?"

"I use *certainty, consistency, control, familiar bias, scarcity,* and *negativity*. This keeps me from having financial security. It seems strange that my fear factors keep me stuck."

"That's a great observation," Wes said encouragingly. "Fear factors can help you, but they can also limit you. Your survival fears are keeping you in a very familiar place that has allowed you to survive all these years. Unfortunately, you view trying new things to improve your financial security as an even bigger threat to your survival. Don't worry. This is more common than you might think, and it is something I'm going to help you with.

"Yesterday we talked about the payoff you receive from your desired experience of sacrifice. It is directly related to your secondary fears. Your secondary fear statements are beliefs, and two of them state that you aren't worthy or lovable. In your coping strategies you listed *punish* and *sacrifice*. This adds two more beliefs: *because you are unlovable and unworthy, you must be punished*, and *the only way to be lovable and worthy is to sacrifice*. Translating this in terms of your survival fears, if you don't punish yourself and sacrifice yourself for others, then you'll die. Even though you don't want to experience the pain and suffering from punishing yourself and sacrificing for others, you do it willingly because it's much better than dying. Does that make sense?"

Elin replied, "Yes, that makes sense. What's even more interesting to me is that I do this without even thinking about it rationally. That doesn't make logical sense."

"Fears are funny that way, and that's why they're so powerful. I'm going to show you how to overcome them soon, but for now, it's enough to be aware that it is happening.

"There's one last thing: **recurring questions**. These are questions we often ask ourselves or others. They are based on our fears and are often focused on the worst-case scenario and regularly lead to stress and even panic. They cause us to change how we behave, to develop bad habits, and sometimes to do things we otherwise wouldn't do.

"For example, my friend Frank was a single parent with three small kids. There was no one around to help him. He lost his job, and there wasn't enough money to pay for food and his small apartment. He was terrified of not being able to feed his kids. He struggled to keep jobs because he was honest and spoke his mind. Some of his managers didn't like that and either fired him or forced him to quit. Frank made the following connections in his mind: *Expressing myself means losing my job, which means having no food to eat, which means starving to death.* In short, *If I express myself, I'll die.*

"One of the recurring questions Frank asked almost every day was, *How am I going to get through today without saying something that gets me fired?* This led him to stay quiet in meetings and contribute much less than he was capable of. After some hard work, he was able to get rid of his fear. He replaced his recurring question with a new empowering one: *How can I use even more of my God-given talents and freely express myself in order to make things better?* I also taught him some more effective ways to communicate his ideas so they would be better received. He began to contribute and added significant value to his employer, which made them both much happier.

"Elin, do you have any recurring questions?"

Elin replied, "I have the following recurring questions:
- How am I going to survive today?
- How am I going to survive to the end of my life?
- What's going to go wrong today?
- What bad things are going to happen to me today?"

"Regarding our discussion today as a whole, how would you summarize how fear keeps you from achieving your goal of financial security?" Wes asked.

Elin took a minute to think. "Well, there's quite a bit actually. Pretty much everything, if I'm really being honest. My primary and secondary fears are unhealthy. My value strategies are limiting. My coping strategies are harmful. My tertiary fears and labels are keeping me from connecting with others. I have a fear of not having enough money to survive but I have an even bigger hidden fear to try to do anything to improve my situation."

"Great work, Elin! We'll come back to this later and turn your unhealthy fears into strengths.

"To summarize, our primal fears drive everything we do. They are so powerful that we will do anything to avoid them, sometimes doing things we wouldn't normally do because it seems better than 'dying.' We use multiple value, coping, anti-belonging, and independent strategies to ensure we belong. Our fears of outsiders and the labels we use aren't aligned with how things really are. We use several of the eight fear factors to improve our likelihood of survival, but there are sometimes harmful side effects. Our recurring questions are based on our fears and drive our behavior. Some fears are healthy, but most of them are harmful and limit us.

"So that's all for today. Are you ready for your homework?"

"Yes, sir! What's my homework?"

"Please make a list of the significant events and experiences in your life. Two examples from your life, of course, are your dad dying and your move from Florida to Colorado. Put them in chronological order. Then for each item on your list, answer the following questions:

1. What do you think happened?
2. What did the other people see, think, feel, say, and do? What were their intentions?
3. What actually happened? What are the facts?
4. What survival and belonging fears were involved?
5. What did you decide about yourself and the world because of this event?

6. How did these new beliefs affect your life?

7. What have you been trying to prove to others since this event? Are you trying to prove that they are wrong or right?

8. What good and bad things resulted from this event, and as life went on?

9. What limiting beliefs do you need to delete? What empowering beliefs do you need to create?

"Let's meet here again tomorrow at the same time. Any questions?"

"No questions. See you tomorrow, Wes!"

Chapter Eight

Significant Events

When Elin arrived at the Cinnabon the next day, Wes was already there. He greeted her with a big smile and said, "Good morning, Elin! How are you today?"

Elin replied, "Good morning, Wes. I'm good. How are you doing?"

"I'm fantastic!" Wes replied enthusiastically. "Let's get started, shall we?" he said as they began their morning walk around the mall.

"Today we're going to talk about significant events which are the defining moments in our lives. They are linked to our primal fears and become an integral part of our autopilot. I'm going to simplify this information and present it to you in a different way than you've probably heard before so that I can make it more impactful for you in the transformation process."

Wes gave Elin a handout titled *Significant Events* and went over it with her.

Significant Events

Significant events are the key experiences in our lives that shape us and, in some ways, define us. Most of these events occur when we are children, but they can occur at any age. They are tied to our primal fears of survival and not belonging. These events can be seemingly mild, or they can be painful and traumatic. It is not necessarily the event itself; it is what we think about the event that matters. When we are younger, our fears are heightened because we are more vulnerable and less knowledgeable about how the world works.

We, of course, want to keep these negative events from happening again, so three things happen: our conscious mind makes a decision about ourselves and the world; our unconscious mind takes this information and stores it in the form of beliefs; and our unconscious mind stores an automatic reaction. Our unconscious mind adds this to our autopilot since it wants to keep us safe, and it wants us to avoid the pain from thinking about this consciously every day.

Sometimes we do not recognize that a significant event occurred until later in life when we become aware of the effects the created beliefs have had on us. Sometimes, a **negative pattern** develops where we repeat similar experiences with different people, and each time the pain and suffering becomes worse.

Sometimes there is not one specific event we can point to, but we become aware that something has happened. This **significant experience** is more likely to happen when we are too young to remember the actual events. We still make a decision, create a belief, and store an automatic reaction as if a specific event occurred. We only become aware of the belief and the automatic reaction as we get older.

Significant Event Perspective

We have a unique perspective of each significant event that is usually different than that of the other participants. We do not know the full story. We only know what we think we saw from our perspective. Unfortunately, our memories are inherently flawed. They are not perfect recordings but must be reconstructed from different areas of the brain. We might think we know for sure what happened; unfortunately, there is always a certain amount of error, which increases over time.

Our perspective of a significant event can also be something that never actually happened. We can draw false conclusions, think we saw something that wasn't there, and add meaning that isn't true. Labels, stereotypes, and prejudice can influence our thinking too. It is easy to create a false narrative. We might change our perspective after speaking with someone we trust or who is in a position of authority and tells us something different. In this way, we throw out what we believe to be true and replace it with something else. False perspectives can also be created when we are intentionally manipulated and lied to by others.

The bottom line is this: Our perspective of what happened will override what actually occurred. We will believe that we are right and everyone else is wrong. In order to see the truth, we have to have an open mind and objectively revisit what happened with people we can trust.

Significant Event Questions

To understand the full impact a significant event has had on our life, we need to ask ourselves the following nine significant event questions:

1. What is my perspective of what happened?
2. What did the other people see, think, feel, say, and do? What were their intentions?
3. What actually happened? What are the facts?
4. What survival and belonging fears were involved?
5. What did I decide about myself and the world because of this event?
6. How did these new beliefs affect my life?
7. What have I been trying to prove to others since this event? Am I trying to prove that they are right or wrong?
8. What good and bad things resulted from this event, and as life went on?
9. What limiting beliefs do I need to delete? What empowering beliefs do I need to create?

Go to www.WiseLovingBeing.com/handouts
to find a copy of this handout online.

"Elin, I know this can be a very uncomfortable exercise. Some of these significant events will be very difficult for you to talk about, especially those you regard as your deepest and darkest secrets. Emotions will surface that you don't want to feel. You may feel embarrassed or be concerned that what you say will in some way make me think less of you. Your fears of not belonging will be active and intense. You might even be afraid that I will reject you. In short, you will most certainly feel that *disclosure is death*.

"I can assure you that you are not going to die because of this exercise. There is nothing you can say to me that will make me feel differently about you. I know you much better than you think. I will definitely not reject you. You belong here. You are good enough. You are smart enough. You are lovable. Nothing you say can change that.

"This is an incredibly important exercise that must be done in order for you to move forward and heal. Awareness and honesty are critical. Everything you say to me will be kept in strict confidence. I will never disclose what you tell me to anyone else.

"Does that make sense?"

Elin nodded, but it was clear that she was uncomfortable with the exercise.

"There are two important concepts that will make this exercise easier for you. The first is **The Perfect Human**. You are perfectly human. You're no different than anyone else. Every human has significant events, successes, failures, secrets, fears, and flaws. Being human isn't easy. Humans are imperfect and make lots of mistakes. A perfect human is perfectly imperfect. As the saying goes, 'If you aren't making mistakes, then you aren't alive.'

"The **Flamingo Analogy** will help make this clearer for you. Visualize a lagoon filled with a million flamingos. They're so pretty, aren't they? As you look at them, you only see flamingos doing what flamingos do. You don't see good flamingos or bad flamingos. All you see are a million perfect flamingos.

"Similarly, you are a perfect human. You are no better or worse than any other human. All humans do what humans do. All humans are just trying to do their best. They make mistakes and then try to learn from their mistakes. Everyone has things that are going well and things they wish were going better. Everyone is imperfect. In this way, *a perfect human is wonderfully imperfect.*

"The second important concept is the Wise Loving Being. For the purposes of this exercise, I want you to pretend that I am a Wise Loving Being."

Wes gave Elin a handout titled *Wise Loving Being* and went over it with her.

Wise Loving Being

A **Wise Loving Being** (WLB) combines the ideal masculine and feminine love into a single, highly intelligent being. You can think of a WLB as someone who treats you with unconditional love and kindness. It is also a great way to treat yourself and others. A WLB would tell you the following about itself:

- I am very wise.
- I am very loving and good.
- I am a powerful creator.
- I am selfless and focused on helping you.
- I know everything about you, including all your secrets.
- I think you are perfectly human.
- I provide unconditional and unlimited love, patience, respect, understanding, acceptance, appreciation, kindness, and forgiveness.
- I am always genuinely positive.
- I am very generous.
- I see your true potential.
- I celebrate your successes and reward you for doing your best.
- I comfort you and help you learn from your failures.
- I never criticize, condemn, complain, or judge you.
- I never reject you.
- I always think you are good enough, smart enough, and lovable.
- I always help you feel like you belong.
- I give you what you need, but not necessarily what you want.
- I have your best interests at heart.
- I want to see you win.
- I love you very much.

Go to www.WiseLovingBeing.com/handouts
to find a copy of this handout online.

"Elin, let me provide you with an example of a significant event story. When my friend Jim was a child, he craved his parents' love. However, his father was not around much. When he was, he criticized Jim, often calling him lazy and stupid. He never spent much time or played catch with Jim like the other fathers did with their sons. Jim felt that his father didn't approve of him. He tried everything to change himself in order to make his father proud of him, but nothing was ever good enough. Jim was rejected by his father and felt unlovable and unworthy.

"Jim's mother was very loving and kind to him. He naturally clung to her and tried to live up to her high expectations. She often said, 'Do it right or don't do it at all.' But Jim sometimes made mistakes and got into trouble. Once, his mother discovered that he stole a softball from his elementary school. Another time, she caught him lying after he destroyed the shower curtain and blamed it on the cat. His teacher caught him cheating on a test and told his mother. Each time, Jim's mother told him that she was very disappointed with him. Because he was sensitive to all the criticism from his father, Jim amplified what his mother said. He hadn't just made a mistake; he had let her down. Therefore he was no longer worthy of her love.

"As a result of these significant events, Jim created the following secondary fears: *I'm not lovable, I'm not good enough*, and *I'm not worthy*. He decided that bad people would lie, cheat, and steal. Bad people were also lazy and stupid. He decided to prove that *he was the good one*.

"Although he was trying to be better, these decisions unfortunately had a detrimental effect on his life, and negative patterns soon developed. Jim worked very hard as an adult. He tried to be smart, perfect, and do the right thing. He often encountered people who did bad things, and he labeled them as bad people. He criticized them and called them out. Wherever he went, he seemed to be able to find these bad people. As you can imagine, since nobody is perfect, he had labeled almost everyone around him as bad. He had no friends and didn't get along with many people at work. Unconsciously, he had labeled himself as bad too.

"As time went on, Jim thought he could detect bad people quickly and easily. Unfortunately, he was about to discover a string of folks who pretended to be good but were a whole new level of bad. By the time he figured out what was going on, they had destroyed his life. He ended up with no friends, no money, and in terrible emotional and physical health.

"I helped Jim understand why he did the things he did. He realized he needed to stop trying to prove that he was the good one, stop trying to be perfect, and accept himself and others as they were: perfectly human. He needed to accept the fact that everyone is free to make their own choices, and all choices have positive and negative consequences. He decided that he still wanted to avoid what he called 'bad activities.' He also wanted to help others do better. But first, he had to commit to being wiser and more loving. The bigger challenge, though, was accepting that he was lovable and worthy, which had a profound effect on improving all areas of his life.

"Let me tell you one more story. My friend Barry was living his dream life with his wife and three young daughters. He worked long hours and was a good provider. Out of the blue, his wife decided to divorce him and received full custody of their children. This included him paying generous alimony and child support payments. In order to keep the children from wanting to see him, she then manipulated them into thinking that their father was a bad man who did bad things. It worked, and he lost contact with them. After they became adults, only one daughter went looking for the truth. It was a critical first step in the healing process for both of them.

"Elin, please go through your significant events in chronological order, one at a time, and answer the significant event questions."

Elin smiled nervously and said, "I have two significant events. The first one happened during the summer when I was nine years old. I was sent off to camp while my dad took my three older sisters to Colorado. He had to work and couldn't take care of me because I was too young. My mom went on vacation with her friend, and my brother went to Boy Scout camp. I cried every day at camp, and my mom had to cancel her plans to come pick me up after only two days.

"The secondary fears I had were *I'm not lovable*, and *I'm not worthy*. When my mom had to come pick me up, I felt guilty about causing problems and ruining her plans. That added to my secondary fears. As a result, I lost my self-confidence and became anxious and fearful. I would physically hang onto my parents all the time. Ever since, I've been acting anxious and fearful so I can get attention and love from my parents, siblings, and others.

"The good things that came out of it were that my parents supported me and gave me attention. The bad thing that happened was that it started my secondary fears of not belonging. I even invented a story that I wasn't related to my family: *I was either adopted or switched at birth*. I need to delete all of my beliefs around this event and replace them with *I am lovable, I am worthy*, and *I belong*.

"My clingy behavior from this significant event created two other limiting beliefs: *I'm bothering others*, and *I don't have anything of value to contribute*. I'd like to replace these beliefs with this new empowering belief: *I make valuable contributions to others*.

"My second significant event happened a few months later in December after I turned ten. My dad died. I didn't understand what had happened. I just thought he went away. At the memorial service, my relatives didn't hug me, but they hugged my mom and older siblings. This was probably because I was too young. I don't think it was intentional. But I did feel rejected and abandoned. I felt like *I wasn't lovable* and *I wasn't worthy*. I again felt like *I didn't belong*. I think that's why I moved around a lot as an adult. Whenever I felt like I didn't fit in, I would move to a new city, hoping I would find a place where I truly belonged.

"As a result of this event, I felt insecure. I was very close to my father, but he was no longer around to provide love, attention, and stability. I naively believed that my dad was still alive but living in a different city. Every time we would visit a new town, I'd check the phone book to see if he was listed.

"The good things that came out of this event? My teacher was very kind to me, and so were my friends and family. The bad things are obviously that I lost the person I was closest to, I lost a parent, I lost stability, and I lost my self-confidence."

"Nicely done," Wes said. He paused for a moment and then added, "Elin, do you remember when we were talking about your beliefs around money, and you told me you believed you couldn't do basic things, including operating a cash register at a fast-food restaurant? I think the underlying belief is that you just aren't a math person. What significant event was involved in creating that belief?"

"Well it's true," Elin replied animatedly. "I'm not a math person. When I was in third grade, I had to switch schools. We didn't move, but the school district redrew the boundaries, and I had to transfer to a new school across town where I didn't have any friends. On my first day, the teacher asked me to use a ruler in a math problem. I was never taught how to read all the lines on the ruler, but all the other kids knew. They laughed at me, and I felt embarrassed and stupid. My teacher never offered to help me learn this skill and was generally not supportive of me afterward. Working at a cash register requires me to ring up the cost of items and then give back correct change. This requires math, and I can't do it under pressure. I would just freeze."

"So you believe you are not a math person and you can't learn math. Interesting. This is a lot more common than you realize. There is a widely accepted belief that you are either born a logical person or a creative person. You are either left-brained or right-brained. You can either do math or you can't. This is unfortunate because it is absolutely not true. People might have different interests and motivations, but everyone has the same ability to learn a new skill. Everyone is a math person. Everyone can learn math. You just need a good teacher and the right method. This false belief typically comes true as a result of a bad experience with math like you had. I'll bet you didn't have this belief when you were in second grade, did you?"

"No, I didn't have any problems with math in either first or second grade," Elin replied reflectively. "As a matter of fact, I think I did pretty well on my math tests."

"What makes this such a strong fear for you is that you were kicked out of your school, your first tribe, and sent to another school or new tribe. You were then basically kicked out of that tribe on your first day. The only way for you to survive was to never make a mistake again, to never do math. In your mind, *math is death*. So how do you think this event affected your life?"

"Well, it kept me from doing any job that involved math. It also stopped me from learning more about managing my finances, and that has obviously been a disaster."

"What's interesting is that you are more motivated by logical activities, aren't you?"

"Yes, I am," Elin agreed. "I love editing. I love to fix grammar and spelling errors. I've done this at several jobs, and I even helped my niece edit a few things she has worked on over the years."

"What new beliefs do you need to create now, Elin?"

"*I can learn anything I want to learn. I am a math person. I am smart enough to work at any company. I am smart enough to work at McDonald's.*"

"I love them! Great job, Elin! When we were talking about your habits, do you remember your third avoided experience of *being socially uncomfortable*, where you didn't know what to say or do? Where do you think that comes from?"

"Do you think it's related to this same significant event?" Elin asked.

"I do. I think when you are in an uncomfortable social situation, your eight-year-old self comes out and you freeze. After all, to this little girl, *talking is death*. Your survival mind probably takes over and produces the freeze response, shuts off your conscious mind, and makes it impossible for you to engage in a rational conversation. It is important to understand where your behavior comes from and why you react the way you do. Don't worry. This is something we can address later on."

"Sounds great, Wes. I can't wait!"

"So, Elin, you gave me three significant events today, and there are still more that you'll discover as time goes on. It's amazing how they can continue to stay hidden. Whenever you remember a new one, just answer all the questions. Sound good?" Wes asked positively.

"Yes. Will do, Wes!" Elin replied with a smile, relieved that this exercise was over. It was difficult, and she felt good about getting through it.

Wes took some time to think about what he was going to say next. He then looked at her and said, "I think the most important personality trait a person can have is **courage**. Courage means feeling the fear and doing it anyway. I love the quote from Brené Brown, 'Today, I will choose courage over comfort.' Without courage, we can't confront the truth. The truth always sets us free. Embracing the truth is required to heal. Taking the courage to act changes our lives significantly. Courage is critical. Do you agree with me, Elin?"

"Yes. I agree. Absolutely."

"Then please be courageous now, Elin. You didn't tell me about all the significant events you actually remember, did you? It is critical that you do this so you can heal. You've got to trust me on this. Please show me how courageous you are."

Elin pretended she didn't know what Wes was talking about and remained stoically silent.

Wes leaned closer to Elin and in a serious but supportive voice said, "You know what I'm talking about, Elin. Tell me what happened when you were seventeen."

Elin looked at Wes in shock, and tears began to roll down her face. Speechless, she put her head down and covered her face with her hand as she continued to cry. There were a lot of emotions connected to that year that she hadn't dealt with. In her mind, those emotions were unresolvable. She had stuffed them deep down and triple locked them so they couldn't get out. She didn't like to think about that year, and she definitely wasn't prepared to speak about it.

Thoughts ran through Elin's mind. How could Wes have known about this? Only a handful of people actually knew, and most of them were now dead. This was her deepest and darkest secret. She had never even told her closest friends about this. Wes was a stranger. How could he expect her to tell *him*? And to speak about this in public? No way!

Wes handed Elin his handkerchief. She gratefully accepted it, drying her tears and blowing her nose. It took her a couple of minutes to compose herself. But before she answered his question, she had a couple of her own.

"How do you know about that, Wes? There are only two people alive who know, and they're sworn to secrecy. Who are you again?"

Wes smiled and in a caring voice said, "It's difficult to explain in terms you would understand. It's really not that important in the context of what we're doing today. Besides, I've already told you everything you need to know. As I mentioned earlier today, you can think of me as your Wise Loving Being. I'm here to help you live a better life. I have your best interests at heart. You can trust me."

"Well, you're right, Wes. I don't understand. And I guess I don't need to in order for us to work together. You've been very helpful, and for some reason I do feel like I can trust you."

Elin paused and tried to compose herself. "Yes, I did leave out an entire year of my life. It was a very difficult and scary time for me. It seemed like significant events happened to me almost every day. I feel so much regret and guilt and shame over what happened that year. It has affected my life so much. Yes, you're right. It needs to be dealt with if I'm truly going to heal.

"Here are some of the major things that happened to me when I was seventeen:

- I got pregnant.
- My boyfriend no longer cared about me and didn't want to marry me.
- Our parents forced us to get married to give the child a name.
- I had to hide my pregnancy by moving to another city.
- I couldn't talk to any of my friends or do anything with them.
- I couldn't participate in all the fun events for high school seniors, including my prom.
- Almost everyone told me to give my child up for adoption. My brother was the only person who said he would support me if I decided to keep my child.
- My uncle died, and I couldn't attend his funeral because I was showing.
- I gave birth.
- I decided to put him up for adoption.
- I had to go to court to do the relinquishment. The judge wasn't very nice and chastised me in front of everyone.
- I filed for divorce soon after I gave birth.

- I had to go to court again for the divorce. A different judge chastised me in front of everyone.
- My ex-husband married someone else soon after our divorce was final.
- My grandpa died.
- I tried to redeem myself by becoming a nurse, but I quit the program after nine months.
- I moved to California to escape everything.

"In the long term, my primary fear was that I wouldn't be able to find a man who would marry and take care of me. I would be poor and would struggle to meet my basic survival needs.

"My secondary fear statements were: *I'm not good enough*, *I'm not lovable*, *I'm not worthy*, and *I don't belong*.

"I decided the following things about myself and the world:

- I was meant to be poor and struggle for my basic needs.
- I would never have more children or get married again.
- All men will abandon me.
- My son probably ended up in a bad home and is living an awful life.
- I'm a bad person and a bad mother.
- I need to be punished.

"These beliefs affected my life in many ways:

- I never married again.
- Whenever things became serious with a man, I would become insecure and cause problems.
- They would break up with me. I'd never break up with them. I always forced them to 'abandon' me.
- I avoided connecting with people because they would always ask about children and relationships. I hated lying. I couldn't open up and be myself.

- If I told people the truth, they would chastise me and no longer be my friend.
- I started to punish myself as I got older. I don't date, have close friends, allow myself to have fun, participate in enjoyable activities, or earn more money than I need to provide for my basic needs. I live in a city with summer weather that is way too hot for me, and I live in a small apartment in a declining part of town.

"I've been trying to prove to others that I'm a good person. I care. I'm giving. I'm thoughtful. I'm worthy.

"I didn't initially think that much good came out of that year. But there were actually quite a few things:

- I became closer with my own family, especially my mother.
- I have a close relationship with my niece, which otherwise wouldn't have happened.
- I am independent and can do whatever I want.
- I didn't end up suffering in a bad marriage like so many of my friends and family did.
- I didn't have all the responsibility of taking care of people who depended on me.
- I was able to help my mom as she got older.

"Which beliefs do I need to delete? All of them! What new beliefs do I need to create? Quite a few actually. How about:

- I belong.
- I'm lovable.
- I'm good enough.
- I deserve to experience the best that life has to offer.
- I'm perfectly human.
- I'm a good person."

Wes said, "I'm so proud of you, Elin. You are much stronger than you give yourself credit for, aren't you?"

Elin nodded in agreement with a slight smile and watery eyes.

"One last question for you before we call it a day. Do you see any repeating patterns in your life, and if so, what happened as things repeated?"

Elin thought for a minute before replying. "Yes, I have had several significant events involving men rejecting, leaving, or abandoning me. My dad, uncle, and grandpa died. My boyfriend left me and quickly married someone else. Two male judges scolded me in public, and an entire male-dominated society rejected me for getting pregnant out of wedlock. I then did to my child what others did to me: I abandoned him. Instead of having the pattern of rejection and abandonment stop with me, I let it continue to the next generation. As time went on, I had a series of relationships where men abandoned me. I stayed in relationships where men treated me poorly. I think I wanted them to punish me. Each time, the pattern involved different people, and each time things got worse. I also have a brother-in-law who constantly criticizes me and treats me poorly. It's abusive behavior and I put up with it."

"Yes, Elin, that's exactly right. Even though you did your best, the pattern continues to get worse each time. It is just too strong for you to stop.

"Patterns are driven by our unconscious minds and the beliefs we store there. When you look at this pattern and the events in your life, can you see what belief was dominating?"

Elin had to think for a minute. "Wow. I didn't see that, Wes. The dominant belief is *I'm a bad person*, which leads to the beliefs that *I deserve to be punished* and *I was meant to be poor and struggle for my basic needs*."

"Well done, Elin. Your conscious mind and unconscious mind were both trying to prove different things: *I'm a good person* versus *I'm a bad person*. You were on autopilot and never took a closer look. We're going to talk about this in more detail tomorrow. Don't worry.

It's common for people to experience significant events, create limiting beliefs, and have challenging lives as a result. And I'm going to help you with this. Promise. So hang in there. You did great work today! And they said it couldn't be done! You proved them wrong again. Hah!" Wes said animatedly.

"To summarize, significant events become a powerful force in our lives by tapping into our fears. They can occur at any age, but most of them occur when we are young. As a result of the event, we make decisions about ourselves and the world. This information is stored in our unconscious mind, which creates new beliefs and automates new behaviors. This sometimes leads to repetitive patterns of negative experiences that get worse over time. In this way, significant events shape and define us. You are a perfectly imperfect human, and courage is critical for the healing process. Be courageous today by saying, 'I choose courage!'

"Are you ready for your homework?"

"Yes, sir! What's my homework?" Elin asked, completely relieved that this session was finally over.

"I realize this was a difficult and emotional day for you, so I'd like to help you better process your emotions. Make a list of the emotions and feelings you often experience. Then for each one, write down what you think about it. Oh, and one more thing. I'd like you to watch a video of a mime trapped in an invisible box. That's it. Let's meet here tomorrow at the same time. Any questions?"

"Seriously, Wes? Mimes?" Elin asked, looking at him somewhat puzzled and a little annoyed.

"Yes, dead serious. It's a very useful exercise. And after today, you could use something to lighten things up."

"Okay then. No questions. See you tomorrow, Wes!"

As Elin walked back to her car, she couldn't help but think about her homework assignment. "Mimes? Seriously? That's just stupid. Why would Wes ask me to do such a ridiculous thing?"

Chapter Nine

Emotions and Feelings

When Elin arrived at the Cinnabon the next day, Wes was already there. He greeted her with a big smile and said, "Good morning, Elin! How are you today?"

"Good morning, Wes," Elin replied. "I'm actually doing better today. How are you?"

"I'm feeling totally superb, thank you very much!" Wes replied enthusiastically. "As you can see, Elin, I didn't reject or abandon you. And I can assure you that I don't in any way think less of you. You are still a perfect human in my eyes. So let's get started, shall we?" As was their routine now, they began their walk around the mall.

"Let's begin with the homework," Wes started. "What emotions and feelings do you experience often, and what do you think about each one?"

"I feel sad, hopeless, and disappointed with myself," Elin said with a sigh. "I had such a great start to life, but I didn't capitalize on it. Now, I'm just waiting for the end. There's nothing very positive going on. I have lots of things I'd like to do, but I don't have any money or anyone to share my life with. I don't think there's anything I can do to improve my situation. I don't like these emotions, I don't want to feel them, and I don't think it's good to feel them."

"Thank you, Elin. You did a great job, as always. We will come back to this later today. To better understand emotions and feelings,

I need to explain how the mind and body work. But I'm going to simplify it and tell it to you in a way you've probably never heard before. It is designed to better help you with the transformation process."

Wes gave Elin the following three handouts and went over them with her: *The Mind*, *Emotions and Feelings*, and *Unconscious Mind Goals*.

The Mind

The **brain** is the three-pound physical organ protected by the skull. It helps manage the many functions of the body. It also provides a place for the mind to operate.

The **mind** is the set of mental processes that operate within the brain. The mind is not physical. It cannot be touched. The mind can be broken into three categories: conscious, unconscious, and survival.

The **conscious mind** is our ego, or **rational mind**. It is our identity. It is used for creativity, decision-making, learning, problem-solving, reflection, and social engagement. It is in charge when we are awake and when we feel safe.

The **unconscious mind** is a very powerful part of our mind to which we aren't completely aware. It houses our beliefs, habits, desired experiences, avoided experiences, fears, triggers, buttons, feelings, and automatic behaviors. It monitors all of our senses. It listens to the words we think and speak. It sees the images we create in our head and knows all the stories we tell ourselves. It learns by repetition: the more we do something, the stronger the habit becomes and the stronger our unconscious mind gets. It has access to our memories that are too frightening or painful to deal with, including our significant events and secrets. It contains all of our guilt, shame, and regrets. It also holds the list of people we have not forgiven or freed ourselves from. It is our autopilot. Carl Jung said, "Until you make the unconscious conscious, it will direct your life and you will call it fate."

Iceberg Analogy
To give a visual representation of the level of power we are dealing with, imagine a large iceberg floating in the ocean. If it represents

all of our mental processing power, the conscious mind is only the 10 percent that is visible above the water. Most people go through life on autopilot, courtesy of the unconscious mind, which has 90 percent of our mental power, or that portion of the iceberg that is below the water. The actual percentages can vary depending on the person. Some people have greater control of their unconscious mind, and a few have harnessed its full power.

Most people try to improve themselves solely through working on their conscious mind. That is what traditional therapy, personal development training, and coaching focus on. In order to make significant progress, improvements need to be made to both the conscious *and* the unconscious mind.

Survival Mind

The survival mind is the basic mind that is similar across all animals. It contains the **survival response system** (SRS) that automates certain functions in response to opportunities and threats. It helps us take advantage of opportunities we encounter, such as food, water, and procreation. It also contains the fight-or-flight response that keeps us safe from danger. It tells our body to release hormones, makes physiological changes, and creates outward facial, vocal, and physical expressions. It generates emotions, which are a positive or negative experience that is associated with a particular pattern of physiological activity. It also carries our instincts and ancestral survival information. The SRS can be triggered by something external or by internal thoughts.

Regarding threats, there is the familiar **fight-or-flight response** that can be more accurately called the faint, freeze, fight, or flight response—or **4F Response** for short. It is an instant, automatic response that is critical for our survival. We don't need to consciously think about anything. Our bodies simply do what is necessary for us to survive. This physiological response lasts ninety seconds. During this time, we are not able to access our conscious mind, so it is impossible for us to think of a practical solution to the threat.

There is a strict hierarchy to the SRS, consisting of three levels. At the lowest level, when our body senses a danger that will most likely end in death, it completely turns off consciousness, causing us to faint. The next level is the freeze response, where it senses that the danger is too great for a physical reaction. This also triggers the camouflage response in an octopus or chameleon that allows them to blend in with their background.

The highest level is fight-or-flight. The SRS tells the pituitary gland to secrete the hormone adrenocorticotropin and tells the adrenal glands to secrete adrenaline and cortisol. This affects the body by increasing our heart rate, breathing, blood sugar levels, speed, strength, and pain tolerance. The blood vessels dilate to the muscles and constrict everywhere else. And our senses hyperfixate on the danger. As you can see, it is a chemical reaction that produces physiological changes.

In our everyday lives, the SRS can activate during stressful work situations. For example, the lowest level response is to faint, freeze is saying nothing, flight is leaving the room, and fight is arguing with someone. If you can wait ninety seconds, you will regain access to your conscious mind and be able to think, speak, and act rationally.

Go to www.WiseLovingBeing.com/handouts
to find a copy of this handout online.

Emotions and Feelings

The words *emotions* and *feelings* are often used interchangeably, but they are quite different.

Emotions are biological, inherited, instinctual, real-time reactions to the present moment. They are automatically generated by the survival mind in response to external stimuli or internal thoughts. We have no conscious control over this. Emotions communicate important information about what is happening in the present moment, both around and within us. Emotions precede feelings.

According to Jaak Panksepp, there are **seven basic emotions**: care, fear, lust, panic/grief, play, seeking, and rage. They are similar across humans and animals, and they facilitate basic communication. For example, when you smile at a dog, it wags its tail.

Feelings are the many words we use to describe how we are doing. They are a mental construct, and there are well over one hundred different words we use to describe our state. Feelings are often used as a measure of emotional well-being and mental health.

A feeling is a mental interpretation of an emotion. Feelings are the meanings we assign to an emotion and vary widely by person. Our feelings and their intensity are unique to us and reflect information from our past experiences and our fears about the future. Emotions and feelings are connected: emotions come first and feelings follow. Emotions are objective while feelings are subjective.

Emotions Are Good

Emotions occur naturally and communicate important information that can help us improve our lives and keep us safe from both mental and physical harm. All emotions are good, whether they are positive or negative. Having a negative emotion isn't the problem; it's how we express that emotion that counts. Expressing a negative emotion in a positive, empowering, and productive way can be incredibly beneficial for everyone involved. Unfortunately, society has told us that negative emotions are bad and we need to control and suppress them. This causes tremendous damage to our mind, body, and life. The longer the suppression goes on, the more pressure builds. It is like a **volcano** ready to explode. We become a Mount St. Helens or Krakatoa with the potential to cause incredible amounts of damage to ourselves and others.

Managing Our Emotions

There are many things we can do to make it less likely that we will react with a negative emotion. We can elevate ourselves by becoming wiser and more loving; take better care of ourselves by getting enough sleep, exercising, managing our stress levels, and giving ourselves extra time to do things; stay well fed and hydrated so we don't get hangry; avoid situations that cause certain emotions or remove ourselves from a negative situation at the first sign of our impending reaction; and receive training to normalize and better handle the situation. If we are angry at someone, it's often best to wait twenty-four hours and calm down before we try to resolve the situation with them.

It is also important to let our emotions out in a productive and healthy manner. Some ways we can do this are through physical exercise, meditation, and breath work. Or you can park your car in the middle of an empty parking lot with your windows and doors closed and scream as loud as you want.

Source of Our Emotions and Feelings

This brings to light a very interesting truth that is quite often denied: we are the source of our own emotions and feelings. We create them. They aren't caused by someone else or something external. As a matter of fact, emotions and feelings can be created immediately by our thoughts. When we think about a fearful event from our past, we immediately feel fear. Similarly, we can feel love by remembering a moment from our past when we felt loved by someone. We are completely responsible for what we think, feel, say, and do.

People Have Different Reactions

Note that the same external stimulus can produce different emotions and feelings in each person who experiences it. For example, when two people see a roller coaster, one person could experience the play emotion and feel excited, while the other person could experience the fear emotion and feel scared.

Go to www.WiseLovingBeing.com/handouts
to find a copy of this handout online.

Unconscious Mind Goals

Our unconscious mind is good and has good intentions. It has **three goals**: to automate our responses, to help us avoid conscious pain, and to help us get what it thinks we want.

Goal #1: Automate Our Responses

Our unconscious mind can automate our responses. This helps free up our conscious mind to do more important things. The unconscious mind gathers data from our senses and interprets the physiological changes and emotions generated by the survival mind. It also takes into consideration our internal views and beliefs about the event. It then maps this information to a **button** or **trigger**, which automates our response. The button decides our feelings and the intensity of those feelings. It then provides us with an automatic behavioral response, including thoughts, words, and actions. Some buttons are based on our fears. The stronger our fears, the more intense the button response will be.

Responses can be positive or negative. For example, a person who smiles, jumps up and down, and gives a joyous greeting to an old friend is giving a positive response. A person who yells at another person and hits them is giving a negative response.

Responses can be considered positive or negative depending on the situation. For example, a soldier who has an intense reaction to a backpack in the road and breaks hard or swerves around it is taking appropriate action in a war zone. They would be rewarded and thanked for taking quick action to save lives from a potential improvised explosive device (IED). However, at home during peacetime, this same reaction would be considered a problem.

Buttons and triggers can produce a wide variety of responses that can be considered either healthy or unhealthy, but we typically hear these terms used in reference to negative responses. In this negative context, a trigger is an intense reaction generally related to post-traumatic stress disorder (PTSD), while a button is associated with less traumatic events. When you see the word *button* moving forward in a negative context, it will have a meaning similar to the phrase, "He pushed my buttons."

For example, let's say you are driving your car and see someone maneuver their car in front of you from the lane next to you. They do it quickly, and their car comes within a foot of yours. Your SRS detects this, starts a physiological response, and sends an emotion of rage. Your unconscious mind interprets the emotion and sensory data and maps it to a specific button. The someone-cut-me-off button is tied to an angry feeling, and the automatic behavioral responses are honking your horn, yelling at the driver, and flipping them off. It also labels the driver as a jerk, or something worse.

Since we are responsible for generating our own emotions and feelings, it also means that we are responsible for pressing our own buttons. Although it feels good to blame others for how they make us feel, we have no one to blame but ourselves. They are innocent. If we truly want to be free and in control of our lives, then we must choose how we wish to respond to the world.

Goal #2: Avoid Conscious Pain

The unconscious mind's most important function is to help us avoid conscious pain and suffering. It wants to help us avoid any emotional pain from our *past* by hiding that information from us. It wants us to feel better in the *present* moment by distorting the information we receive from our senses. It helps us avoid doing things that might cause us to feel rejection, failure, guilt, shame, or embarrassment in the *future*.

Our conscious mind always provides **intellectual justification** for what the unconscious mind does. For example, if our unconscious mind wants us to avoid pain from an activity we need to do, it will have us do escape activities instead. If we try harder, it will make us tired, give us a headache, or get us sick. We consciously justify this by saying we are depressed, tired, stressed out, lazy, or some other "logical" reason. Blaming circumstances or blaming others for our own problems is another common intellectual justification we use.

The **Horse Blinder Analogy** will help illustrate this point. Horses know they are a basic food source for predators. They are constantly looking around for any evidence of threats to their safety and survival. As a result, when horses are working in a city, they are easily spooked by cars, people, dogs, and loud noises that are everywhere, and which are all things that rarely cause them harm. To keep horses calm, blinders are put on either side of their eyes. This restricts their view to what is immediately in front of them. Your unconscious mind similarly uses blinders to focus you on only what it wants you to see, hiding what it doesn't want you to know.

Goal #3: Get What It Thinks We Want
The third goal of our unconscious mind is to help us get what it thinks we want. It has a built-in **radar** that can help it quickly find things. It will find what we ask it to. Be careful. Are you looking for problems, or are you looking for positive outcomes?

The unconscious mind also makes sure we act consistently with who we think we are, our identity. It has an **unconscious compass** by which it navigates life. In many ways, it becomes our **autopilot** and manages our life without us even knowing it. The stronger our fears, the stronger our autopilot.

Unfortunately, in many people, the unconscious mind becomes an unseen force, creating obstacles and causing problems due to a **faulty compass**. We think a compass is never wrong so we conclude that ours must also be correct. But it's not. We have limiting and false beliefs about ourselves, our identity, our tribe, and our world; negative and conflicting desired and avoided experiences; and memories of traumatic events that have created deep-seated fears around survival and belonging. There is knowledge we hold to be true that sometimes isn't. This creates obstacles to success and causes us to repeat negative patterns.

World View
Our unconscious mind can alter our view of the world to be aligned with our beliefs. Our senses see the truth, but our unconscious mind hijacks the information. If the information is aligned with our beliefs, then the unconscious mind allows our conscious mind to receive it. Otherwise, it ignores, changes, distorts, or hides it. We thus develop an imagined view of the world that is different from the actual truth.

Conflict in the Mind
Over the course of our lives, a conflict develops between our conscious and unconscious minds. The bigger the conflict, the more pain, suffering, and hopelessness that develops in the conscious mind. In order to heal, we must do the following:

- Become aware of the unconscious mind, what it contains, and how it is managing our life.
- See the actual truth instead of the imagined truth.

- Clean up our unconscious mind by throwing out all the limiting and false information.
- Update the unconscious mind with empowering beliefs and habits, and the truth.
- Train the unconscious mind to work in harmony with our conscious mind.

Body-Mind Connection

There is a link between our mind and body. A negative emotional state can cause serious damage to our body. We sometimes get sick when we are experiencing a difficult time filled with fear, negative emotions, conflict, stress, or worry. Over a longer period of time, living with high levels of guilt, shame, and fear can lead to obesity and other chronic conditions. The body can also develop aches, allergies, migraines, skin problems, and digestive tract issues. In fact, it is possible to guess the emotional state of a person by the way their body looks and by asking them how their body feels. Our body is always trying to communicate with us. Therefore it is important to listen. Improving our emotional state can help reduce or even eliminate these issues from our body.

The reverse is also true. When the body is not doing well, it negatively affects the mind and makes us feel worse about ourselves. We may feel depressed, agitated, or impatient and have difficulty concentrating or thinking logically. Conversely, when the body is happy, it produces endorphins, which make us feel and think better.

Go to www.WiseLovingBeing.com/handouts
to find a copy of this handout online.

"Elin, I know that was a lot of information to absorb. Let's talk more about the source of our emotions and feelings. Think about how ridiculous this statement is: 'I will feel loved when I get a boyfriend.' A boyfriend has nothing to do with it, and quite often actually produces the opposite feeling after a few dates. The good news is that we can learn to take control of how we feel by creating feelings of love at any time."

Elin laughed and nodded in agreement.

Wes continued. "It's interesting to note that the good feelings we have after achieving a goal only last for a short time. Sometimes the experience of working toward our goal isn't as rewarding as we thought it would be. It is quite a waste if we don't enjoy the process *and* the end result. There is definitely some wisdom in the classic saying, *It's the journey, not the destination.* What matters is how you feel right now. That's what determines the quality of your life.

"Any questions, Elin?"

She shook her head, indicating she had none.

"Let me give you an extreme example of the unconscious mind's power to help us avoid pain. My friend Aubrey was prostituted and abused by her mother in every way possible, from the moment she was born until she turned eighteen. Her mother controlled her with fear, drugs, and threats of events even more horrific than the unimaginable horrors she had already suffered. The trauma was so severe that Aubrey suffered from dissociative identity disorder. Her unconscious mind went to great lengths to protect her from the intense pain and keep her alive. Her unconscious mind created different identities to hide specific traumatic events. Each identity kept that specific trauma to itself, allowing Aubrey to be free of it and live a somewhat normal life. The unconscious mind knew that if the trauma leaked into the conscious mind, then Aubrey wouldn't be able to function.

"This strategy kept Aubrey from needing to escape. It also kept her from falling into a downward spiral of drugs, alcohol, and further abuse. By protecting her from having to relive these traumatic events over and over again, it most certainly kept her from committing suicide. She graduated junior high school, high school, and college with honors. She is a lovely person who is the kindest and bravest person I know.

"Let me give you an example of how your habits are driven by your unconscious mind. My friend Daniel genuinely loved to exercise, but he rarely did. He invested in a nice home gym but always had an excuse for not exercising: I'm too hungry. I'm too tired. I don't feel well. I worked too many hours today. I don't want to bother my family. There's not enough time to do a real workout that takes at least one hour. My commute was too long today. I need to do something for my family. I need to spend quality time with them.

"They were all very reasonable excuses. Interestingly enough, years later after he divorced, his kids moved out of the house, he started working from home, and his income increased, he still didn't exercise. The funny part was that he couldn't use any of his normal excuses. In fact, he had none. He was simply choosing not to exercise.

"Daniel knew that he was much more productive at work and much better at home when he exercised. He knew that exercise was critical for his long-term health. But whenever he tried to start exercising again, he would end up getting sick or injured.

"Daniel told me that for the first thirty years of his life, he had put his health first. He loved to play various sports, he enjoyed backpacking, and he trained for marathons. Exercise, healthy food, and plenty of sleep were his highest priorities. All of this changed shortly after the birth of his first child. He lost a high-paying job and had challenges meeting the financial needs of his family. He worked more than seventy hours a week at two low-paying jobs, stopped exercising regularly, and gained a lot of weight.

"I helped Daniel understand that he had experienced a significant event that was attached to a very powerful fear: the survival of his family. It was basically, *Make money or die.* He made a decision to put work first, then his family, and to only allow himself to exercise when those first two goals were met. And since he was a perfectionist, 'financial success' morphed into something that wasn't really attainable for him given his current circumstances and beliefs, and exercise meant 'the perfect hour-plus workout.' His unconscious mind took that information and made one minor adjustment: *Exercise is a threat to your survival.* The effective translation was, *If I exercise, I'll die.* From that moment on, his automatic pilot made sure he didn't exercise regularly, and his conscious mind always delivered intellectual justification with one of his many excuses. What a team!

"I helped Daniel create a new belief for his unconscious mind that said, *I need to exercise regularly so I can live longer, have higher financial security, and take better care of my family.* In short, *Exercise is life.* He changed his habits, prioritized his workouts, and changed his exercise routine so it supported his primary goal of financial success so he could take care of his family. As a result, he began to exercise regularly, improved his diet, lost a significant amount of weight, improved his finances, became a much better father, and became much happier with his life.

"My friend Gustavo developed a conflict in the mind following a significant event that happened in elementary school. His parents saw that he was having a difficult time academically. He was currently enrolled in the best private school in the area, which placed a lot of pressure on its students to perform. His grades were typically the lowest in the class, and his teachers were concerned. His parents decided to transfer him to a public elementary school that was regarded as much easier, hoping to give him a better overall school experience.

"From this significant event, Gustavo concluded that people thought he wasn't smart. He decided to prove them wrong. He created a belief that only smart people—who attend the best schools, have the best grades, have the best major, and have the highest degree—are worthy. He added to this by creating a desired experience of success, with AND Rules that also said he had to make a lot of money, own a big house, drive a nice car, work at the best company, have the best job title, work on the latest research, and be married to a woman of similar status.

"When I met Gustavo, he was in his early forties. Although he was a very positive person, I could tell that it masked a lot of pain. He had a major fear of failure and rejection that was connected to his elevated primal fear that he didn't belong. His secondary fear statements were that he wasn't smart enough and wasn't worthy. This had been causing problems throughout his life. He was overweight, out of work, and his marriage was starting to develop problems. Although he told me he had done a lot of great things, when I asked him to review the major events in his life, he saw that it was really a long string of failures. When I asked him if he achieved his desired experience of success every day, he said he didn't and never had.

"I took Gustavo deeper into the awareness process and helped him see there was a major conflict in his mind. From that same significant event from his elementary school where he believed he was told by others that he wasn't smart, his conscious mind decided to prove they were wrong, while his unconscious mind decided to prove they were right. And the unconscious mind always wins.

"I was able to help Gustavo create new beliefs about what success currently meant to him, which turned out to be almost the opposite of what it had been. Family, health, charity, and spirituality now topped the list. I then helped him create a new conscious compass that still had a vision of doing meaningful work that has a positive impact on society, but this time the driving force wasn't about personal wealth and status. I helped him fix his faulty unconscious compass and reprogram his unconscious mind so it worked in concert with his conscious mind. He was finally able to find a great job that aligned with who he really was, proving that he was smart and capable. But he was even more proud of his personal accomplishments. His emotional and physical health improved, and so did his marriage and family relationships.

"For the next example, I would like to use the most common scenario of being overweight in order to demonstrate the link between the unconscious mind and the body. When I first met my friend Melissa, I noticed that she was quite heavy. She never told me her weight, but she said she was more than double what she weighed in high school. No matter what she tried, she just couldn't lose the weight. If she did manage to lose a few pounds, after a short period of time, she would gain it all back and then some. She said she just didn't have enough willpower. She was frustrated but had resigned herself to the fact that she was just meant to be overweight. It was in her genes.

"I told her about the **Weed Analogy**. Every gardener knows that the only way to get rid of a weed is to remove what is above the soil *and* its roots. If you only remove what is above the soil, it makes the roots stronger, and the weed will grow back bigger than before. Similarly, if you don't completely deal with the root of an issue, it leads to the issue returning, and in many cases, getting worse. Replacing the root of an issue with new empowering beliefs and habits is crucial for lasting change.

"Melissa was doing all the standard weight-loss activities, and she was failing like almost everyone does because she was trying to get rid of a weed without removing the roots. Diets and willpower don't work because they don't address the root cause of the weight gain. The overweight body is like the weed we see above the ground. It is trying to tell us there is a problem. The roots are the unconscious mind. The best way to make permanent changes and remain at your optimal weight is to address the underlying emotional issues in the unconscious mind that are causing the problem in the first place. It can't be done at the conscious level. The unconscious mind must be addressed because in the end, the unconscious mind always wins.

"I helped Melissa understand how her body, conscious mind, and unconscious mind interact. I told her how it was extremely difficult for her conscious mind to win this game in the short term, and nearly impossible to do it in the long term. Melissa embraced an equal partnership between her conscious mind, unconscious mind, and body. Instead of fighting her body, I suggested she listen to it and hear what it had been trying to tell her for many years.

"I helped Melissa find what was hiding deep in her unconscious mind that was the root cause of the weight gain issue. She said there was a significant event that happened in college where she was assaulted, and she felt a combination of fear, guilt, shame, and regret over it. She had created the belief that she could keep a similar event from happening again if she wasn't physically attractive, and she made an unconscious decision to be heavier. I helped her create the new belief: *I can be safe regardless of how I look.* I then helped her make new decisions on how to stay safe, which included taking a self-defense and weapons training course, buying a gun, and getting a trained, intimidating watchdog. Once she was able to clean up the mess of disempowering beliefs, fear, guilt, and shame that had been festering in her unconscious mind for a long time, she was finally able to love herself and find peace, joy, and freedom.

"Melissa could now look at her diet objectively and see that she had been eating foods to soothe her emotions. She was eating for her unconscious mind, not her conscious mind or body. A conflict had developed. Her unconscious mind wanted to keep her aligned with the beliefs and decisions she created from the significant event, while her conscious mind and body wanted to lose weight. She could now see that her unconscious mind craved foods that tended to be high in fat, sugar, and salt, which made her gain more weight, which then led to more emotional distress and conflict with her conscious mind. It was a vicious circle.

"I recommended that Melissa feed her body the nutritious foods it needed to be healthy. In addition to drinking lots of water, I recommended she switch to organic, non-GMO foods. I asked her to eat lean protein, healthy whole-grain carbs, and have at least half of each meal consist of fresh fruit or vegetables. This is basically the caveman diet and only includes foods that were available to them. No processed or packaged foods. Nothing in a box, can, or jar. I also recommended she give her body the exercise it needed. She chose to walk, lift light weights, and do yoga. As a result of all these changes, the weight started to fall off without much effort. She became much happier, and other areas of her life started to improve too.

"Elin, our bodies are always trying to tell us things. If your body could speak in words, what would it tell you right now?"

Elin thought for a moment and then spoke. "My digestive and sinus issues are telling me that I'm not dealing well with all the stress in my life. My body wants me to positively deal with or eliminate all the stress and worry in my life. The major stressors are money and dealing with a certain difficult person I can't avoid."

"Nicely done, Elin. We will work on improving this soon. I'm sure your body is happy to hear that you are finally listening to it. Returning to our conversation from yesterday about your significant events when you were seventeen, can you see now how the conflict between your conscious and unconscious mind developed? Can you better understand why your life turned out the way it did?"

"Yes, Wes. It all makes sense now. Even though I consciously wanted money, my unconscious mind put me on autopilot and created a life that was aligned with the beliefs *I'm a bad person, I need to be punished,* and *I was meant to be poor and struggle for my basic needs.* It gave me what it thought I wanted. It shielded me from reality to help me avoid conscious pain about my past as well as my daily life as I was living it. My conscious mind provided intellectual justification and had me focus on thinking about how I was a good, caring, giving person. It justified that I needed to be poor by presenting the false belief that good people are poor and rich people are bad. This conflict also led to the chronic health problems I have. My body has been trying to communicate with me, but I haven't been listening."

"Excellent job, Elin. I can see you've had a big moment of clarity, which is critical to your healing and transformation.

"To summarize what we have learned so far, all emotions are good. They are automatically generated and are out of our conscious control. They are providing valuable information to us, and it is important for us to use that information productively. Feelings are generated by our unconscious mind, which contains important information about us. We are completely responsible for what we think, feel, say, and do, including pressing our own buttons. Our unconscious mind is good and is only trying to help us. We can change our lives by changing what is in our unconscious mind. Conflicts can arise between our mind and body, and between our conscious and unconscious minds. Resolving these conflicts helps us live much better lives.

"Regarding the second part of your homework, did you get anything useful out of watching the mime-trapped-in-an-invisible-box video?"

"Nope. Nothing. I still think mimes are stupid. Everyone thinks mimes are stupid."

Wes chuckled. "I certainly understand your view. A lot of people feel that way. As a matter of fact, I used to feel that way too. Then one day I figured them out. It was genius what they were doing, really."

Elin interrupted, "You've got to be kidding me, Wes. Have you completely lost your mind?"

Wes smiled. "No, I still have my mind. Patience, please. I'm going to have to ask you for an extra helping of trust and a side of open mind."

Elin rolled her eyes and said, "Okay. Please proceed."

"The **Mime-in-a-Box Analogy** is a metaphor for life. We are all mimes trapped in an invisible box. The mime can't see the walls, and neither can anyone else. The walls only affect the mime. He is stuck, but he doesn't know why. He suffers in silence and wears a fake smile. He tries as hard as he can to get out, but he can't improve his situation. In the end, he gives up and accepts his fate. Henry David Thoreau made this observation in 1854 when he wrote in *Walden*, 'The mass of [people] lead lives of quiet desperation.'

"The challenge for the mime is to see the walls and the information contained in them. Only then can the walls be removed. Only then can the mime escape the box. The mime represents us, or our conscious mind, and the walls represent our unconscious mind. So what is within the walls? The walls contain all the information in our unconscious mind, including the fears and beliefs that automate our lives.

"Any questions, Elin?"

"No questions. After all, I'm basically the queen of mimes trapped in a box," Elin said with a laugh. "But I do have a newfound respect for them."

"Who knew that mimes could be so cool and smart? They've provided us with this incredible wisdom for centuries, but we just haven't been paying attention. I blame their presentation and silly outfits. I mean, it's really hard to take them seriously!" Wes said with a giggle. "Let's take a look at the first part of your homework again. What do you think about your emotions and feelings now?"

Elin replied, "I have a much more positive view of my negative emotions and feelings now. Even though they are negative, there is a positive message underlying them. My unconscious mind was just trying to help me make important changes, but I didn't hear the positive messages. I only felt the obvious bad feelings on the surface. I've been dwelling on the negative instead of looking for the positive, probably because I've accepted the belief from society that negative emotions are bad and shouldn't be expressed. We should stuff them down and ignore them."

"Excellent observation, Elin. Let's take a closer look at your habits. Do you remember the patterns in your avoided and desired experiences? You achieved none of your positive desired experiences, but you achieved all of your negative desired experiences and all of your avoided experiences. This shows you the power of your unconscious mind. It is currently in almost complete control of your life. Why is it so dominant in your life? Let's take a look.

"When we talked about your habits and you presented me with your list of avoided experiences, you didn't mention rejection and failure. By the way, you also didn't mention guilt and shame. Do you remember?"

"Yes, I do," Elin replied. "It was strange. Clearly rejection, failure, guilt, and shame should have been at the top of my list."

"Agreed. The reason is that your unconscious mind is trying to protect you from all the pain you have suffered from the many traumatic and significant events in your life. Remember that rejection, failure, guilt, and shame are connected to your secondary fears around not belonging, and your cavewoman mind is hardwired to believe this equals certain death. You are absolutely terrified. Your unconscious mind is trying to remove any hint of rejection, failure, guilt, and shame from happening on a daily basis.

"Another example I'd like to bring up is around your goal of financial security. You're consciously very motivated to achieve this goal, yet you spend twelve hours a day on activities that take you further from that goal. You know you are a hard worker, but something is holding you back. You have rationalized this by thinking you were 'lazy' because you didn't work on your goal. But there is much more to it than that. Your unconscious mind knows from experience that anything you try to do to improve your situation will likely end in failure and more pain. Its priority is to protect you from pain, so it has been taking control of twelve hours of your waking day.

"Your unconscious mind also gives you what it thinks you want. What is the message you have been sending it? Up until we started working together, your identity was *I am an old, poor, lazy woman without hope who deserves to be punished.* Your beliefs have been largely negative. Three of your secondary fear statements are: *I'm not worthy. I'm not lovable. I'm not good enough.* Your four negative desired experiences are no companionship; having an unhealthy emotional well-being; sacrificing; and thinking negative thoughts, including your guilt, shame, and regrets. One of your avoided experiences is around receiving positive things from others. In other words, you don't feel worthy of receiving compliments or help. Your unconscious mind has heard you loud and clear, and on a daily basis, it helps you achieve all of this.

"Similarly, your unconscious mind helps make your beliefs come true whether you are aware of them or not. Yesterday, we were talking about a repeating pattern where men abandon or reject you. This was caused by a belief you created when you were only ten years old. You were somewhat aware of that belief. When we were talking about your general beliefs, I mentioned you had two deep, dark, disturbing hidden ones: *There is nothing I can do to improve my situation,* and *I don't deserve to live a nice life.* You weren't even aware of those two beliefs, yet they were coming true for you every day. That's just how powerful the unconscious mind is.

"The good news is that your unconscious mind is working perfectly. It protects you from pain, automates your life, and gives you exactly what you are asking for. It is creating your world exactly how it thinks you want it to be. Unfortunately, that's also the bad news. You've got to give your unconscious mind new directives if you want to live a better life. And we're going to fix that very soon. There's just one more day of awareness to go, so hang in there, Elin!" He gave her an encouraging smile.

"Once again, you did a great job today. I really appreciate your hard work, your open mind, and your honesty. Are you ready for your homework?"

"Yes, sir! What's my homework?" Elin asked.

"Relationships are the biggest contributors to our emotions and feelings. I want you to make five lists:

1. Things you need to forgive yourself for.
2. Good people you need to forgive so you can improve the relationship.
3. Good people you need to apologize to so you can repair the relationship.
4. Bad people you no longer want in your life, from whom you want total freedom.
5. People you need to set better boundaries with.

"Let's meet here tomorrow at the same time. Any questions?"

"No questions. See you tomorrow, Wes!"

Chapter Ten

Forgiveness and Freedom

When Elin arrived at the Cinnabon the next day, Wes was already there. He greeted her with a big smile and said, "Good morning, Elin! How are you today?"

"Good morning, Wes," Elin replied. "I'm good. How are you doing?"

"I'm outstanding!" Wes replied enthusiastically. "Let's get started, shall we?"

As they began their morning walk around the mall, Wes began speaking. "We are social creatures. We need to have positive relationships with others, even if we are introverts. Relationships are important for our personal growth and our emotional well-being. Sometimes we find ourselves in challenging situations or in unhealthy and abusive relationships that can cause us a tremendous amount of pain. Freedom and forgiveness are an incredibly important solution. Done correctly, they can help us make dramatic improvements to our lives. Otherwise, we remain trapped in the past, fearful about the present, and worried about our future. We remain trapped in our invisible mime box."

Wes gave Elin a handout titled *Freedom* and went over it with her.

Freedom

What Forgiveness Is Not

Forgiveness can't be used in cases where bad people did bad things to us. You are not going to:

- Pardon or condone a person's bad or abusive behavior.
- Let that person off the hook without exacting penalties and negative consequences.
- Forget the event ever happened so something worse can happen to you in the future.
- Get closure by having an honest discussion with the person about what happened.
- Reconcile and create a new positive relationship with the person.
- Get the person to admit what they did wrong, tell them about the pain they caused you, and have them say they are sorry.

Sometimes we may mistakenly think that a bad person is good. This is more common than we might think, especially if they are good at controlling others. It is always a good idea to ask someone we can trust to get their independent view of that person. If they really are a bad person, then we must use the **Freedom Process**. The **Forgiveness Process** will only make matters worse for us.

Freedom

When we remain negatively affected by someone, two things happen. First, we remain attached to them and are unable to move forward with our life. Second, we give them power to control our thoughts, feelings, words, and actions without them having to do anything. We are actually recreating the past trauma in the present moment instead of letting it remain in the past. In doing so, we are harming ourselves, not the bad person. It is important to take our power back. What is needed in this case is called *freedom*. Note that if we still need to interact with this person, then in addition to the Freedom Process, we can set healthy boundaries with them. This is discussed in a separate handout.

Carl Jung said, "What you resist persists." When you hold on to your anger and remember a painful past experience, you are keeping the negative feelings alive. By resisting the need to forgive, forget, and move on, the painful past experience persists because you are reliving it over and over again in the present. To make this clearer, let's use the **Chained Together Analogy**. Imagine you are chained to the bad person, ankle to ankle. Wherever you go they follow, and vice versa. Naturally, you want physical freedom from them and to get as far away from them as possible. In real life, of course, you want physical, mental, and emotional freedom from them.

The Freedom Process

The Freedom Process is done in a safe place. There is no interaction with the bad person. They are nowhere near you. Note that you don't need to do the entire process at once, and you can take as much time as you need for each step. Everyone is different, so please do not rush this process. The basic steps are as follows:

1. Write a letter to the person telling them what they did wrong, how it affected you, and what they should have done instead. This letter is never to be sent to them. It is for your private use only and will be needed again in a future exercise.
2. Now imagine they walk into the room toward you in an unthreatening manner, willingly accepting your invitation to speak with you.
3. They sit down in front of you while you remain standing. You have the power and are in control.

4. Read the letter to them.
5. Feel the emotional pain you suffered as a result of what they did to you.
6. Express your anger. Let it all out.
7. Grieve. It is important to grieve over all that you have lost.
8. Repeat these words: "I am taking my power back. I will no longer let you control how I feel. I am free from you. I am a wonderful person. I choose to create a great life."
9. Imagine that they tell you they are sorry and will no longer try to harm you. Watch as they say goodbye and leave the room.
10. Release yourself from them by cutting the invisible chain or cord that connects you. There is no longer any physical, mental, or emotional attachment to them.

Note that there are some cases where you want freedom, but you still need to maintain some form of harmonious relationship. In that case, you can do the Freedom Process without the final cord-cutting step. They become **lovingly disconnected** by setting a boundary that gives you what you need while still maintaining the relationship. You remove the negative and dysfunctional parts and create something positive that is better for both of you. Setting boundaries is discussed in a separate handout.

Also note that when you are attached to a bad person, you are constantly trying to push them away. Since there are always equal and opposite forces, as defined by Sir Isaac Newton's **third law of motion**, they are also pushing back toward you. When you cut the cord, you stop pushing. This results in them temporarily getting closer to you. This could result in you unexpectedly running into them or them reaching out to you in some way. So be prepared for that possible conversation. It usually takes a couple of weeks for the energetic forces to stabilize. The energy between the two of you is very real. When you seek to distance yourself from them or to disconnect from them entirely, then you will both notice a change.

Go to www.WiseLovingBeing.com/handouts
to find a copy of this handout online.

"Elin, here's an example. My friend Alexander was really angry with his ex-wife, who had prostituted and abused their children for more than a decade. He traveled a lot with his job, and when he was home, he worked long hours at his office. He burned the candle at both ends so he could provide for his family and was shocked when he discovered what she had been doing. He didn't even think it was possible for a mother to do that to her own children.

"Alexander was also angry at himself for not seeing what was going on. After all, it was his job to protect his kids, and he had clearly failed in the worst possible way. This anger and guilt ate away at him every day for many years and began causing problems in every area of his life. He finally decided to make a change. He forgave himself and then went through the Freedom Process with his ex-wife. Since he still had to interact with her in person, he set a new healthy boundary with her. He is now at peace. Instead of being stuck in the past, he can focus on the present moment and help his kids heal.

"Do you have any questions about the Freedom Process, Elin?"

"No, I don't. I can't wait to try it and break free from all those jerks on my freedom list."

"Great! Let's talk about forgiveness."

Wes gave Elin a handout titled *Forgiveness* and went over it with her.

Forgiveness

Forgiveness is used for good people. It is used to forgive others, apologize to others, and to forgive ourselves. In the simplest terms, forgiveness is about treating yourself and others as you would if you were a Wise Loving Being. Any relationship can be saved and transformed if both parties are motivated to do so. Relationships can also be improved if only one of the parties works to improve themselves and the relationship.

There are many **reasons to forgive**. You can choose any of the following statements that resonate with you:

1. All humans are imperfect and make mistakes.
2. People are defined by their totality, not solely by their worst moments.
3. Good intentions are sometimes more important than failed outcomes.
4. People are doing their best, given their knowledge and abilities at the time.
5. It is best to separate the behavior from the person.
6. Everyone is dealing with trauma, fears, limiting beliefs, and automatic behaviors.
7. People just need to apologize, learn from their mistakes, and move forward.
8. Although what they did was bad, it led you to a better place you would not have found otherwise. They made you who you are today. If you blame them for the bad, then you also have to blame them for the good.
9. You are no better than they are.

The last item on the list deserves a little more attention. There is a **natural bias** in our thinking that makes us look better than others. When we see someone doing something bad, we say they are a bad person. When we do something bad, we might say it was an accident, a one-time thing, a bad hair day, or caused by external circumstances. It's not who we are. We are still a good person. We unfairly judge others and label them as bad people while giving ourselves a pass.

Similarly, when something goes wrong in our life, we tend to blame others instead of looking first at ourselves. In many cases, we not only contributed to the problem, but we bear most of the responsibility. Finally, we tend to see the imperfections in others while viewing ourselves as near perfect and good. We see their mistakes but fail or refuse to see our own.

Of course, there are other people who only see their faults and view others as perfect. This is called a **reverse bias**. They need to understand the limits of their responsibility and better understand how the other party contributed to the issue. In both cases of bias, we need to take a balanced view of things.

The Forgiveness Process

The Forgiveness Process is really a conversation and is usually done in person. Here are the steps:

1. Start from a positive place. See the good in yourself and others.
2. Tell the other person that you care about them and that you'd like to work with them to improve the relationship.
3. Ask them if they are interested.
4. If they are not, then respect and accept their choice and go to the last step.

5. If they are interested, then first try to understand their point of view by asking questions.
6. Confirm your understanding by summarizing what they said.
7. Help them understand your view.
8. Apologize for your contribution to the problem.
9. Collaborate with them on how to create a better relationship.
10. Thank them for their time.

Note that if the person says no, has passed away, is unable to be reached, or perhaps apologizing would harm them or others, then you can write a letter and read it to them as if they were sitting in front of you. Imagine that they forgive you. What might they say to you? This letter is for your private use only and will be used in a future exercise.

Also note that this Forgiveness Process focuses on an issue between two parties. When a group of people do something wrong together, it is important for everyone to acknowledge how they contributed to the problem. You can follow the same process with everyone in the room.

Forgiving Ourselves

The most important person to forgive is ourselves. For some reason, it is easier for us to forgive others than it is for us to forgive ourselves. We like to beat ourselves up for all the mistakes we have made, hoping that if we remind ourselves often enough, then we won't do it again. And sometimes when we forgive others for the bad things they have done to us, we blame ourselves for letting them do that to us. We tell ourselves that we knew better or that we should have known better. We punish ourselves. We do all of this so we can avoid experiencing future guilt, shame, and regret.

Unfortunately, our "clever" solution causes more problems. We stay focused on our past and worried about our present and future. We relive past events instead of letting them stay in the past. We create painful negative experiences in the present moment instead of creating new positive experiences. Staying focused on the past keeps us from effectively creating an empowering future.

We need to forgive ourselves for anything where we feel regret, guilt, shame, or embarrassment. The goal is to eliminate these unhealthy feelings so we can be at peace with our past. Said another way, the goal is to love, understand, accept, appreciate, and forgive ourselves unconditionally without limits as our WLB would do. Forgiving ourselves completely also allows us to have a much deeper, authentic, and loving connection with others.

Self-Forgiveness Process
Select all the relevant items from the Reasons to Forgive list and apply them to yourself. Follow the Forgiveness Process. When you are done, say the words, "I love and forgive myself."

Go to www.WiseLovingBeing.com/handouts
to find a copy of this handout online.

"Elin, I have an example for you. My friend Harvey wanted to receive forgiveness from his mother. They had been close when he was a child, but he started to pull away as he grew up. He started to spend more time with his friends and his dad. Harvey thought he should have treated her with more respect, been nicer to her, and spent more time with her. He actually had quite a bit of guilt and regret around this, even twenty years after she died. He thought he was a bad son and a bad person. He hated himself and thought he needed to be punished. Every night before going to bed, he would say to his departed mom, 'I am sorry. I love you. I miss you. I wish you were here.'

"Harvey decided to write her a letter letting her know how much he loved her, how sorry he was for the way he treated her, how kind and loving she was to him, and how grateful he was to have her as his mother. He then read the letter to her and imagined her forgiving him and giving him a big hug. Afterward, he got this feeling that she always knew how much he loved her, that she knew this was a normal part of life, and that she had done something similar to her mother. He then forgave himself.

"Harvey told me that going through the Forgiveness Process made a huge difference for him. He could stop punishing himself; start loving himself, which allowed him to love others better; stop trying to prove he was good and others were bad; and accept himself and others as they were. Before, he felt there were obstacles that kept him from improving his life. Now that he was free of this obstacle, his life began to get a lot better.

"Here's another example. My friend David chose to forgive his dad, who had been very critical of him, telling him to act like a man, and bullying him. He even kicked David in the balls once. David felt rejected as both a son and a man. As an adult, David was polite, but he never went out of his way to do anything with his dad. He harbored a lot of anger and hatred toward him.

"David told me that all the items on the *reasons to forgive* list were helpful during his Forgiveness Process with his dad. David had recently learned about the trauma his dad had suffered as a teenager and was able to understand why he acted the way he did. He realized that his dad had good intentions and was just doing his best. David also realized that as hard as he tried to be a better father to his own kids, he still did similar bad things that his dad had done. If David were to be really honest with himself, he would have to acknowledge that in some cases, he had actually been a worse father than his dad.

"David decided to forgive his dad, but not in person. He wrote a letter and read it to his dad as if he were sitting in front of him. He imagined his dad apologizing to him and telling him what a bad father he had been. This allowed David to achieve a higher level of peace so he could move on. As a result, their relationship improved. They spent more time together and became a lot closer. His dad never apologized to him, but that didn't matter anymore.

"Elin, normally these forgiveness conversations happen in person, online, or over the phone, but I wanted to show you a few other options. Do you have any questions about the Forgiveness Process?"

"No, I don't. I'm a little bit nervous about doing this, but I can see the benefits if both parties are willing to work on the relationship."

"Sounds good, Elin. Yes, you might be a little nervous initially, but once the conversation gets going, you'll probably feel more comfortable. And, when you have completed the process, you'll feel a lot better."

Wes thought about her answer for a little bit and then asked, "I'm curious. Who will you be doing the Forgiveness Process with? Who is the most important person you need to apologize to and seek forgiveness from?"

"Well, I was thinking about my niece or my cousin Carl. I guess my niece is the most important person."

"I don't think that's right. I think the most important person you need to apologize to and seek forgiveness from is your son. You have a tremendous amount of guilt from abandoning him. Please write him a letter and then follow the Forgiveness Process even though he's not here in person. You can follow my friend Harvey's example."

"You're right, Wes. For some reason I was just thinking about people who I interact with."

"What do you need to forgive yourself for? Which of the reasons on the *reasons to forgive* list can you use?"

Elin thought for a bit before speaking. "There are two big things I need to forgive myself for. The first one is relinquishing my child for adoption. I have a tremendous amount of guilt about this because I abandoned him, and I think he probably ended up in a bad situation with his new family. The first four reasons on the list are very helpful. I'm perfectly human, which means I make mistakes. I did my best and had good intentions. I've done a lot of good things in my life, and I need to give myself credit for that.

"The second thing I need to forgive myself for is my immaturity. I've behaved like a child whenever I've been stressed or in bad situations. I feel like I'm stuck in time as a ten-year-old. The first seven reasons are helpful. I think it also helps me understand how big of an impact my dad's death had on me."

"Excellent!" Wes said. "Forgiving yourself takes time, but it is a critical step in the healing process. It has to be done. You can't transform without it.

"I'd like to address your 'stuck ten-year-old self' for a moment. This is very common and is sometimes referred to as **regression**. We are hard-wired to survive and avoid what we fear. When we have a significant event when we are young, our solution is to run to that experience of life before that event when we felt safe. In your case, you had two significant events that were close to each other: summer camp and your dad dying. So your solution was to return to being the nine-year-old just before these two events happened.

"What that also means is that your nine-year-old self has been running your life ever since. After all, everything was just fine when she was in charge. You don't want to mess with success, right? That's why you still feel and act immature sometimes. Your nine-year-old self has been doing the best she could and has been asked to do much more than she should have. It isn't easy trying to be a grown-up when you've never learned all the skills needed to act like a mature adult. From the perspective of a nine-year-old, you don't know how the world works, you don't feel strong, you don't feel safe, you don't know your rights, and you don't know how to protect yourself. You also don't know you have the power to change yourself and to influence others. You don't know that you can be a leader. We are going to help your nine-year-old self retire soon so she can run off and play. She has definitely earned it! Does that make sense, Elin?"

"Yes, it does. When you explain it like that, it makes perfect sense."

"Good. Then it should be a lot easier for you to forgive yourself for being immature sometimes. Now let's talk about boundaries, which are important for maintaining healthy relationships."

Wes gave Elin a handout titled *Boundaries* and went over it with her.

Boundaries

It is important to set **healthy boundaries** with others. Boundaries are used to let others know what is acceptable behavior to us and what is not. Sometimes we don't set boundaries. Sometimes we set boundaries but don't enforce them. The result is that we tolerate situations and allow people to abuse us. This harms the relationship, causes us problems, and keeps us from elevating. It is critical that we set and enforce healthy boundaries.

Reasons We Don't Set Boundaries

There are two primary reasons why we don't set boundaries. First, we worry about how the other person will react. We are afraid they will not accept our request. We don't want to offend them, and we don't want to make the relationship worse. We want to avoid conflict. But we have no control over how someone else feels; we only have control over how we feel. Second, we don't know how.

Set an Effective Boundary

You can set an effective boundary by doing the following:

- **Positive:** Be positive and assertive.
- **Clear:** Clearly describe the old behavior you don't want and the new behavior you need.
- **Needs:** Tell them why their behavior doesn't match your needs.
- **Actionable:** Make sure it is something they can do.
- **Love:** Deliver the message from a kind and loving place.
- **Sandwich Technique:** Deliver it with the negative message sandwiched between two positive messages. Start with good news, then tell them the bad news, and end with good news.
- **Confirm:** Ask them if they accept your request, reject it, or would like to make a counteroffer.

Note that we have a fundamental right to choose how we want to live. If they can't accept our boundary request, then it is time to reconsider how we will interact with them in the future, if at all. Reasonable people will usually welcome a boundary conversation. Difficult people may not want to have the conversation, but they will generally respect a boundary we set with them.

There are other people who will not react favorably to a boundary conversation. We don't necessarily need their approval. It is really just a courtesy notification to inform them of how you will be interacting with them from now on. Instead of setting the boundary you want to set that could cause more problems for your relationship, you might set a different **harmonious boundary** that appears to be reasonable and positive, yet accomplishes the same goal. You can maintain harmony and still get what you want.

Remember that you only have control over changing yourself. You can't control others or force them to behave differently. Some people don't want to change or think they can't. Just like you can't expect your dog to act like a cat or your turtle to fly like a bird, you can't expect others to do what you want them to do. It is important to accept them as they are.

Go to www.WiseLovingBeing.com/handouts
to find a copy of this handout online.

"Elin, let's apply this to your life. For example, with your cousin, you could say something like this: 'Hi, Carl. You have a lovely home, and I love spending time with your cat. Unfortunately, I will not be able to take care of your house or your cat next summer because I will be working. I wanted to make sure you had enough notice so you can find someone else. I am glad that I could help you with this over the past several years, and I appreciate your friendship.'

"What do you think, Elin? Is that something you can do?"

Elin confidently replied, "Yes."

"Is there anyone on your boundary-setting list you need help with?"

"I have a person on my list named Richard, who is extra difficult to deal with, and I can't avoid him," Elin offered. "I'm guessing that if I push back in any way, it will cause tremendous problems. We kind of need each other's help right now, and the relationship will definitely be coming to an end in the next year or two. I think my best course of action is to figure out what I can do to improve the situation now. I need to find a way to set a boundary that helps me but in no way looks like it is focused on him. That way I can start preparing for what happens after the relationship ends. Let me think about this for a bit."

"That sounds like a good idea, Elin. Great work today!

"To summarize, freedom and forgiveness are critical to the healing process. They free you from the past and allow you to make the most of the present. The most important person to forgive is yourself. Setting healthy boundaries is valuable for both parties. Freeing yourself from others, forgiving yourself and others, and setting healthy boundaries all have to be done if you want to transform.

"Now, from a high-level perspective, you've officially made it through the very difficult and uncomfortable awareness process. Congratulations!"

Elin responded by clapping her hands with a big smile on her face.

"Elin, I know you like the comics. In Walt Kelly's comic strip *Pogo*, the title character said, 'We have met the enemy and he is us.' The bad news is that, for the most part, it's our fault. That's also the good news. We have complete control over ourselves, and we can choose to make things better.

"Let me tell you about the **Sculptor Analogy** to give you a visual representation of where we are in the transformation process. Most people see a block of marble as an obstacle. The sculptor sees the marble block and visualizes its highest potential. She sees the amazing statue hiding inside and wants to let it out. She then chips away at the block and transforms the marble into a work of art.

"We've been doing the same thing in our work together. You've become aware of what is blocking your full potential, and now we are going to transform your obstacles into strengths by discovering that incredible part of you that is just begging to be let out.

"Tomorrow, we will start exploring some new concepts and perspectives that will help you see the world in a different way. This will lay the foundation for your transformation. Are you ready for your homework?"

"Yes, sir! What's my homework?" Elin asked.

"Please make a list of the top-ten things you would have liked to have achieved by this time in your life. For each one, write down what obstacles have been in your way. Let's meet here again tomorrow at the same time. Any questions?"

"No questions. See you tomorrow, Wes!"

Part Three:

New Perspectives

Chapter Eleven

Universal Elevation

When Elin arrived at the Cinnabon the next day, Wes was already there. He greeted her with a big smile and said, "Good morning, Elin! How are you today?"

"Good morning, Wes," Elin replied. "I'm doing pretty good. How are you?"

"I feel truly amazing today!" Wes replied enthusiastically. "Let's get started, shall we?"

As they began their morning walk around the mall, Wes began speaking. "Let's go over the homework. What are the top-ten things you would have liked to have achieved by this time in your life? For each one, list what obstacles have been in your way."

Elin took out her homework and replied, "My ten items are:

1. *Have a nice, close-knit family, including a husband, children, and grandchildren.* The obstacles were my immaturity (stuck as a nine-year-old), my challenges growing up, my failed first attempt at family life, and my fear of rejection and abandonment.

2. *Have financial security.* The obstacles were wanting to avoid math, being ignorant about finances, not getting training for better-paying jobs, lack of confidence, immaturity, and not developing a healthy respect for money.

3. *Have a variety of good friends.* The obstacles were shame, fear of rejection, difficulty meeting other people with common interests, and not being able to be open with others.

4. *Pursue a job or volunteer in archaeology and geology.* The obstacles were lack of money, fear of rejection, physical demands of the job, and my allergies.

5. *Earn a master's degree and receive field training in archaeology and geology.* The obstacles were lack of money, physical demands of the job, lack of confidence, and my allergies.

6. *Be involved with the community and do volunteer work.* The obstacles were fear of rejection, lack of confidence, lack of money, and my allergies.

7. *Good dental health.* The obstacles were lack of money and lack of insurance.

8. *Own a safe and cozy home.* The obstacles were lack of money and the fear of entrapment, meaning I can't move or escape when I feel I need to.

9. *Travel, dine out, and explore America with a compatible companion.* The obstacles were lack of money and lack of friends or a companion.

10. *Live on a ranch and operate a rescued animal facility.* The obstacles were lack of money, fear of entrapment, and lack of family."

"Great job, Elin! I'm so impressed by how well you do your homework. One of the obstacles you mentioned multiple times was the word *fear*: the fear of rejection, abandonment, and entrapment.

"The second obstacle that you either mentioned or implied was the word *lack*. You mentioned the lack of maturity, knowledge, training, confidence, understanding, money, health, insurance, friends, and family.

"The third issue is a disconnect between your abilities and your career interests. You didn't take everything into consideration. In other words, you were pursuing something that wasn't a good fit for you due to the physical demands and your allergies. You didn't have enough money to pay for the program. But the bigger issue is that you wouldn't be able to earn enough income from that career to cover the cost of the education and your living expenses.

"The fourth issue you implied is that you didn't make any progress toward many of these goals. You didn't evolve and get better. There is definitely a lack of commitment and resourcefulness here. I also think there is a lack of both drive and purpose.

"The final issue, which you didn't mention but underlies all ten items, is your fear of not belonging. When we were talking about fears, you listed the following as your secondary fear statements: *I'm not lovable. I'm not good enough. I'm not smart enough. I'm not worthy. I'm an outsider. I don't fit in.* When you add your core belief and identity that *I'm a bad person and I need to be punished*, it becomes quite clear why you haven't been able to achieve any of these ten items. Are you aware of this?"

"No. Not like this," Elin replied. "It's obvious when it's all laid out in front of me though."

"Indeed. Awareness is critical in this process. You've done a lot of work over the past week, becoming more aware of your invisible walls, which have been the obstacles preventing you from achieving your goals. The good news is that you are about to escape the walls of your invisible box. But now there's a new challenge. Where are you going to go? What is right for you? What is even possible? What is the most important and impactful thing you can do now?

"Let me illustrate my point with the **Cardboard Box Analogy**. Imagine that you have lived in a cardboard box your entire life. You can't see through the walls. You can't hear or smell anything outside the box. In fact, nothing gets through. You don't even know if there *is* anything on the other side of the walls because this is all you've ever known. You don't have access to the internet or any other knowledge. Given these circumstances, what can you imagine is possible for your life? It's quite limiting, for sure."

Elin nodded her head in agreement.

"Now let's say I come along, open the box, and let you out. You are now in a basement, which is a lot better than the small box. I then take you upstairs so you can see the rest of the house. Then I take you on a tour of the neighborhood, the city, the state, the country, and the entire world. Then I point out the moon, the planets, the galaxy, and the universe. Finally, we visit the planet Neptune. With this newfound awareness, what can you imagine is possible for your life now? It's almost limitless, isn't it?"

Elin nodded her head in agreement, this time with more excitement.

"Great! The purpose of today is to help you see life from a different perspective and discover new possibilities. Are you ready, Elin?"

"I am, Wes. Bring it on!"

"First, I'm going to share with you a very powerful concept called Universal Elevation."

Wes gave Elin a handout titled *Universal Elevation* and went over it with her.

Universal Elevation

Universal Elevation is a concept that helps you see the world in a different way. There are twenty-one powerful principles that, when practiced completely and consistently, can transform your life, family, company, community, government, and the world. The Universal Elevation principles help you achieve better results in a shorter amount of time. The word *universal* means "all." The word *elevation* means "moving higher, getting better, improving, or transforming."

Standard vs. Universal Thinking
Standard thinking is how people normally think today, and it is fear-based. Universal Thinking is how a person would think using one of the Universal Elevation principles, and it is love-based.

#	PRINCIPLE	UNIVERSAL THINKING	STANDARD THINKING
1	**Abundance**	There is more than enough to go around. There are no limits. Be more resourceful and creative.	**Scarcity.** Limited. Lack. There isn't enough for everyone.
2	**All**	All parts need to be included and addressed. Complete. Diversity. Examples: all living things, all areas of your life, all generations, complete solution, diverse viewpoints.	**Some**. Incomplete. Uniformity. Some members are chosen; others are excluded. Everyone must think and act the same.

#	PRINCIPLE	UNIVERSAL THINKING	STANDARD THINKING
3	**Balance**	We can't have too much of one thing and not enough of another. Examples: balance of power, balanced ecosystem, balanced view, balanced life.	**Unbalanced.** Off balance. One group or person dominates and controls all others.
4	**Collaborate**	We create better solutions together than either side can create alone. We all win when we work together. Peace.	**Fight.** Argue. Ignore. Discount. Us vs. Them mentality. Conflict. Mediate.
5	**Connected**	All parts affect each other. What I do to you, I do to me. Interdependent.	**Disconnected.** Independent. Separate and unaffected.
6	**Equal**	All parts are equal, equally important, and need to be treated equally.	**Unequal.** Levels. Hierarchy. Segregation. Some are arbitrarily viewed as better.
7	**Evolve**	Get better, elevate, improve, innovate, or transform.	**Decline.** Stagnate. Get worse, stay the same, or elevate slower than others.
8	**Excellence**	Competent, effective, efficient, expert, experienced, knowledgeable, and skilled.	**Incompetence.** Ineffective, ignorant, or unskilled.
9	**Fair**	Justice. Everyone is treated fairly.	**Unfair.** Unjust. Discrimination.
10	**Freedom**	Everyone is free to choose how they want to think, feel, speak, and act. We make our own choices and allow others to make theirs. We are tolerant of others.	**Enslaved.** Dictate. Cancel. Censor. Control. Intolerant. Exert power over others.

#	PRINCIPLE	UNIVERSAL THINKING	STANDARD THINKING
11	**Generous**	Give. Help others in need.	**Greedy**. Hoard, take, cheat, and steal.
12	**Internal**	We can only change ourselves. We can't change others. Focus on what we can do better.	**External**. Focus on things we can't change.
13	**Lead**	Lead by example. Take initiative. Inspire and empower yourself and others.	**Follow**. Oppose. Resist. Stop. Do nothing and complain.
14	**Love**	Seek the highest form of energy, purpose, and belonging. Accept, appreciate, respect, and forgive yourself and others. Be kind and positive.	**Hate. Fear**. Judge. Disrespect. Reject. Discount. Mean. Negative.
15	**Present**	Be present and focus on what is happening now. Do the most important thing in the present moment that is aligned with your desired future.	**Absent**. Distracted. Preoccupied. Stuck in the past or focused on the future without taking meaningful action now.
16	**Required**	All parts have a unique purpose, are valuable, and are required.	**Expendable**. Some parts are not needed.
17	**Responsible**	Have integrity, take ownership, be productive, work hard, and do the right thing.	**Irresponsible**. Shirk. Lazy.
18	**Serve**	Help and add value to others. Valuism is adding maximum value to all stakeholders. Profit and wealth are an incomplete measure of success.	**Exploit**. Take. Extract the maximum amount from others. Take advantage of others.

#	PRINCIPLE	UNIVERSAL THINKING	STANDARD THINKING
19	Spectrum	A spectrum consists of two opposite endpoints and everything in between. Instead of black or white, it is black *and* white *and* every shade of gray in between.	**Binary**. There are only two opposite values: good or bad, right or wrong, black or white.
20	Truth	Be honest and humble. Seek wisdom, truth, and understanding. Keep an open mind. Be authentic. Discover, think, and verify. Listen.	**False**. Lie. Prejudge. Label. Naïve. Blindly accept. Talk but don't listen.
21	Win	We all need to win. This is known as win/win thinking.	**Lose**. Win/lose thinking. I win when others lose actually becomes lose/lose.

Go to www.WiseLovingBeing.com/handouts
to find a copy of this handout online.

"Elin, the world would look much different if more people consistently practiced Universal Elevation. It would lead to the end of abuse, conflict, crime, environmental disasters, global warming, human trafficking, murder, poverty, prejudice, starvation, terrorism, and war.

"Our whole legal system is set up to fight and argue in court. There are arbitration agreements and companies who specialize in conflict resolution. Marriage counseling leans more toward mediation. With *collaboration*, we aren't looking to mediate a conflict where we split the difference and neither side (or only one side) is happy. Instead, we're looking to create something new that both sides are happy with and that is better than either party could come up with on their own.

"Imagine what would happen if companies focused on *valuism*, which is creating the maximum possible long-term value for all stake-holders, instead of just short-term profit that focuses on extracting the maximum possible value from everything. Profit is an incomplete measure of success. It is a one-dimensional measurement of a multidimensional world, which includes employees, customers, communities, suppliers, partners, and the environment. The lifetime value of an organization is maximized when profit is balanced with all other competing needs. Moving from capitalism to valuism by applying Universal Elevation would completely change the world, and those companies would see better financial results over a much longer period of time.

"The founders of the United States created a government that was founded on the principles of Universal Elevation. Unfortunately, many of today's politicians have lost sight of this and have switched to *standard thinking*. The results speak for themselves.

"Here is a real-world example of how to apply the principles to your personal life. My friend Billy always put work first. He worked long hours and had a long commute on top of that. He focused on making money and getting to the top. In his mind, though, he wasn't successful. He wasn't a millionaire, and he wasn't an executive in a big company. He left home as a teenager to prove himself to the world and to his parents. He didn't feel he could return home until he met his expectations of success. At fifty-four years old, Billy felt he was out of time. Every one of his childhood friends, who was worse off as a kid, was now doing much better than he was. He wasn't married, and he had no kids or close friends. He was out of shape, overweight, and didn't get much sleep. He consumed a lot of coffee and sugary foods during the day to keep himself going. His favorite 'restaurant' was the vending machine. He was depressed and lonely.

"Billy studied the principles of Universal Elevation and realized a few things. All these years, he had only been focused on his career. He had been abusing his body and wasn't excelling in the other areas of his life. As a result, he was off balance and his life didn't work. He was always focused on being successful in the future. He was always unhappy in the present moment, yet he thought he would be happy when he met his goals and expectations. He tried to do everything on his own, and he rarely connected with others at work or elsewhere. He thought money was scarce and the positions at the top of the company were few. For him to win, he believed others had to lose.

"Billy decided to embrace all the principles of Universal Elevation. He first started to treat his body as an equal partner with his mind. Clearly, his body was a necessary tool to improving his life and served a purpose. So he decided to listen to it and give it what it needed. He gave it enough sleep. He fed it nutritious foods. He gave it exercise, and eventually he lost weight. His soul also was an equal part of him. He decided to slow down, spend more time in nature, enjoy the moment, and connect with others. He started donating his time to help others in need. Slowly, he began living a more balanced life.

"Billy decided to get a new job close to home, which saved him over an hour each day and greatly reduced his stress levels. He made a career change that was better aligned with his skills, abilities, purpose, and vision. He saw that the decisions he made were often win/lose or even lose/lose, and he was often the biggest loser. He focused on adding value and looked for ways everyone could win. He accepted that he didn't have all the answers, and this humility motivated him to gain important knowledge and wisdom.

"After a year of following this new path, Billy told me that one of the biggest revelations he had was around his view of himself. Since he didn't feel successful in his eyes, the only logical conclusion he could draw in a binary world was that he was unsuccessful and bad. He hated himself, was very critical of his own mistakes, and was angry all the time, taking it out on those around him. Of course, the source of this outrage was his unconscious anger at himself. He said that realizing life is a spectrum made a huge difference for him. He wasn't bad. In fact, he was good. He was simply in a different place than he had expected he would be as a teenager. He was finally able to accept himself, forgive himself, and, more importantly, love himself.

"Billy is much happier today. He is healthy. He has new friends and is doing fun things. His career is taking off like he had always hoped. Life is now full of abundance for him. Everything is connected. Improving his health improved his mind and all other areas of his life.

"Here is a business example. My friend Bob applied the Universal Elevation principles when he joined a company that wasn't doing well. The company was not meeting its financial goals and was losing customers. Their products were of increasingly poor quality and were falling behind the competition in terms of functionality and technology. The top executives were removed by the parent company, and Bob was brought in to help turn the company around.

"Bob conducted a detailed assessment of the company to see how it was truly doing. He discovered the things it did well, where it was failing, and everything in between. Bob could see that it suffered from standard thinking. The different departments were fighting with each other about everything, and each thought they were the most important department in the company. Each department worked to make the others look bad while concealing their own faults. They were fighting over limited resources.

"Of course, the reality was that every department had major performance gaps and needed to focus on how they could improve. If the employees didn't turn things around immediately, the company was going to go out of business and they would all be out of a job.

"Bob met with each employee to understand their view of the company. He gathered their ideas on how they thought the company could do better, and he took inventory of their skills, interests, and knowledge gaps. He asked them about their career and life goals. He reorganized the company and sent his employees to training so they could deliver higher value. He formed a new strategic group with a representative from each department. Their purpose was to speak about challenges, issues, and strategies. Their goal was to find solutions where everyone could win.

"Bob then met with the other stakeholders, including the parent company, customers, partners, and suppliers. He asked them for their feedback on what the company did well and how it could do better. He set up quarterly meetings where they could discuss issues and provide their requests for future functionality. He created a three-year strategic plan based on everyone's input that met their highest priority needs.

"Every stakeholder, including the new strategic group, was able to submit requests for functionality to be included in the next product release. Everyone was treated equally. Each one was allocated a fair number of development hours for which they could submit a prioritized list of work they wanted done.

"Bob created a new company culture, as well as a new mission, vision, and values statement. The new company culture required everyone to treat each other equally and respectfully. They were all one team; therefore they needed to work together. The new mission was to deliver products on time with the best functionality and the highest quality. The new vision was to become the vendor of choice for customers needing a similar system. The new values were placed into the acronym *I VOTE*, which stood for *Innovation, Value, Ownership, Truth,* and *Excellence.*

"Bob held a company meeting where he drew a line in the sand. What happened in the past stayed in the past. Everyone was forgiven, and they all had a clean slate. He explained to his employees what was expected of them moving forward. He went over the new culture, mission, vision, and values. He talked about the strategy, the reorganization, the new strategic group, and the scorecard that would track their daily progress on key metrics. He talked about the principles of Universal Elevation. He laid out what the new incentives, rewards, and consequences were. He told everyone that he was going to be holding them accountable, and that they also needed to hold themselves accountable.

"Bob held team-building events. Each team was composed of one member from each department. He assigned a problem to each team to solve. As they worked together, they became more aware of how they could better utilize each other's strengths to solve the problem. They realized they could achieve much better results when they helped each other and worked together as one team.

"As a result, the company transformed itself. Bob's results were quite amazing, but they weren't unique. He applied Universal Elevation to his next company and a nonprofit sports team, all with similar results.

"Elin, what new possibilities do you see for your life if you practice Universal Elevation? How would it affect your ability to achieve your goals?"

Elin answered excitedly, "Where do I begin, Wes? I mean, this represents a huge shift in my thinking.

"With *abundance*, I can see there are numerous ways for me to achieve my goals. I just need to be more resourceful and creative. If there is no scarcity of money, then I don't have to feel guilty that others will starve when I eat. I can find friends and companions. I can find a job and make enough money to support myself.

"With *all*, I see it is important that I improve all areas of my life. I can't leave anything out. *All* means helping others today, as well as future generations. All means looking for complete solutions and making sure everything is addressed.

"With *balance*, I see that I actually need to spend time earning money *and* improving my health. I have ignored these two areas, plus others. I'm so off-balance that nothing works. Instead of focusing on my faults, I need to have a balanced view and acknowledge that there are some things I do well and some things I can do better. I also need to have a balanced view of the world. I tend to only look at what's wrong. I need to spend more time asking what's right with the world. What I find odd is that I often have an overly positive view of people when I first meet them. I then become disappointed when reality appears and they eventually let me down. I need to have a balanced view here too.

"With *collaborate*, I understand that I need to work with others. I've been trying to do things on my own. I can get where I want to go much faster by speaking with experts who have done something similar. Instead of arguing and fighting with certain people, I can look for how we can work together. By increasing my circle of friends, I can improve my life in many ways.

"With *connected*, instead of being stuck not knowing what to do next, I can just pick something on my list. No matter what I do, all areas of my life will benefit. If I want to receive love, then all I have to do is give love. As my dad used to tell me, 'If your feet are cold, then put on a hat.' When I spend time helping others in need, it actually helps me. Likewise, if I help others who should be helping themselves, then I am only harming both of us. Connected also reinforces my use of the Golden Rule. When I treat others well, then I also benefit.

"With *equal*, I need to believe that I'm not less than anyone because of my age, lack of wealth, or gender. I am equal with others, and I will require that they treat me equally. I'll have more confidence speaking with others I once saw as better than me.

"With *evolve*, I see that I need to be constantly improving myself by learning new things and then putting that knowledge to use. I need to always think about how I can get better instead of trying to maintain my current state, or getting worse, which is what I've been accustomed to doing. I can spend some of my extra twelve hours a day working on bettering myself in some way.

"With *excellence*, I will become an expert in personal finances and gain skills and experience in an area where I can make money. I can become more knowledgeable by reading books from the library, searching for information online, and talking to others.

"With *fair*, I will make sure I treat others fairly; likewise, I will insist that they treat me fairly. I will also make sure I treat myself fairly instead of putting everyone else's needs before mine.

"With *freedom*, I will be comfortable thinking, feeling, speaking, and acting as I choose. I will remove my expectations of how others should act, and I will respect their decisions. This will give me greater peace of mind, and I might actually learn something from them.

"With *generous*, I will continue to help others while also being generous with myself.

"With *internal*, I will focus my energy on improving myself and will stop trying to change others. I will stop focusing on things that I can't control. One of the biggest things I can do is stop the news feeds that play on my emotions and fears and distract me from the important things I need to do.

"With *lead*, I will take the initiative to improve my life and inspire others to improve theirs. I will lead the way in making things better for myself and others. I will blaze my own trail.

"With *love*, I will improve my relationships with myself and others. It will also guide me. When I'm not sure which direction to go, I can simply choose the path that results in the highest form of love. By loving myself, I can manage my fears around not belonging. I will also see the best in others.

"With *present*, I can stop focusing on the regrets, guilt, and shame from my past. I can stop obsessing about the things I fear will happen in the future that are unlikely to occur. I'll be much more productive when I focus 100 percent of my energy on doing my best in the present moment that is aligned with where I want to be in the future. When others speak, I will be focused on what they are saying instead of thinking about what I want to say. That will improve all of my relationships.

"With *required*, I see that I am valued, I have a unique purpose, and I am needed. I think this is incredibly powerful and motivating. I need to move quickly to help those who need my help.

"With *responsible*, I see that I need to finally take ownership of my life. I think I've had this fantasy that someone was going to save me, and I wouldn't need to do anything. I see now that the only person who is going to save me is me. I need to work hard. I need to make a choice to go down a different path.

"With *serve*, I know that helping others and adding value is very important. That's something I've always believed. But now I see that I can't help others when I can't even help myself. Focusing on serving others will help me be more positive, feel better about myself, and make each day more fulfilling and meaningful. But I have to balance that with receiving value too. I need to stop preventing others from helping me.

"With *spectrum*, I can see all of me: the good, the bad, and everything in between. I am not defined by my worst moments. I can accept all of me. I used to think that if I wasn't perfect and good, then I had to be bad. Now I see that my behavior exists on a spectrum. I have rarely done anything truly bad.

"With *truth*, I can see the importance of verifying that what I think is true really is. This is a big job since there is so much misinformation out there. Instead of prejudging groups and using labels, I can spend time understanding others as individuals. I can also give up being 'right' about things I really don't know enough about. Instead of blindly accepting the news feeds as true, I can verify them and discover what is really going on to the best of my ability.

"With *win*, I can make sure that everyone wins, including me. This will be a tremendous help in changing my desired experience of sacrifice. It's important that I also benefit. I didn't see that I was always creating a win/lose situation where I was the biggest loser."

"Great work today, Elin! You're on fire! I love this side of you. I can see the bright light inside you shining even brighter!" Wes said ecstatically.

"To summarize, by shifting from standard thinking to Universal Thinking, we can transform our personal lives, families, communities, companies, organizations, government, and the world. Universal Elevation helps us achieve superior results quickly by providing better ways for us to approach the world.

"I want to tell you one more story that I think will help you to better understand how Universal Elevation can help you transform. My friend Nico had a difficult childhood. His parents were alcoholics, and the house was filled with constant disfunction, conflict, and violence. His parents had difficulty keeping jobs and were so caught up in their own survival mess that they couldn't take care of themselves, let alone him.

"Nico learned how to take care of himself early on. He lived a very different life than his friends did, and he never felt like he belonged. His clothes were not only too small, they were also torn and dirty. He didn't get to participate in after-school sports because he couldn't afford the uniform and he didn't have the time. He had to take care of his parents and do the work they should have been doing. He didn't get good grades because he didn't have much time to do his homework, no one at home helped him, and he was focused on survival instead of seeing the importance grades would have on his future.

"Nico was an outcast. Most of the other kids at school teased, bullied, and excluded him. But there were a few kids who treated him with respect and kindness. They went out of their way to treat him equally and helped him feel like he belonged.

"When I met Nico, he was in his early thirties. He was out of work and was totally lost. He didn't think he had any valuable skills and didn't know what he was going to do for work. He told me he never felt like he fit in anywhere. He believed he wasn't lovable, worthy, or smart enough. He didn't think like other people did and therefore believed there was something wrong with him. He didn't have much confidence in himself, nor did he have much hope that things would get better.

"When I introduced Nico to Universal Elevation, he was surprised to see how much standard thinking held him back, especially *scarcity* and *absent*. He thought jobs he could do were scarce, and he was always focused on his terrible past experiences or worrying about the future. He was also surprised to see that so many of his beliefs around how we should treat others aligned with Universal Thinking. I was able to help Nico see that his upbringing gave him a unique perspective on life that helped him think differently. It was far from a curse. It made him much stronger than he realized. Yes, he was a terrible follower and never fit in. But that was because he was a leader with a lot of empathy.

"I helped Nico understand his value; together, we created a vision and purpose for his life. I helped him understand that his life mattered, and there were people who were desperately waiting for him to show up and lead. I helped him realize that a fulfilling and meaningful life would only happen when he used all of his talents to help others. He enjoys being a leader now, helping others, and living a life he loves.

"Perspective is a funny thing. You look at a life from one angle and it looks terrible. But you look at that very same life from a different angle and it's fantastic. That's what Nico learned.

"Elin, I'd like to follow up on one thing you said earlier. For the principle of *connected*, you mentioned the Golden Rule. Have you ever heard of the Platinum Rule?"

"No. What's that?" Elin replied.

"The Golden Rule says to treat others as *you* would like to be treated. The **Platinum Rule** says to treat others as *they* would like to be treated. It's a subtle difference but it becomes very important in relationships. For example, my friends Bella and Jay had been married for seven years. They said they didn't feel loved by their partner anymore. They said the love was gone and they would probably need to divorce.

"I let them know that this was a very common challenge they could overcome. In fact, they could create a much stronger and higher love if they chose to work on their relationship.

"I walked them through the process. There are three steps to creating a loving relationship: understand yourself, understand your partner, and change yourself. The last step is the most important and difficult to do. Remember, as hard as you try, you can't change your partner; you can only change yourself. So focus on yourself. Ask what you can think, feel, say, or do to help your partner feel more loved.

"It seems simple, but they couldn't start the three steps until they improved their communication skills and created a safe, authentic environment where they could speak openly and honestly. I taught them several techniques and coached them until they mastered the new skills. I then introduced them to *The 5 Love Languages* by Gary Chapman. He found that people give and receive love in the following five ways: acts of service, gifts, physical touch, quality time, and words of affirmation.

"Jay was giving lots of compliments, but Bella needed acts of service to feel loved. She had past relationships where people had said one thing and done the opposite so acts of service were the only things she trusted. Bella did lots of things for Jay, but he didn't appreciate these acts of service; he needed words of affirmation. He had past relationships where people did nice things for him to compensate for the bad things they said to him. They both thought they were giving love, but it wasn't being received by their partner because they were using the Golden Rule and using the wrong love language.

"Bella and Jay continued to work on better understanding them-selves and each other. They talked in detail about the different ways they felt loved, and they discovered that sometimes circumstances changed things. For example, Jay felt loved when she made dinner for him when he was too busy and stressed at work. Bella said that in difficult times, what she needed most was just hearing something positive and supportive from him.

"I showed them how giving love also produces the same feeling as receiving love. They were in charge of creating the feeling of love inside themselves. I explained that love, in its highest form, is a selfless act with no expectation of receiving anything in return.

"They both learned how to adjust how they showed love so it would better match their partner's needs. Now when they receive love in their preferred language, they appreciate it even more, knowing their partner was making a special effort for them. The Platinum Rule transformed and elevated their marriage, and they are much happier today.

"Elin, you might try using the Platinum Rule with some of the important people in your life and see how it affects your relationships."

"Sounds good, Wes. I think my good intentions will have an even bigger impact on others when I try this."

"Agreed. It's amazing how making small changes to yourself can have such a big impact on everyone involved.

"Let me provide you with another perspective on life, which is based on the **Forest Fire Analogy**. There is a process in nature where destruction leads to a new and better world. One example is how a huge forest fire can destroy vast acreage. It looks like it kills all the plants and animals in its path, but that's not entirely true. It does clear out all the old debris and the weak. However, it also nourishes the soil and opens the pinecones to release their seeds. This results in a new, healthy, vibrant forest being created in its place. The animals that escaped the fire soon return. Sometimes the animals and plants need to evolve so they can better adapt to their new environment. It's the survival of the fittest. And it is nature's way of cleansing, growing, and transforming itself.

"Several of my friends have gone through something similar in their lives. Something happened where they lost their spouse, their job, their health, most of their friends, and almost everything they owned. They reached rock bottom living in a shelter, on the street, or in their car. It was a very humbling experience, but they didn't give up. They were able see the good both in their 'loss' and in their new living situation. They were able to learn and adapt and eventually transformed their lives into something that was much better than before.

"They've also realized that sometimes the only way to grow and get to a better place is to lose everything. They are then free to totally recreate themselves from the ground up. From this **Naked Perspective**, they're not trying to replicate what they had. They're not going backward; they're moving forward. It's an internal and external cleansing, and it's a time for evolution, revolution, and transformation.

"In many ways, they're grateful. As the title of The Fixx song says, they were 'Saved by Zero.' Losing everything was the best thing that ever happened to them because it allowed them to discover the truth and see new possibilities they couldn't have seen otherwise. Being hungry and uncomfortable provided the extra motivation they needed to take action. It allowed them to do something they wouldn't have done before because they were too comfortable with the way things were. With a blank piece of paper, starting from nothing, they were then able to create something better and move forward, unencumbered by their past.

"Elin, something similar is happening to you right now. There is hope. Something better is possible if you choose to learn, grow, and act. Of course, nothing will happen on its own, and no one is going to do the work for you. It's time to recreate yourself and transform. It's time to fight for what you want. Stay positive and don't give up. This is only temporary. Does that make sense?"

Elin nodded her head, still thinking about the magnitude of what Wes had said. "Yes. It makes sense. And it's comforting and inspiring to hear that others go through this too. I thought I was the only one."

"Yes, it's easy to think that we are unique and that all the bad things that are happening to us are making things worse. We think there is something wrong with us, and we focus on what we have lost. With the **Perspective of Time**, we can look back on our lives and see how the challenges made us stronger and smarter. Instead of thinking life was better before, we can see that life is much better now. We can focus on what we have gained and how we have grown.

"Note that disaster isn't required for this transformation process. Some of my friends have created this naked perspective proactively by backpacking through Europe, India, or the Pacific Crest Trail. One of my friends got into a boat and sailed around the world. The key is to step out of your current life and comfort zone. The goal is to do something you haven't done before, and give yourself plenty of time for self-reflection. Living a simple life helps you avoid external distractions so you can focus internally.

"This transformation process can also happen more than once in a person's lifetime depending on how much growth they have to do. My friend Glenn had gone through this process four times and was on his fifth go-round when I met him. He felt like a total loser when he compared himself to his friends and family. Being judged and hearing negative comments from those around him only reinforced this view. I helped him see that each of these 'dumpster fires,' as he called them, were evolutionary forest fires. They were critical, beneficial events and were required for him to make the tremendous personal and spiritual growth he had made. While his friends and family had basically stayed the same, he had completely transformed his life. And I let him know there will probably be a few more forest fires in his future as he continues to grow. They are definitely something to be welcomed and valued."

Wes saw that Elin had completely digested this lesson and was more at peace with herself. "There's one more perspective I need to teach you today that will better help you understand what taking action looks like, especially given your default behavior of 'waiting for your prince to arrive and save you' without you having to do any work. The **Poodle Perspective** is the view of a domesticated dog, who waits patiently to be fed, looks for ways to please her owner, and begs for food when she's hungry. She is completely subservient to her owner. She has effectively turned off her mind since there is nothing important to think about. She is lazy and simply waits for her owner to come home and take care of all her basic needs. She is always waiting for a handout and feels entitled to her comfy lifestyle.

"On the opposite end of the spectrum is the **Wolf Perspective**. The wild wolf is a very effective hunter who practices his skills every day. He is a self-reliant survivor who is proactive and highly intelligent. He doesn't wait for someone to feed him, nor does he wait for something to die like a vulture does. He takes ownership. He goes hunting and doesn't stop until he has successfully killed and eaten something. He observes his prey with an intense focus, looking for opportunities and weakness. He creates a plan that has a good chance for success and then attacks with the help of his pack. The only measure of success is whether he is able to kill something and eat it.

"Let me give you an example to help you better understand this. My friend Viktor had been looking for a job for the past nine months. He was out of money and living in his car. He had sent out over four hundred job applications but still had not landed a job. He kept hoping that someone would hire him, and he made sure to present himself as a positive, nice, hard-working person who would make a great addition to the team. He thought jobs were scarce and thus resigned himself to take any job he could find anywhere in the United States. He applied for entry-level jobs at fast food restaurants all the way up to senior management positions he had held in the past, and a wide variety of different roles in between. He was basically begging for a company to give him a job. He was depressed, desperate, and felt like a total failure.

"Then one day after receiving yet another rejection, Viktor snapped, and he turned into a wolf. He realized that he was very talented and that none of the companies he applied to deserved him, nor would they appreciate him and pay him what he was worth. He decided that instead of waiting around for someone to hire him, he was going to create income on his own. He looked at the different options available to him, picked the one with the best chance of success, and then took massive action. He basically hired himself. He gave up begging for jobs and finally started hunting for income.

"Elin, does that help you better understand where you are today versus where you need to be regarding taking action?"

Elin replied, "Yes, that really puts things into perspective. I realize there is an action spectrum here, but I need to move myself far away from being the pampered poodle I am today and get closer to being a wild wolf."

"Agreed. You can even have some fun with this. Whenever you don't know what to do, just ask yourself, WWWD? What would Wolfie do?"

Elin laughed. "Sounds good to me!"

Wes paused momentarily as he thought about all the information he had covered. "Elin, today was our first day of looking at life from new perspectives. We covered quite a few, and each one needs to be practiced as you would any new skill. They aren't just something to know; they are to be acted upon repeatedly over time. Tomorrow we'll continue this with my favorite: The Play Exercise. You're going to love it! Are you ready for your homework?"

"Yes, sir! What's my homework?"

"First, I want you to make a list of all your skills, abilities, and resources. We so often look at what is wrong with us. This is an exercise in looking at what is *right* with us. Second, I want you to think about a theatrical play. Who writes the script? What are the elements of the story? Who are the actors? How is it performed? Let's meet here again tomorrow at the same time. Any questions?"

"No questions. See you tomorrow, Wes!"

Chapter Twelve

The Play

"When Elin arrived at the Cinnabon the next day, Wes was already there. He greeted her with a big smile and said, "Good morning, Elin! How are you today?"

"Good morning, Wes," Elin replied. "I'm doing great! How are you?"

"I'm incredible!" Wes replied enthusiastically. "Let's get started, shall we?"

They began their morning walk around the mall as Wes spoke of the lesson for the day. "Let's talk about a play."

Wes gave Elin a handout titled *The Play* and went over it with her.

The Play

Elements of a Play

In order to put on a play, you need a script, a director, a set, and some actors. When a play is performed, there are usually multiple acts. For this exercise, the play will have two acts with one intermission.

Chronological Storyline

The chronological storyline for this script follows these ten stages:

1. In the beginning, everything is great for the main character, you, the protagonist.
2. Then a bad event happens to you. It is usually some kind of loss delivered by an antagonist, also known as the bad guy or villain.
3. You are determined to fix things.
4. You leave home and go on a journey filled with challenges and tests.
5. You find a wise being who usually knows the antagonist and what is needed for you to win.
6. The wise being sees your potential and offers to help you.
7. You become a student of the wise being. The training is intense. You work very hard for long hours and get little sleep. You learn, train, and elevate until you master the new skills. Sometimes the student becomes better than the master. The more powerful the antagonist, the more you need to rise.
8. You start the journey to confront the antagonist and are met with more challenges, yet you continue to learn and grow.
9. You battle the antagonist and win.
10. You live happily ever after.

Go to www.WiseLovingBeing.com/handouts
to find a copy of this handout online.

"Are we in agreement about what a play is?"

Elin nodded her head and said, "Yes. Agreed."

"Great. And if your life were a play that followed this same storyline, where are you on your journey?"

"I'm at stage four. I've left home, but I think I might have lost my determination to fix things along the way, from step three."

Wes smiled and said, "Yes, I agree that you are missing that strong determination to improve things right now. You mentioned yesterday that you needed to finally take ownership of your life. So it sounds like you never made it to stage five because you were looking for someone else to save you because you never decided to save yourself, correct?"

"Yes. You're right. I've had this childhood fantasy that a handsome prince on a white horse was going to ride up and save me. We would live happily ever after, and I wouldn't have to do a thing. I think I've always been looking for others to rescue me, and I've never taken ownership of my life and my problems. In many ways, I still feel like a scared nine-year-old girl whose parents take care of everything. All I have to do is play and go to school."

"That's a great observation, Elin. Are you ready to grow up and take ownership now? Are you highly motivated to improve your situation?"

"I'm ready, Wes!" Elin replied enthusiastically.

"Excellent news! You're now at stage seven, so listen up," Wes said with a smile and a wink. "One of my favorite quotes is from a play written in 1599 called *As You Like It* by William Shakespeare. You've probably heard it. 'All the world's a stage, and all the men and women merely players.' It turns out that a play is a perfect metaphor for life, and I want to spend our time today going through **The Play Exercise**. So hang on. It's going to be a wild ride!"

Wes gave Elin two handouts titled *The Rules* and *Act One* and went over them with her.

The Rules

Overview

In order to get the most out of The Play Exercise, you will need an open mind and you will need to think within the rules of the play. This is a foundational step in your transformation. If you map the play to a **caterpillar's journey** then Act One is the caterpillar, the intermission is the chrysalis, and Act Two is the butterfly. Your goal today is to take the first step toward identifying your purpose in life and your vision for the second act.

Disclaimers

Here are some disclaimers to help you with The Play Exercise.

- This is not a spiritual or religious exercise. It does not espouse a particular belief system, nor does it ask you to change your current belief system or atheistic or agnostic views. Please do not try to map the concepts here to your current belief system, including your definitions of God, soul, spirit, reincarnation, heaven, and hell.
- This exercise does not promote the view that we are in any way responsible for all the negative things that happen to us. There are bad people who do bad things, and they should be held responsible for their actions.
- This exercise does not promote the view that everything and everyone you interact with is a message from a higher being.
- This exercise also doesn't promote the view that our lives are predetermined. You have free will and complete control over what you think, feel, say, and do. You can react and respond to the events of the play as you choose. Everyone is free to make their own choices, which all have positive and negative consequences.

WLB Role

Let me give you some more details on the Wise Loving Being, or WLB, we talked about when we were working on significant events. You are obviously aware that you are a human being, consisting of your mind and your body. There is another part of you called your WLB. A WLB is a highly intelligent and loving entity. It is indestructible, it will still exist after you die, and it cannot be harmed in any way. A small part of your WLB resides in your body, while the vast majority of it remains in an area that is beyond this physical world.

For The Play Exercise, you can think of me as your WLB. You and I are a team. I love you very much, and I only want what is best for you. Today, I am interrupting your life and giving you a time-out so I can share some important wisdom with you.

The Script Framework

Your life has actually been a theatrical play this whole time. I wrote the script framework for your play before you were born on this planet. It is **intermission** time. The first act is over, and the second act is about to begin.

You are the **protagonist**. Instead of a script that predetermines your life from start to finish, I created a framework for you. It provides the underlying structure for your life, but it also allows you to create what you want. You have free will.

The **Car Frame Analogy** can help illustrate this point. In very simple terms, all cars share a basic frame. Car manufacturers then customize the frame to create different models of cars; they use different engines, interiors, and exteriors. The same car frame can result in a sedan, a sport utility vehicle, a luxury vehicle, or a sports car.

Similarly with your life, you can take the framework I have provided and create who you want to be.

The framework I have provided includes the following:
- The setting,
- Your circumstances,
- The main events that occur in your life,
- A series of lessons for you to learn, and
- The main characters or humans who will help you learn the lessons.

Objectives in Life

You only have two objectives in life. Both objectives are equally important. Note that the second objective is clearly dependent on the first.
- **Elevate Yourself:** Your **first objective** in life is to elevate yourself as high as possible, given your life's circumstances. You can think of this like you are playing a video game; you are basically leveling up as far as you can.
- **Elevate Everything Else:** Your **second objective**, also known as your **Big Strong Why**, is to help elevate everything else: all other humans, all living things, and the planet. They desperately need your help, and they are patiently waiting for you to show up. The more you elevate yourself, the more you can impact others. Realistically, you can't elevate everything, but you can focus your efforts on the areas that are important to you. The bigger and stronger your why is, the more value and impact you will have on others, the more motivated and fulfilled you will be, and the more value you can receive in return in terms of income, influence, knowledge, market share, or success. Note that your efforts do not always need to be big. Even the

smallest, seemingly inconsequential acts of kindness can grow to be something much bigger. If you can't plant a whole forest right now, then start by planting one seed.

Equivalent Value and Impact

It is critical that the amount of value and impact you receive is roughly equivalent to the value and impact you give, in order to maintain a healthy, circular flow. This is referred to in engineering as the **continuity equation**. The **Hose Analogy** can help demonstrate this. The volume of water entering the hose must be the same as the volume of water exiting it. If you partly cover the end of the hose with your thumb, then you produce a smaller, harder stream of water that moves much faster than it did before. The output water volume of the faster speed and the smaller opening must always equal the input volume of the slower speed and bigger opening. If this equality is not maintained, then something will break. If you aren't getting back as much as you are giving, then the thing that will break is *you*. Likewise, if you are receiving more than you are giving, then you will end up breaking the other person.

The Actors

I hired other WLBs as actors to play the humans in your life. They have the following characteristics:

- All WLBs are good.
- All WLBs are friends.
- WLBs are in constant communication with each other.
- All WLBs are talented and experienced actors.
- The WLBs are just doing the job they were hired to do, whether they play good or bad humans.
- Just as in any play, when it is over, the WLBs, or actors, will stop playing their roles on stage and will go do what WLBs do.

- All WLBs have unconditional love for you. They want you to learn and grow. They want you to win, and they are doing their best to help you.
- Anger, fear, regret, guilt, shame, and other negative feelings only exist at the human level.
- The WLB world is a positive place filled with pure love, peace, joy, freedom, and fulfillment.
- The other humans do not know they are in a play, and they do not know what I am telling you.

The Fine Print

Here are a few more important details about the play.

- Earth is a place that allows WLBs to experience life. For example, WLBs can't fully understand the concept of love until they experience what love *is*—and also experience its opposite: hate and fear.
- You are a part of me sent to experience life.
- You actually helped me write the play, and you agreed to be the protagonist.
- The birth process requires you to enter a new body with a new, empty conscious mind. You are not able to bring any memories with you. You are required to forget about me and who you are.
- Your life is usually difficult and challenging as you learn to be a perfectly imperfect human.
- I cannot communicate with you directly (this intermission is a rare exception), but I can arrange for things to happen with the help of my fellow WLBs. This appears to you as luck, coincidence, or fate.
- The ultimate goal is for you to remember who you really are: a WLB.

- Your next task is to think, feel, speak, and act like a WLB, powerfully creating your vision and helping others who desperately need your help.
- Death is just a simple, painless transition back to the WLB world; there is nothing to fear in this.
- When your life ends on Earth, you leave your body behind and return home. You bring your memories and identity, and you reintegrate with me. You now become a combination of the person you were on Earth and a WLB, who is very wise and loving.

Grade School Analogy

This process of experiencing life on Earth is like attending a specific grade in school. There are a series of lessons you must learn, and there is knowledge you must put into action before you can move on to the next grade. If your life ends before you learn the lesson, then you have to repeat that grade. If you are living an unpleasant life, then you will essentially have to relive a similar life again until you learn the lesson. If you end your life, then you will have to relive a worse life, as a penalty, and then you still have to learn the lesson. Do you really want to do this again or something worse?

Go to www.WiseLovingBeing.com/handouts
to find a copy of this handout online.

Act One

Today, I am interrupting your life and giving you a time-out so I can share some important wisdom with you. You have just completed Act One.

Act One Questions

Ask yourself the following questions about your present situation, the WLBs, and their humans:

- How has your current situation helped you become open to speaking with me, your WLB?
- What do you think about me?
- What do you think about Act One of the play?
- How are you doing on achieving your two objectives in life?
- Looking at how you live your life today:
  - What are the main habits that define your experience of life?
  - What are your major beliefs?
  - What have you been trying to prove?
  - Where did this need to prove yourself come from?
  - Who are you trying to prove this to?
  - What are you trying to accomplish by proving this?
  - Do you still need to prove this, or is it time to let it go and create something else?
  - How will your life be better? How will you benefit? How will others benefit?
- Looking at the WLBs who are the actors playing their parts:
  - How do you feel about them?
  - Are they doing a good job?
  - How do you feel about the humans they are playing?
- What are the humans and your current circumstances really trying to teach you or tell you?

- Which of the humans do you no longer need in your life because you have learned what you need from them?
- How can you find freedom and empowerment by releasing yourself from these humans?
- How does knowing that your loved ones are WLBs help you with the grieving and reconciliation process?
- How does knowing what you know now about the play and the actors help you release yourself from your shackles of anger, fear, regret, guilt, and shame?
- How does knowing what you know now free you from anxiety, stress, and worry?

Dealing with the Other Humans

Let us separate the humans from the WLBs now. Some humans have done great things and have been good friends, while others have done bad things and should receive the appropriate consequences. I am not suggesting the bad humans should be forgiven, nor am I saying that you are in charge of giving out punishment. You can use the following Human Release Process to free yourself from the bad humans, and you can use the Human Resolution Process to resolve any outstanding issues between you and the good humans.

Human Release Process

Here are the steps to release yourself from the bad humans in the play:

1. Speak directly with the WLB of the bad human. You can assume that they can hear you no matter where they are.
2. Thank the WLB for doing such a great acting job and for being such a great friend.
3. Thank the WLB for helping you learn and grow. Be specific about what you have learned and how you have benefited.

4. Now imagine you are speaking directly to the integrated entity consisting of the human and its WLB. They are a very wise and loving version of the person you know.
5. Read the letter you wrote them in the Freedom exercise.
6. Blame them for all the bad things they have done, and also give them credit for the good that has resulted.
7. Listen to them as they ask for forgiveness and let you know they did not enjoy doing what they were assigned to do, but it was necessary to get you to where you are today.
8. Listen to them as they impart important wisdom to you, tell you how proud they are of who you have become, tell you how much they love you, and talk about the brilliant future you will be co-creating with them.
9. Thank them. Let them know you are proud of who you have become and where you are going.
10. If their human is still alive, let the WLB know what you are requesting from their human going forward. Set a healthy boundary. If you want complete freedom from their human, let the WLB know that you now release their human and no longer need their services.

Human Resolution Process
Here is the process to connect yourself with your loved ones who are no longer in your life. It can help you resolve feelings of loneliness, sadness, and depression. It can also help you remove feelings of loss, grief, regret, guilt, and shame. Your loved ones might have died, or they might be living but you are no longer in contact with them. It doesn't matter if their human bodies are gone or if they still exist. The mind of the person you knew always exists and has been integrated with their WLB. They are a very wise and loving version of the person you knew, and this is who you will be speaking with.

Here are the steps to connect yourself with your loved ones and resolve anything that has been left undone:

1. Speak directly with the WLB of the good human. You can assume they can hear you no matter where they are. Your WLB and their WLB are in constant communication.

2. If you wrote them a letter in the forgiveness exercise, you can read it to them now.

3. If they died, let them know how happy you are that they are in a place of pure love.

4. If they are still alive, then wish them the best and let them know you are here for them if they choose to reconnect in a healthy manner.

5. Tell them how much you miss them, share all the great things you remember about them, and express how they have impacted your life. Thank them for helping you on Earth.

6. Understand there is nothing negative between you both because it doesn't exist for WLBs; everything that happened is part of the valuable experience process you are all doing.

7. Apologize to them for anything you feel you need to.

8. Listen to them as they forgive you, apologize to you for anything they need to, tell you how much they love you, tell you how proud they are of the person you have become, and talk about the brilliant future you will be co-creating with them.

9. Listen to them as they give you important wisdom.

10. Tell them you love them and are looking forward to seeing them again.

Go to www.WiseLovingBeing.com/handouts
to find a copy of this handout online.

"Elin, I know that was a lot of information, so let me start off with an example. My friend Edward had a very challenging life. As a child, his father regularly beat him while his mother stood by and watched. His parents were always working and made it clear that the most important thing was money. This caused him to believe he wasn't important, lovable, or worthy. Not only was he afraid for his life; he was also afraid he would be kicked out of his family. With his primal fears highly activated, he found a new tribe to belong to where he felt safe: a gang whose members had similar childhoods. They enjoyed their time together, did some crazy things, and always had each other's backs. They also committed almost every crime you can imagine. Not surprisingly, they experienced trauma in the local gang wars, dealing with the deaths of some of their fellow gang members, family, and friends.

"Edward had a lot of anger toward his parents, and this was often displaced on others, with him easily getting angry or upset. He also felt quite a bit of guilt and shame around some of the things he had done. He believed he was a bad person who needed to be punished and it wasn't possible to become a good person: once bad, always bad, and forever defined by his worst moments. He was also concerned that trying to be good was a waste of time because karma would catch up with him. He was depressed, hopeless, and participated in a lot of escape activities, including drugs and alcohol.

"I let Edward know that there was hope; he could change and become whoever he wanted to be. He wasn't defined by his past. He could learn from his experiences and do something good with this knowledge. I also reminded him that he was a kind, innocent child when he began this life. He started out good but went down a different path as he tried to survive his brutal childhood.

"I explained that karma is a limiting belief that doesn't exist, and it is harmful for both the receiver and the sender. Yes, there are consequences for your actions, but karma labels the person as bad

215

instead of focusing on their actions. It implies the receiver will be punished without consideration for their circumstances, intent, and capacity for good. Karma means they cannot create something good out of their bad actions. They are forever defined by their worst moments and are unable to elevate, and there is nothing they can do about it. There is no hope, so why bother trying to be better?

"For the sender of karma, they are focused on wishing bad things and revenge on others. This violates several Universal Elevation principles, including *connected*, *love*, and *win*. It also keeps them attached and unable to seek freedom or provide forgiveness. They experience negative emotions, which only affect them, not the 'bad' person. They go into victim mode and become helpless to improve the situation since they are waiting on that 'karmic force' to do the work. They don't look at how they might have contributed to the problem, nor do they become part of the solution. The end result is that the sender receives negative consequences too.

"I took Edward through the transformation process and helped him see the good that was inside him. I reminded him that he was the protagonist in the play. He was the good guy! I showed him that he became a tough guy so no one would be able to scare him and hurt him like his father did. I explained that in many ways, his scared little five-year-old self was still running his life. He realized he had accomplished his goal of being tough and intimidating. Everyone was afraid of him. He saw that he no longer needed to play that role, and it was actually keeping him from creating the close family relationships he wanted.

"I reminded Edward that he was a magnificent WLB and told him to start acting like one. I also helped him see how the WLBs of the other humans in his life were on his side and were helping him, including his father. I helped him explore how his experiences brought him to this moment in time and how he could use them to co-create a positive and compelling future along with his supportive

WLBs. I asked him how he could maximize his second objective in life to add the most value and have the biggest impact on others.

"With this new knowledge and perspective, he resolved his fear, anger, guilt, and shame. He forgave himself and went through the Human Resolution Process to seek forgiveness from others. He created a new vision and purpose for his life and started a charitable organization to help others only he could reach because of his background. He ended the terrible cycle of violence of fathers abusing their children that had been handed down over many generations to him. Even more amazing was that he was able to transform the terrible relationships he had with his family into strong, loving, and supportive ones, including the relationship with his parents. Edward turned his trauma and 'bad karma' into a powerfully positive force for good that otherwise wouldn't have been possible."

Wes could see that Elin was completely engrossed in this story and was deep in thought. With a simple look he indicated that he was curious about what she was thinking.

"Wes, that was an amazing story. I'm not a gang member, but I am struck by the many things I have in common with Edward. If he can change, then there is definitely hope for me."

"Yes, we have a lot more in common with others than we think. Recognizing this simple fact can help us be more kind toward ourselves and others." Wes smiled and paused for a moment to let Elin finish processing her thoughts.

"Elin, when you are ready, please answer the Act One Questions about your life so far."

"Interesting questions, Wes. Let's see here. I am now open to speaking with you, my WLB, because I literally reached rock bottom, injured and laying on the floor, with no money and no food to eat. I am glad you are here to help me and am comforted that you are always looking out for me. I can't say I have really enjoyed much from Act One. I'm stuck and haven't learned the important lessons or made the necessary changes to my life that will help me elevate and graduate to the next grade. I haven't made much progress toward achieving my two objectives in life.

"Looking at how I live my life today, the habits that define my experience of life are escaping, doing things for others without allowing anything good to come back to me, not working, not trying to improve my life, and spending a lot of time thinking negatively. I believe I should be poor and should be punished. I've been trying to prove that I am helpless and hopeless. This came from my childhood experiences in school and from my dad dying. I originally tried to prove this to my family, but since then, I've been trying to prove this to everyone, including myself. I've been hoping that someone would just show up and take care of me. I don't need to prove this anymore. I can see that I've survived on my own without any help, and I've done a decent job for the most part, especially when you consider how little effort I put in. There is hope for me if I actually try. I can now focus on improving my life. I will obviously benefit, but so will others around me.

"Looking at the WLBs who are the actors playing their parts, I see that all the WLBs are good and are on my side, even though it appears that their bad humans are my enemies. The WLBs are doing an amazing job. In fact, I don't know how they could do a better job. They've created humans who seem to know exactly how to trigger my primary and secondary fears. The humans and my current circumstances are telling me that I need to grow up, take ownership, take action, stop punishing myself, resolve my issues, and start living my life. I now understand that I need to love myself, treat myself with respect, and embrace the fact that I am a powerful WLB.

"I no longer need a person named Richard in my life. Being angry at him only keeps me stuck. I need to set boundaries with him and let him know that his behavior is no longer acceptable. By releasing myself from him, I can regain my power, unshackle myself from him, and move on.

"It's a real game-changer knowing that so many people are here to help me learn and grow instead of harm me. I know the WLBs see me as perfectly human. Knowing that they unconditionally love me is a great feeling. My feelings of grief, anger, fear, regret, guilt, shame, anxiety, stress, and worry only exist in my mind, and removing them from my mind frees me to do whatever I want."

"Good job, Elin. Let's look at the next two exercises. The Human Release Process is more powerful than the Freedom Process we discussed the other day. And the Human Resolution Process is much more powerful than the Forgiveness Process we discussed. Please go through them both on your own later today.

"There is an abbreviated version of the Human Release Process I'd like to do with you now. Please go through the first three steps and the last one for anyone you want to release who is still alive."

"I'm speaking to the WLB of Richard. Thank you for doing such a great job and being such a great friend," Elin began. "Thank you for helping me learn and grow. You taught me to stand up for myself, be independent, and take responsibility for my life. Going forward, I need your human to be supportive and respectful. I need him to let me interact as I choose with Beverly and stay out of my way. I release Richard and no longer need his services."

"Is there anyone else you need to release?" Wes asked.

"I don't think so."

"How about the guy who stole your wallet two weeks ago?" Wes asked.

"Good idea. Let me try it on him." Elin paused to think. "I'm speaking to the WLB of the guy who stole my wallet. Thank you for doing such a good job and for being such a great friend. Thank you for engineering that encounter. It was exactly what I needed from you. Without it, I never would have met Wes, and I never would have taken steps to improve my life. If it weren't for you, I'd still be living a miserable, desperate existence. Going forward, I need your human to leave me alone and to do no more harm to me. I now release your human and no longer need his services."

"Excellent job, Elin. I want to talk about the first Act One question a little bit more. WLBs are always trying to communicate with their humans, but humans rarely listen. It sometimes takes quite a lot to get through, as you now understand. Many a WLB has asked themselves, *Seriously? What do I need to do to get their attention?*

"My friend Doug lost his job and couldn't find work for more than a year. None of the businesses he started produced any income, and he depleted all of his savings. Eventually, he lost his house and his car. His wife left him and took their kids. Only after he was living in a shelter did he start to listen to his WLB. The good news is that he finally listened and created a compelling vision for his life. And that's exactly what I am going to help you do.

"Let's move on to the next part of The Play, which is focused on creating your future."

Wes gave Elin a handout titled *Act Two* and went over it with her.

Act Two

Fundamental Drivers

Everyone has two fundamental drivers. The first, of course, is to avoid the pain associated with our primal fears. This is our highest priority. Our second fundamental driver is to experience elevated levels of our **fundamental needs**: *love, peace, joy, freedom,* and *fulfillment*. Everything we think, feel, say, and do is in some way motivated by our primal fears and fundamental needs.

How Life Works

The following are the rules for living your life in the play:

- The play is not fixed. Your life is not predetermined. Everyone has free will.
- You were involved in writing the script and agreed to be the protagonist.
- You are equal with all other humans. No one is better or more important than you.
- You have unique gifts, talents, skills, experiences, and challenges.
- A villain or adverse situation can sometimes serve as a catalyst for your elevation and success.
- Life is about opposites. For example, you can't completely know what good is until you know what evil is.
- Life has lessons.
  - The primary way to learn a lesson is to experience things and feel pain or joy.
  - The sooner you learn your lesson, the sooner you can move on to another lesson.
  - If you don't learn your lesson, then you do not elevate. You will get stuck in a pattern, encountering similar situations, each time with different humans, and each time it will get worse for you.

- Your unconscious mind is a powerful force.
  - You are subject to the invisible forces of your unconscious mind, both harmful and beneficial.
  - The biggest challenge you face is the internal conflict between your conscious and unconscious mind.
  - You have the power to overcome the limitations of your unconscious mind and harness its full power. You will learn how to do this in later lessons.
- Life is happening for your benefit, even the bad things; it is not trying to harm you.
- You will never want for anything if you use your creativity and resourcefulness.
- You can only change yourself. You can't change others; you can only inspire others to change.
- All of your fundamental needs of love, peace, joy, freedom, and fulfillment come from within. They do not come from external sources. When you fully understand this, you will be able to experience your fundamental needs regardless of what is happening to you externally.

How to Improve Your Future

Here is how you can improve your future in the play:

- Take ownership and responsibility for your life.
- Take action. You must work hard and smart to succeed.
- Maximize your creativity and resourcefulness.
- Elevate yourself through learning, continuous improvement, and seeking the truth.
- Experience the highest levels of your fundamental needs: love, peace, joy, freedom, and fulfillment.
- Understand your true power, potential, and limitations.
- Reprogram your unconscious mind so it empowers you to succeed.

- Reduce (ideally eliminate) your unhealthy fears, guilt, regret, shame, stress, and worry, and embrace your healthy responses to life's circumstances.
- Establish and enforce healthy boundaries so you do not allow others to harm you.
- Ignore your *sunk costs* and focus on how to best move forward.
- Do your best in the present moment that is consistent with your purpose and vision.
- Follow the principles of Universal Elevation.
- Remember who you really are: a WLB. Think, feel, speak, and act like a WLB.
- Find a Big Strong Why. Imagine a future where you deliver the highest possible amounts of value and impact to help those who desperately need your help, and also receive equal value in kind.
- Be a powerful creator. Create your vision with your thoughts, words, and actions.
- You are co-creating with your fellow WLBs in a powerful collaboration, and it is okay to ask for their help.

Resourcefulness

Resourcefulness means maximizing the use of all the resources available to you. This includes the people you know; your skills, abilities, strengths, knowledge, and experiences; and any other assets you own or have access to.

Sunk Costs

Sunk costs refer to the money and time you have already invested in something up to this point that you can't recover. Management theory says that sunk costs should be ignored when determining how to move forward. Yes, there might be something valuable there that can help you achieve your future goals, but it should not constrain your decision-making. In other words, your past should not dictate your future. The key is to maximize your creativity and resourcefulness in order to create your best possible future. This also means that if you have behaved badly in the past, there is nothing stopping you from being a good person now and in the future. It also means that if you have had a difficult life in the past, there is nothing stopping you from having a great life now and in the future.

Big Strong Why

Creating a Big Strong Why can sometimes be scary, intimidating, and overwhelming. We sometimes feel powerless, small, and unimportant. We think other people can do this better than we can. It is difficult to imagine how we can instantly go from zero to the speed of light. Luckily, we do not have to. We can take baby steps and make small changes that are consistent with where we want to go. It takes a lot of time and practice to be a great athlete, and achieving a Big Strong Why is no different. Every act matters. Even small, seemingly insignificant encounters can yield big results. Many small impacts can add up to something big. All you have to do is leave something better than you found it.

Vision Questions

The intermission is almost over and the second act is about to begin. Answer the following questions about your vision for your future to help you achieve your highest potential in the second act and live a life you would love to live. Think of this exercise as defining your purpose and vision in life, your Big Strong Why, or your compelling reason to get out of bed each day.

1. What unique experiences, skills, abilities, relationships, and resources do you have?
2. What has life prepared you to do, that is unique to you, that no one else can do or wants to do?
3. How will you leverage your uniqueness to add the most value and impact to this planet?
4. How can you experience more of your fundamental needs?
5. How can you play a much bigger game?
6. Who or what is desperately waiting for you to show up and what value will you receive?
7. How can you be more creative and resourceful?
8. What empowering beliefs, experiences, and habits can you create?
9. What obstacles do you need to free yourself from?
10. What choices can you make that will change your future?
11. What smart actions can you take to create that future?
12. How can you add value and impact that continues after you die?

Go to www.WiseLovingBeing.com/handouts
to find a copy of this handout online.

"Elin, I have an example for you. My friend Jennifer had worked for her company for a long time. She had a good income and was able to be a good provider for her family. It was a safe choice since the company was doing well and was Amazon-proof. Unfortunately, she'd been having a difficult time the past couple of years. Quite a few people seemed to be against her, and she was miserable.

"Jennifer decided to apply the lessons of The Play Exercise to her life. When she saw that the WLBs were good and were just doing their job, she realized how great they were as actors. Their humans were bullying and abusing her, and they could push her buttons with ease. She was then able to understand what her coworkers were trying to tell her: she needed to leave the company. She was able to free herself from her coworkers and asked their WLBs to have their humans support her in making a career transition.

"Jennifer examined her unique experiences, skills, and abilities, then looked at what she enjoyed doing and where she felt most fulfilled. With the facts in hand, she determined how she could maximize her value and impact on the world. She identified the perfect customers who desperately needed her help. She decided to start her own business, which was a much better use of her talents and would provide her with a much better income.

"Jennifer talked with experts, created a plan, overcame both internal and external obstacles, and committed to taking smart action. Today she is much happier, more fulfilled, and loves helping her customers. And she is very grateful for the great work the WLBs of her former coworkers did. She has forgiven her coworkers and is now at peace. She realized they were just trying to help her live a much better life, and being nice to her wasn't working.

Wes could see that Elin was deep in thought and waited for her to indicate that she was ready to move on. "Elin, please answer the Vision Questions. Tell me about the life you'll be creating in your second act, the one you'll be thrilled to live. Tell me what your purpose and vision will be."

"My *unique experiences, skills, abilities, relationships, and resources* are that I have empathy for people who are dealing with trauma, I'm a good listener, and I am kind and supportive of others. Since I'm older, I've experienced the struggles many people of my generation face today. I also have the new knowledge and perspectives that you've taught me.

"The second question trips me up a bit: *What has life prepared you to do that is unique to you, that no one else can do or wants to do?* I'm sorry, but I don't really have an answer to this. I can't think of a thing. I'm finding it difficult to translate this new knowledge into action. You know, I've never been good at this process. I think I missed that day of school.

"I *can* tell you what I can do next. I can choose adult thinking over child thinking; create a path to financial security by getting a job; develop a healthy respect for money; be more creative and resourceful in getting income; participate in activities that interest me; find compatible friends; continue to learn from those who have different viewpoints; set boundaries and enforce them with unavoidable and difficult people like Richard; strive to be more positive; practice gratitude; and enjoy the love that is all around me when my walls come down.

"The third question is, *How will you leverage your uniqueness to add the most value and impact to this planet?* By helping myself and others level up and achieve Universal Elevation.

"The fourth question is, *How can you experience more of your fundamental needs?* By having enriching relationships and becoming more involved with others who have similar interests and goals.

"The fifth question is, *How can you play a much bigger game?* By going down a path of Universal Elevation.

"The sixth question is, *Who or what is desperately waiting for you to show up and what value will you receive?* Everyone and everything. I can help others help themselves by providing access to community resources. I can teach people how to fish instead of just giving them the fish. I will benefit by accessing these same community resources and by connecting with others.

"The seventh question is, *How can you be more creative and resourceful?* By getting a job and interacting with organizations that have a positive impact on the lives of others. I can also talk with others about how I might be able to improve my financial situation.

"The eighth question is, *What empowering beliefs, experiences, and habits can you create?* I can work on self-forgiveness, experiencing life in the present, and being grateful. I can do positive things with the twelve hours I have available each day.

"The ninth question is, *What obstacles do you need to free yourself from?* I need to reduce and hopefully eliminate the fear, regret, guilt, shame, escape activities, and limiting beliefs that are negatively affecting my life. I need to grow up and take responsibility for my responses, actions, and thoughts.

"The tenth question is, *What choices can you make that will change your future?* I need to choose empowering beliefs, stay in the present moment, and interact with others. I need to choose to improve my life.

"The eleventh question is, *What smart actions can you take?* I need to leave my house and find work. I can prepare my resume for a job search, reapply for additional prescription benefits, reduce negative talk through awareness and feedback, continue to learn new things, and incorporate this new knowledge into my life.

"The twelfth question is, *How can you add value and impact that continues after you die?* I can help others elevate themselves using Universal Elevation. They can educate and help others, and so on.

"What do you think, Wes?"

"This is a good start, Elin. On a scale from cardboard box to Neptune, I'd say you're somewhere in the basement, maybe heading up the stairs to the main house. This is great progress, but I was thinking of something much bigger for you. I'm after that something-great-shining-bright-inside-you type of thing. You also gave me general answers instead of specific things you could do. I'd like you to have answers that are actionable, ones you can easily create a goal around. You're playing it safe, and I need you to be much more courageous.

"Furthermore, I thought your answer to the second question was quite interesting: *What has life prepared you to do, that is unique to you, that no one else can do or wants to do?* There is a huge limiting belief here attached to your fear of not belonging: *I'm not worthy.* Let's take a closer look. You're probably thinking that if you honestly answer that question, you'll either embarrass yourself or make mistakes. People will laugh at you, and you'll get kicked out of the tribe. In short, you still believe this statement: *If I try, I'll die.* It's clearly a very powerful fear for you, one that you'll need to work on more. So let me help you here.

"When I look at your past and your present, I get different answers than the ones you gave me. Let me frame what I'm about to say by focusing on the second objective in life, which is to help elevate all others, all living things, and the planet. Note that this doesn't mean sacrificing yourself. You will receive a similar amount of value in return.

"Here is a list of characteristics that you share with other people, but when they are all combined, they make you unique:

- Your answer to the first question was that you have empathy, you're a good listener, you are kind, and you are supportive of others. You also mentioned that you have the new knowledge and perspectives you've learned from me.

- In several of your answers, you mentioned that you want to connect with and help others.
- Yesterday, you mentioned that you have always wanted to create an animal rescue facility and have a large family.
- When we were talking about your significant events, you mentioned that you tried to redeem yourself by going to nursing school.
- When we were talking about habits, you mentioned that one of the ways you've made life better for yourself is by taking care of your cousin's cat. In doing this, you experienced firsthand how animals can help humans feel better.
- When we talked about your beliefs around money, you mentioned you could be more resourceful and even live on a farm.
- You have gone through a lot of difficult times recently, and you're obviously not the only one. You have lots of empathy here.
- When we first met, you hadn't eaten in two days, and you weren't able to buy groceries for the week.
- You live in an area with a large population of people who have similar experiences, challenges, and needs.

"To help you with this process, let me tell you about the **Puzzle Analogy**. All of your characteristics and resources are like the pieces to a puzzle. When you put them together, the image on the puzzle represents your purpose and vision, and it's unique to you.

"Elin, when you put together all of your resources, what do you see as your purpose and vision for your life in Act Two? What is a much bigger game you could play that is closer to Neptune than your cardboard box?"

Elin took a moment to think. She didn't want to let Wes down. She was really putting in the effort when all of a sudden, she had that look of realization on her face, as if the proverbial lightbulb of inspiration had gone off in her head.

"I think I've got it, Wes. What if I was able to create a place where people could connect with each other and elevate their lives by learning what you've taught me. We could take care of rescued animals and help them find new homes. The facility would make money and provide jobs by charging an adoption fee, taking donations, selling pet food, and running a small cafe. This would ensure that everyone had enough to eat. I can help create a foundation so these activities can continue after I'm gone. I'd be meeting both of my life objectives this way: improve my life while improving the lives of others and animals."

Wes was impressed. "Nicely done, Elin! Thank you for your courage today. I know this isn't easy for you, but it will get much easier as time goes on. This is a good answer, and I'd like you to think more about it because we'll be refining it tomorrow.

"To summarize, a play is a great metaphor for life. Life is aspiring to help you elevate. There are two objectives in life: elevate yourself and elevate everything else. You are much more powerful than you think. There are many things you can do to improve your life. You can discover your purpose and vision by seeing what your life has prepared you to do, that is unique to you, and that no one else can do or wants to do. Furthermore, the value and impact you have on this planet can continue even after you die.

"There's one last thing I want to talk with you about before we end our session today. The last item under How Life Works states that *all of your fundamental needs of love, peace, joy, freedom, and fulfillment come from within. They do not come from external sources.* Let's take love as an example. People sometimes say they don't feel loved by their partner. When one relationship ends, they often scurry off to find someone new who they think will give them the love they crave, but that feeling only lasts for a short period of time before it's gone again. People become even more desperate for love when one of their secondary fear statements is *I'm not lovable.* They search everywhere outside of themselves for love, but they never find love that lasts.

"If you want to find true, lasting love, then you have to look within. That's the only place you'll find it. As I mentioned before, you create your own feelings and emotions. You can generate the feeling of love when you feel loved by someone, when you are being loving to others, and simply by remembering a time when you felt loved. You are the only one who can generate this feeling of love. It happens when you receive love *and* when you give love. There's an important truth behind the saying, 'It's better to give than receive.' You have control over giving love and both you and the receiver of your love benefit by feeling loved.

"I'd like to take you through the **love bubble exercise** to help you learn how to generate love whenever you need it. Please sit down on this bench. Close your eyes and imagine a time when you felt loved. As you remember this moment, notice how the feeling of love is generated inside you. Now think about another time when you were filled with love. Notice that the feeling of love inside you is getting stronger. Feel it build more and more until your body can no longer contain it. Imagine that a golden light is completely surrounding you, a golden bubble of love. Enjoy this feeling of love. Feel the unconditional and unlimited love you have created. Repeat to yourself over and over again, *I love myself; I love me.*"

Wes waited a couple of minutes to let Elin fully enjoy this experience before he interrupted her. "When you're ready, slowly count to five, open your eyes, and return to our conversation." He waited for her to slowly open her eyes and look at him. "How do you feel?" Wes asked.

"I feel amazing. I've never felt this good. I'm filled with feelings of love, peace, and joy. I don't want this to end!"

"Yes, it's an amazing experience you can do any time you like. When you become more comfortable with this exercise you can take it to the next level and send love out into the world. You start by creating the love bubble around you. Then you make it bigger so that it contains the whole room, then your building, your neighborhood, your city, and so on until you've expanded it to surround the entire world. Everyone can benefit from a little love, don't you think?"

"Agreed. Thank you, Wes. I look forward to trying that."

"Perfect. Are you ready for your homework, Elin?"

"Yes, sir! What's my homework?" Elin asked.

"Tomorrow, we start the transformation process. There are three parts to the homework. First, I'm going to give you a magic wand. You can create anything you want with it without fear of failure. There are no restrictions, so don't let anything get in the way, including time, money, age, or gender. Go through all eight areas of your life and write down what you would like to create. Friendly reminder that the eight areas of life are *charitable, emotional, financial, intellectual, physical, professional, relational,* and *spiritual.* Note that this isn't an exercise in fantasy. For example, don't use your magic wand to create a fire-breathing dragon. Instead, use the magic wand to create real things here on Earth.

"Second, please write down what you think your highest potential is. What do you think is the most you can accomplish in your life? What is the maximum value and impact you can have on this planet?

"Third, please review your list of fears and think about which ones you want to transform. Bring your list with you so we can work on it together.

"Let's meet here again tomorrow at the same time. Any questions?"

"No questions. See you tomorrow, Wes!"

As Elin walked back to her car, she thought about the play, her homework, and everything Wes had talked about. "He makes me think about things I would never think about on my own; things I never would have thought were possible. Two weeks ago, I was thinking my life was over. Now I'm thinking that my life is just beginning!"

Part Four:

Transformation

Chapter Thirteen

Transforming Fears

When Elin arrived at the Cinnabon the next day, Wes was already there. He greeted her with a big smile and said, "Good morning, Elin! How are you today?"

"Good morning, Wes," Elin replied. "I'm excited. How are you?"

"I'm extraordinary!" Wes replied enthusiastically. "Today is Transformation Day! Are you ready to create Elin 2.0? This is going to be a very exciting conversation! Let's get started, shall we?" They began their morning walk around the mall in a noticeably more positive state and at a faster pace than normal. "Before we start, I'd like to ask you a question. What have you tried in the past to improve your life, and what were the results?"

"I've tried everything I could think of to improve myself that I could afford: books, seminars, mentors, coaches, therapy, and meditation. I've explored every topic I could find, including personal development, leadership, metaphysics, self-help, and spirituality. I made some good progress in the beginning but had difficulty improving beyond my initial success. I sort of plateaued. From that point forward, the various improvement methodologies I tried seemed to help me somewhat in the short term, but they didn't produce lasting change. I lost hope that I would get better and decided it was just my fate."

"You're not alone, Elin. The self-improvement methodologies available today can be expensive and they have five fundamental flaws." Wes gave Elin a handout titled *Five Fundamental Flaws* and went over it with her.

Five Fundamental Flaws

The traditional books, videos, seminars, coaching, counseling, therapy, and other self-improvement methodologies available today are only able to get people so far. Yes, they are effective at helping people get to a certain level at the beginning of their learning journey, but after that, they are only able to help people make small, incremental improvements at best. At their worst, they cause problems. People become frustrated and stuck, their bad behaviors get reinforced, they give up on trying to improve themselves, and they start causing problems for others.

The Five Fundamental Flaws of today's self-improvement methodologies are:

1. **Singular.** They focus on only one aspect of ourselves. Business books focus on work. Personal development and self-help books focus on the conscious mind. Spiritual books focus on our soul, and so on. We can only improve one aspect of ourselves so far before our system becomes unbalanced and has difficulty making further improvements.

2. **Conflicting.** They often declare that one aspect of us is more important. What's worse is that they sometimes pit one aspect of us against another, like the mind-over-body willpower shenanigans. This creates inner conflict and long-term damage for most people.

3. **Superficial.** They don't address the root cause of the problem. They give us aspirin for a headache that stops the pain temporarily. They address the symptoms of the problem without fixing what is causing the headache. In other words, they give us tools to fix something that shouldn't need fixing in the first place. Once the root cause of the problem is addressed and the problem is resolved, the tools become obsolete.

4. **Temporary.** They don't address the most powerful part of us, our unconscious mind, which typically accounts for over ninety percent of our mental processing power. The conscious mind may have short-term success using willpower, but eventually it is completely overwhelmed by the unconscious mind, and we return to our old habits, often without realizing it.

5. **Regressive.** They have the unintended negative effect of strengthening our limiting behaviors. There is a repeating pattern: We look for a way to get better. Get excited by their claims. Hope they will help us make the large, lasting, and positive changes we've always wanted. We become motivated during the event or while reading the book. We may even implement one thing we've learned. But after a month or two, we return to our old ways. We may feel better in the short term, but that usually wears off quickly. This pattern that ends with us falling back into our old ways only makes our unhealthy behaviors stronger. Practice makes perfect, but certainly not what is wanted.

Go to www.WiseLovingBeing.com/handouts
to find a copy of this handout online.

"The unintended consequence of these five fundamental flaws is that people become worse and then stop buying self-improvement books, attending seminars, going to therapy, and hiring coaches. They start to believe they have become the best they will ever be. If they believe all the science and hyperbole around the vendor's claims and that other people are getting results, then they must conclude, in the usual binary fashion, that there is something wrong with them. They stop trying to improve themselves, give up, and call it fate.

"Alternatively, they might believe that there is something wrong with the material. They might conclude that self-improvement methodologies are all the same and just don't work. Even worse, they might conclude that they know everything and, by just reading the book or taking the seminar, they have somehow become smarter and better. Without implementing any of the knowledge, making any changes, and taking any action to improve, they conclude that they are the best that any human can get and are superior to others.

"The bottom line is this: people are staying the same or getting worse, and they stop trying to make themselves better.

"In general, when people who have big dreams for their life believe they are unable to get better, feel stuck, and conclude their dreams are unattainable, they may become frustrated and depressed, seek escape activities, develop addictions, and participate in destructive behaviors. Their inner pain can boil over, and eventually they may start creating problems for others. Evidence of this happening is all too common in today's world: homelessness, addiction, suicide, political and social discord, cancel culture, prejudice, hate, high divorce rates, environmental destruction, abuse, crime, violence, mass shootings, terrorism, and war.

"Let me give you an example of how this works. My friend Charlotte was overweight. She went to a weight-loss expert who taught her how to count calories and exercise. She was told to just use her willpower to stop eating bad things and to exercise every day. She lost about ten pounds on the program but stopped doing it after three months. Within six months she had regained the ten pounds she lost and added five more. She concluded that because she had worked with an expert, wasn't able to sustain the discipline, and had gotten worse, it was just her fate or bad genes, and there was nothing she could do to get better. She became more depressed and proceeded to steadily gain weight over the next ten years. She stopped working and was lucky to live in a small unit behind her sister's house.

"My friend Julio had a drinking problem. He got help and was taught how to use his willpower to keep himself from drinking. He stayed sober for about a year. After a confrontation with a family member, he then started drinking again and concluded that there was nothing he could do to make things better. This was just who he was. Things got worse. He started using drugs. He became more confrontational at family gatherings and got into fights at bars. One night he drove home drunk, crashed his car, and put someone in the hospital. When he was arrested, he punched the police officer and ended up in jail on additional charges.

"As you can see from both cases, today's self-improvement methodologies can help people in the short term, but they have their limits. The five fundamental flaws can sometimes cause unintended consequences. Does that make sense, Elin?"

"Yes, it does. It's crazy to think that I've spent so much time and money to actually get worse."

"This isn't what we're going to be doing today. I'm going to take you through the same process I took Charlotte and Julio through so they could transform their lives. I'm going to show you how to make positive, permanent, and powerful changes using all aspects of yourself. It is important to address all aspects of you: mind, body, and soul. All eight areas of your life: charitable, emotional, financial, intellectual, physical, professional, relational, and spiritual. Both parts of your mind: conscious and unconscious. And both parts of your brain: left brain and right brain.

"Everything is connected. When you improve one area of your life, it helps improve other areas. For example, when you exercise, it improves your emotional well-being and helps you think better. When you take action to improve your health, it gives you confidence to work on other areas of your life.

"In laying the foundation for your transformation, we will first work on all of your mind. Both the conscious mind and unconscious mind have to be addressed. And, as we have discussed before, the unconscious mind always wins over the conscious mind because it is much more powerful. In order for real change to happen, the unconscious mind has to be part of the solution, and all parts of you need to be improved and aligned together in a way that is consistent with your identity, purpose, and vision.

"Let's talk about what **transformation** is. It's about making small, important changes that make a huge difference in the quality of your life and in the lives of others. The changes are so powerful that, in many ways, you actually feel like a different person, and people who know you take notice and see the profound changes taking place. Think about a caterpillar transforming into a butterfly. Think *revolution* not evolution. Imagine making positive, permanent, and powerful changes where life will never be the same, and where you won't want to return to the way things used to be. Today is about taking the first steps in creating a critical internal transformation that will lead you to make major external transformations in all areas of your life.

"Now let's go over the homework. In the first exercise, I gave you a **magic wand**. The purpose of this exercise is to remind us that *we are powerful creators*. People have created many amazing things throughout history. Even more impressive is what people have created in just the past one hundred years. It's nothing short of incredible. The magic wand is a simple metaphor for the power of our creativity and resourcefulness.

"You can create anything you want with your magic wand without fear of failure. There are no restrictions or limitations, including your time, money, age, and gender. The idea is to think about what you would like to create by the end of your life in all eight areas of your life. Please remember that this isn't an exercise in fantasy, so use the magic wand to create real things here on Earth.

"So tell me, Elin, what will you create with your magic wand in all eight areas of your life?"

Elin took out her homework and said, "I choose to create the following things with my magic wand:

- Charitable: I have a shelter to care for people and rescued animals. I create a foundation so this facility can carry on after I'm gone.
- Emotional: I feel incredible amounts of love, peace, joy, freedom, and fulfillment every day. I am very happy and free of disempowering worry, stress, fear, guilt, shame, and regret.
- Financial: I am financially secure. I own a house and farm that is completely paid for. I have a new car and take amazing vacations every year.
- Intellectual: I read and participate in classes regarding my interests in archaeology, geology, financial management, and many other subjects.
- Physical: I am in great health. I eat fresh organic foods, drink clean well water, and breathe clean country air. I no longer need to take any medications.
- Professional: I have a meaningful and fulfilling career with no age limit that meets my financial needs.

- <u>Relational</u>: I have a life partner. We have lots of close family and friends we interact with in positive and meaningful ways.
- <u>Spiritual</u>: I host workshops to help others learn how to elevate themselves and practice Universal Elevation."

"This is a good start," Wes said. "I'd like to see you create even bigger things with your magic wand. Instead of giving you subjective phrases like 'play a bigger game' and 'on a scale from cardboard box to Neptune,' let me try giving you an objective way to measure yourself. The **Absolute Contribution Scale** is a twenty-point scale that goes from minus ten to ten; it measures your contribution based on what humans can actually contribute. Negative ten is for people who destroy the world and kill millions of people. Zero is for humans who add no net value. In other words, when you look at their negative and positive contributions and add them all up, they end up with a value of zero. Positive ten is for humans who help millions of people and add incredible amounts of value to the world.

"Let me give you some examples. I won't dignify the list of humans scoring negative ten on the scale, but I'm sure you can name a few. On the positive ten side of the scale is a big list, and some of its more famous alumni include Abraham Lincoln, Buddha, Jesus, Mahatma Gandhi, Martin Luther King, Mother Teresa, and Nelson Mandela.

"Elin, on the absolute contribution scale, how do you rank your current life? How do you rank your future life based on your list from the magic wand exercise?"

"Ouch. I'd probably rate my current life as positive, but close to zero. I'd rate my future life around two," Elin replied.

"Agreed. There is so much untapped potential in you. I can see it, and I'm hoping that you are starting to see it too. So please go back to the exercise and add more contributions.

"The second exercise from your homework was to imagine what your **highest potential** is. I realize this question can be a bit overwhelming. It can also be depressing when we think about the dreams we had for our life when we were kids. When we look at what we've accomplished so far and see what we've settled for and given up on, it can feel utterly bleak. Then there is the stress that comes from seeing what we are doing today and thinking we need to do a lot more. The fear of failure and the corresponding fear of embarrassment creeps in if we actually try to do more. But there's also the excitement associated with the many possibilities.

"So Elin, what do you think is the most you can accomplish in your life? What is the maximum value and impact you can have on this planet? I'm curious. What is your highest potential?"

"Wes, before I give you my answer, I need to preface it with a couple of things. I know that after our conversation yesterday, you're going to think my initial answer is a copout. I know you'll think my fear—*If I try, I'll die*—is active, but it's not. And I think from our discussion today about my answer to the magic wand exercise, you're going to think I'm being short-sighted. Yes, I was playing it safe again. So please be patient with me as I answer your question. I spent a lot of time thinking about this. In fact, I barely got any sleep last night because I was so excited about all the things that were really possible for me.

"With that said, I'm going to start by saying that I really have no idea what my highest potential is. It's actually totally impossible for me to know that from where I stand today. I'm just getting out of the cardboard box, after all. I don't know what I don't know. And as the world continues to evolve, what is impossible today suddenly becomes possible tomorrow. But I see that the key is to focus on my two objectives in life: elevate myself and elevate all. I need to look for ways to add as much value as I can on a daily basis so that I can have the biggest possible impact on the world. When I go down that path, it will surely lead me to achieve things that I can't even imagine are possible for me today.

"By helping others, I can't possibly imagine all the good things they will do for the people in their lives, and so on. Even seemingly small acts of kindness can lead to big changes. If each person helps just two other people, then it leads to a chain reaction which is exponential. I can also create a charitable organization that carries on my work after I'm gone. It can continue to grow and increase its reach and impact as the years go by. Andy Andrews wrote a great book about how our life affects the future called *The Butterfly Effect*.

"That made me think about the quote from Russell Crowe's character, Maximus, in the movie *Gladiator*: 'What we do in life echoes in eternity.' The bigger my efforts are today, the bigger my echo will be. The more people I can help today, the more long-lasting impact I will have.

"I also remembered the fun I had as a kid in Colorado making snowballs. My friends and I would create a base snowball and then roll it down a big hill. By the time it got to the bottom, the snowball grew from a few inches in diameter to a few feet, just like you see in the cartoons. This is similar to what I'm doing with my purpose in life: I'm rolling a snowball down a hill that never ends. Who knows how big it will get!

"So my long-winded answer to your question, *What is my highest potential?* is really simple: my highest potential is truly unlimited."

Wes smiled and gave a slight bow to Elin. "You are very wise and powerful, Elin. You have discovered the secret to life that very few humans truly understand: maximize your value and impact to all, now and forever. Most humans only achieve a tiny sliver of their full potential. It is an honor to be in your presence. I am so glad that we are finally on the same page."

Elin was a bit surprised by Wes's words and actions. She smiled and bowed slightly to him. "Thank you, Wes. I'm so happy to hear you say that. Thank you so much for helping me see the truth."

"You're very welcome, Elin." Wes waited for her to completely soak in this wisdom before continuing.

"Today, we are going to create the foundation for making you even more powerful," Wes said excitedly. "In doing so, you can add more value and have a greater impact. This will help make your vision a reality much sooner.

"When we talked about your beliefs over a week ago, I asked you what your identity, purpose, vision, and values were. You said you didn't have a purpose or a vision. You did give me three values. And I won't bother to repeat the negative identity you had.

"Individuals can seldom answer these questions. Businesses, on the other hand, almost always have them written down and posted for everyone to see, although they often don't reflect reality. Note that all four of these elements are required for you to live your best life."

Wes gave Elin a handout titled the *Conscious Compass* and went over it with her.

Conscious Compass

The conscious compass helps our conscious mind find its way in life. It defines who we are, where we are going, and what is important to us. It consists of our identity statement, purpose, vision, and values. Unlike a regular compass that can only find the magnetic north pole, we can change our conscious compass at any time to find whatever we want. It is forward-looking and is in no way constrained by our past. As a matter of fact, it can't even see our past. That is why the first step in creating your new conscious compass is to start with a blank sheet of paper. By starting from scratch, you are free to create a new you and a new future. Our conscious compass provides us with a new **definition of success**: acting in each moment consistent with our identity, purpose, and values, and taking another step toward fulfilling our vision.

Our **identity** is our definition of who we are. It defines how we think, feel, speak, and act. There are several **ways to define ourselves**:

- **Career:** The most common way we define ourselves is by our career: accountant, chef, doctor, lawyer, parent, teacher, etc.
- **Past:** Unfortunately, some people define themselves by their past, and sometimes by the worst thing they have done. As Samantha said in the film *Her*, "The past is just a story we tell ourselves."
- **View:** We can define ourselves by how we view ourselves or how others view us.
- **Future:** A better way to define ourselves is by our future. Muhamad Ali, the famous boxer, defined himself before he was a champion by saying, "I am the greatest!"
- **Value Strategy:** We are always trying to prove our worth to the group, which often defines our roles and behaviors. We can use one or more of our value strategies as our identity.

- **Purpose:** We can define ourselves by our mission or purpose.
- **Vision:** We can define ourselves by our vision.

An **identity statement** brings our identity definition to life. It needs to be a positive, empowering statement that begins with "I am" in the present tense, which is much more powerful than saying *I'm*. Make your identity statement creative by adding adjectives. Visualize it by choosing a mascot or picturing yourself in a superhero costume as you say it. One of the most memorable identity statements comes from the movie *Stripes*. John Candy's character, Dewey Oxburger, who was an overweight and out of shape Army recruit, defined his future self by saying, "[I am] a lean, mean, fightin' machine!"

Note that there are a lot of **negative identity statements** we use on a daily basis: *I'm an idiot. I'm lazy. I'm a bad person. I'm selfish. I'm so stupid. I'm a failure.* Our habits regarding what we think, feel, say, and do define both our present well-being and our future. Words are the first step in the creation process. So we need to be careful with the words we choose to use and be more positive, balanced, and accurate. Better statements are: *I am doing my best. I am making mistakes and learning from them. I am getting better every day in every way. I am excited about mastering this new skill. I am a perfect human. I am perfectly imperfect.*

Our **purpose** defines why we exist on Earth. It defines how we add value on a daily basis. It is the path we are on. Businesses refer to this as their **mission** and define this using a **mission statement**. Unfortunately, most individuals do not know their purpose in life, but it is a critical part of the conscious compass.

Our **values** define what is important to us as we live our life, fulfill our purpose, and walk down the path toward our vision. They guide our choices and our habits of how we think, feel, speak, and act. They define how we want to live our life on a daily basis and how we want to treat ourselves and others. We can live according to our values regardless of our circumstances. It is completely within our control. When we prioritize them, our values become an even more powerful guide. Around five values are needed to create an effective guide. Most individuals have just a few values, which are rarely prioritized. Note that the word *values*, in this context, isn't asking if we are a good person; it is only asking us to define what is valuable to us, and not in a materialistic sense.

Our **vision** defines where we want to go. It is an inspirational and emotional view of the future we want to create. It is something that is bigger than us and does not exist today. It defines the direction we are headed, where our path will lead us at the end of our life, and perhaps how our efforts will impact the world after our death. It is the most important component of the conscious compass. Unfortunately, most individuals don't have a vision other than to be rich and famous.

Bicycle Analogy
Looking at a bicycle can help us better understand this process. A bicycle consists of many different parts: chain, handlebars, frame, pedals, seat, spokes, tires, wheels, etc. Each part is identified by a name and has a purpose, a vision, and values. The seat proudly says, "I am a seat. My purpose is to provide a place for a human to sit. I value being clean, dry, and comfortable." The chain says, "I am a chain. My purpose is to efficiently deliver the force from the pedals to the back wheel. I value being oiled, clean, and flexible." The seat and the chain share a common vision along with the rest

of the parts of the bicycle: to provide a safe, green, and healthy method of transportation for humans and their belongings for generations to come.

Discover Your Conscious Compass

If you are struggling to see the future and create your new conscious compass, then it might help to look at the past. Steve Jobs said, "You can't connect the dots looking forward; you can only connect them looking backwards. So you have to trust that the dots will somehow connect in your future. You have to trust in something—your gut, destiny, life, karma, whatever. This approach has never let me down, and it has made all the difference in my life."

In other words, if you take a look at where you have been and what you have experienced in life, you might find that a path already exists that you simply were not aware of. Connect the dots from your past experiences and extrapolate it to where you could go in the future. It does not matter if you have had negative experiences or accomplished very little. What does matter is the value you can take from your experiences and how you can best use them in the future.

Another way to identify your path is to ask yourself the following questions:

- What do I enjoy doing so much that I lose track of time?
- What would I do even if I didn't get paid for it?
- What energizes and empowers me?
- What is a great fit for my skills, abilities, experiences, opportunity areas, and limits?

If you still do not know what your path is, then ask your friends and family members. They may be better at objectively connecting the dots for you and recommending options they think would be a good match for you. Sometimes those closest to us know us better than we do.

Go to www.WiseLovingBeing.com/handouts
to find a copy of this handout online.

"Let's try this, Elin. What is your identity, purpose, and vision? What are your values?"

Elin reflected for a moment, then said, "I know I'm going to need to revise these, but here is what I have so far:

- Identity: I am a powerful force for compassion, helping others, and teaching people how to fish. I picture myself saying this while wearing a fisherman's outfit and a red cape.
- Purpose: My purpose is to provide basic needs, training, and opportunities for myself and others.
- Vision: My vision is to create institutions that help millions of people and animals through the end of time.
- Values: Love, courage, truth, service, and resourcefulness, in that priority order."

"Great job, Elin. Now that you've created your conscious compass, it's time to update your unconscious mind and create a new unconscious compass."

Wes gave Elin a handout titled the *Unconscious Mind Cleanse* and went over it with her.

Unconscious Mind Cleanse

In order to live our best life, we need to do an unconscious mind cleanse. This simply means getting rid of the harmful, false, and limiting information and replacing it with useful, true, and empowering information. It is necessary to eliminate our unhealthy feelings of fear, guilt, regret, and shame while keeping what is healthy. In doing so, our unconscious compass will be aligned with our conscious compass, and our radar will find what we truly desire.

The goal at this time is to create what we want our unconscious mind to do. At a later time, we will work on implementing it. Think of this as creating the blueprint for a house. We will build the house later. There are twelve basic steps, which can be done in any order.

1. Turn your unhealthy primary fears into strengths.
2. Turn your secondary fear statements into empowering beliefs.
3. Create a new set of belonging strategies.
4. Turn your limiting tertiary beliefs into empowering beliefs.
5. Turn your general limiting beliefs into empowering beliefs.
6. Create empowering recurring questions.
7. Make a new list of aligned and empowering desired and avoided experiences.
8. Create new empowering habits.
9. Create an environment where you can be authentic.
10. Reprogram your buttons.
11. Find peace through forgiveness and freedom.
12. Set healthy boundaries.

**Go to www.WiseLovingBeing.com/handouts
to find a copy of this handout online.**

"Elin, the first step in the unconscious mind cleanse addresses our primal fear of death. We are going to work on that today and do the remaining steps tomorrow. Let's take a look at how to transform our primary fears into strengths in more detail."

Wes gave Elin three handouts titled *Fear Transformation*, *Managing Fear*, and *Childhood Fears* and went over them with her.

Fear Transformation

Two Sides of Fear

Fears can be either healthy or unhealthy. **Healthy fears** or **beneficial fears** are the normal fears we experience as a result of what is happening around us. They come and go and are of an appropriate intensity for what is happening to us, and most people react in a similar manner. They help us do better in life when we listen to them and take action, and they should definitely be viewed as strengths. They can keep us safe and alive in the present when we encounter danger. Stress and worry about the future can help us prepare for challenges ahead. Fear allows us to function better in groups by helping us avoid things that might cause us embarrassment, guilt, or shame. Fear in the moment can improve our alertness, performance, and ability to focus.

Healthy fear, guilt, regret, shame, stress, and worry help and empower us. We benefit from them. For example, feeling nervous before public speaking is just our body getting us ready to do our best. Feeling stressed about a project tells us that we need to take action to fix something. Feeling guilty that we are not doing enough inspires us to work harder. Feeling embarrassed about our dirty house motivates us to clean it before others visit.

Unhealthy fears can harm us. They cause us physical problems, such as migraines, rashes, weight gain, and other health issues. They sometimes keep us from doing important things we need to do. They can also disempower us and keep us from participating in activities most people regard as safe and normal. Unhealthy fear, guilt, regret, shame, stress, and worry must be reduced and ideally eliminated from our lives.

Turn Unhealthy Fears into Strengths

How do we convert an unhealthy fear into a strength? The simple answer is that we need to do the following:

- **Aware:** Become aware of our unhealthy fear and the problems it causes us.
- **Understand**: Understand what triggers the fear and where the fear originally came from.
- **Confront:** See the benefits of getting over the fear and make a commitment to confront it.
- **Manage:** Find ways to manage, reduce, and eliminate our fear.
- **Elevate:** Learn new skills and develop new abilities that elevate us and make us better off than we would have been if we didn't have the fear in the first place. This creates a strength.

Any unhealthy fear we can manage, reduce, or eliminate will make us better. Having the courage to overcome a fear gives us more confidence, which empowers us to do other things we wouldn't have considered before. Replacing fearful behaviors with empowering behaviors makes us more powerful. Learning new skills because of our fear gives us new abilities and new perspectives; it also gives us an advantage over those who have not experienced and overcome this fear. As a result, we turn our fear from a weakness into a strength.

Follow the Fear Path

Sometimes it is difficult to know if we are on the path that will take us to our vision in the fastest way possible. In the **Stone Path Analogy,** we must jump from one stone to the next in order to get to our destination. There are thousands of stones and many ways to go. But all paths eventually lead to one of our unhealthy fears. We must overcome our unhealthy fears to arrive at our destination. The fastest path requires us to jump on the stones that represent our greatest fears. In this way, fear highlights the fastest path to our vision.

Overcoming our unhealthy fears is scary. Instinctively, we want to avoid or run away from them. Facing our fears is also our best source of growth and elevation. Overcoming just one of our fears creates an upward growth spiral and changes our mindset. We develop more courage and confidence and become motivated to confront another fear, then another. With each triumph, we begin to enjoy the challenge of overcoming our fears and start looking for more.

Open the Door

Jack Canfield said, "Everything you want is on the other side of fear." It makes for a great metaphor: **fears are doors** with treasure on the other side. The bigger the unhealthy fear, the bigger the treasure. The feeling of fear is just an invitation to open the door. We need the courage to face our fear and open the door. Though the door looks scary, it is just a regular door. Fears are simply doors to opportunities.

Visualize each fear door and ask yourself the following questions:
- What is the treasure behind the door? How will I be rewarded by overcoming my fear?
- What will happen if I do not overcome my fear?
- Why is it more important for me to open the door than to not?
- Why is opening the door important for others?
- Why do I need to open the door now?

Go to www.WiseLovingBeing.com/handouts
to find a copy of this handout online.

Managing Fear

Manage, Reduce, or Eliminate Unhealthy Fears

Here are some ways to manage, reduce, and even eliminate your unhealthy fears. Depending on the specific fear, some of these methods may not be a good fit, and some will work better than others. You may choose to combine several methods to help you overcome a specific fear.

- **Ask an Expert:** Work with an expert who can help you better understand, reduce, and eliminate your fear. Learn from others who have already done what you want to do.
- **Ask a Friend:** Things always seem easier when someone is there to show you the way and hold your hand. When things get scary, find a friend who does not share your fear, and ask for their help.
- **Baby Steps:** Take small steps toward resolving your fear. Gradually expose yourself to more of what you fear until you become comfortable with it. Start with what is easier for you and then work your way up to what is more difficult.
- **Breathe:** Deep, slow breathing activates our body's relaxation response. Taking several slow, deep breaths tells our body that everything is fine and there is no danger.
- **Endorphins:** Endorphins fight pain and make us feel good. So try doing one or more of the following the next time you feel fear coming on: connect with others, hug, smile, laugh, sing, dance, jump up and down, move your hips, exercise, walk in nature, or watch a funny video.
- **False Evidence Appearing Real:** This is a fun *FEAR* acronym. Sometimes what we think will hurt us cannot. Some of the reasons for this are the following: the data is wrong, our interpretation of the data is wrong, or things have changed and it is no longer a problem.

- **Fear Is Your Friend:** Fear can be very helpful for you. For example, death is your friend. People who think death is the enemy tend to play it safe and live small lives. People who embrace death as their friend tend to have very exciting and fulfilling lives. They realize that life is short, everyone dies, and they could die today. So why not live their best life before it is too late?

- **Forget the Tribe:** If you get kicked out of the tribe today, you are not going to die. You do not need them. Find another tribe that fits you better. With over eight billion people on the planet, you are likely to make a new friend and find a place where you belong. In the United States, there are many programs designed to take care of you if things go wrong, such as churches, homeless shelters, Supplemental Nutrition Assistance Program (SNAP), unemployment benefits, Social Security, Medicare, and Medicaid.

- **Growth:** Remember that overcoming what you fear helps you grow as a person, and it is the shortest path to achieving your vision.

- **Harmful Effects:** Fear can hurt us mentally by keeping us away from our fundamental needs: love, peace, joy, freedom, and fulfillment. Fear can also hurt us physically by helping to create illness and other health issues.

- **Information:** Fear is feedback. And feedback is just information. It can be helpful because it is simply voicing its concerns. For example: *You are not prepared. You are not ready. This is not a good idea.* Listen and see what you can learn.

- **Invitation:** Fear is an invitation to try something new and receive a great reward in return.

- **Laugh:** Making fun of the situation and of ourselves can lighten the feelings of fear and help us put our fear into the proper perspective.

- **Leave:** As soon as you feel your body start to react to a situation, proactively remove yourself from the situation before your 4F Response has a chance to begin.

- **Magnified Fears:** Some of our strongest fears originated in our childhood. Something scared us, and we thought we were going to die. We did something wrong or embarrassed ourselves, and we thought we would be kicked out of our family or tribe. We quickly associated this event with our primal fears. As a child, we can magnify a small issue into a humongous, scary monster. But if this same event happened to us for the first time as an adult, it most likely would not phase us.

- **Modern Medicine:** Life is not as dangerous as it used to be living in a cave. Some of us will live to be over 120 years old, and modern medicine can fix us up quickly, or it will soon find a way. So the odds are, we are going to be just fine.

- **No Fear:** Fear does not actually exist in the world external to us. You can neither see it nor touch it. It is completely internal to you. What may be fearful to you is not necessarily fearful to someone else. In fact, what you fear, others may crave.

- **No Meaning:** Just state the facts and forget the meaning you attached to the fear. For example, if you ask someone out on a date and they say no, that is all that happened. They did not reject you. They did not say you were unlovable. It is easy to attach a meaning to an event where no meaning actually exists. Similarly, if you make a simple request to someone and they react negatively, it usually has nothing to do with you and everything to do with them.

- **Opposite Day:** Flip your fear-thinking around. Instead of looking at how your fear can harm you, ask yourself how doing what you fear can benefit yourself and others, why it is important to confront your fear now, and how not doing it actually harms you.

- **Practice:** Practice makes perfect. You may get a little nervous the first time you do something, but that disappears after you have done it successfully a few times. Olympic athletes train their entire lives for an event. So get a coach. Practice doing it correctly in a positive, safe environment. Then go and do it in the real world. Keep the training wheels on your bike until you outgrow them.

- **Prepare:** Take action now to minimize the chances of the fearful event happening and to mitigate any potential problems that could occur. What are all the smart actions you can take right now? What is the appropriate amount of effort needed compared to the probability of the event happening and the severity of the expected problems?

- **Reframe:** Reframe your fear so you see it from a more positive perspective. Instead of saying, "This is scary," say, "This is exciting." A roller coaster is a good example. For some people, the fear of heights and falling creates a fun and exciting ride. The higher and faster the better!

- **Reward:** Reward yourself with something valuable whenever you overcome a fear, as well as for each time you try to overcome it.

- **Time-Out:** Give yourself a time-out. Look at your watch and wait ninety seconds. This will help you separate yourself from your automated physical response to fear. The 4F Response will have completed by then, allowing you regained access to your rational mind. Yay!

- **Try It:** Face your fear head-on. Do what you fear doing right now, and you might see that it wasn't as scary as you thought. You might even like it. As the Nike slogan says, "Just Do It!"

Go to www.WiseLovingBeing.com/handouts
to find a copy of this handout online.

Childhood Fears

Heal Fears from Childhood

There is a special process you can use on fears you acquired when you were young. When you were a child, you were small, defenseless, and did not understand how the world worked. This amplified your fears and made you more susceptible to trauma. As an adult, you are no longer small and powerless. You are stronger and more knowledgeable. However, you still carry inside you a child who holds onto those fears and experiences, including the wounds of the past. Your inner child desperately wants to be heard and to feel safe. The more you ignore them or shut them out, the stronger they get and the bigger the fear becomes. In many ways, this frightened inner child still runs your life. You can help them heal by using a visualization exercise.

Visualization Exercise

Close your eyes and take several slow, deep breaths. Picture an imaginary door in front of you that will lead you to your inner child. Open it and walk in. Picture your inner child in your mind. Walk up to them and sit down next to them. Let them know you are the adult version of them. You are big, strong, smart, and powerful. You are here to keep them safe like a healthy adult should. You will make sure that nothing harms them moving forward. Let them know you love them, that they are more than good enough, and that they belong. Connect with them. Ask them if there is anything they want to tell you or ask you. Listen, validate their concerns, and comfort them. Let them know that nothing will be able to harm them again. Give them a big hug, and let them know you love them. Give them a teddy bear, and let them know it will keep them company and is filled with your love.

Place a protective bubble around them, and let them know that it will protect them. Nothing will be able to get in and harm them ever again. Tell them that everything is going to be okay. Thank them for doing their best to run things for so long. Tell them how impressed you are with all that they have been able to accomplish. Let them know how proud you are of them. Let them know that you are taking over now; they are finally free to just be a child and play. Tell them how much you love them. Tell them you have to go be an adult now, but they can always contact you if they need anything. Then wave goodbye, walk out, and close the door behind you. Open your eyes and return to your world where you can act like the mature, strong, and capable adult you are. You are now free to act from a place of love and courage where before you were coming from a place of fear.

Go to www.WiseLovingBeing.com/handouts
to find a copy of this handout online.

"Elin, please do the exercise to heal your nine-year-old inner child later today. It should help you feel more confident in your abilities to make important changes to your life. You are not stuck. Other people have overcome similar challenges. There is hope. It should also help you better understand why you do what you do and why you are where you are."

"Thank you, Wes. I think this will be a big help."

Wes smiled and continued. "Let me give you an example about transforming fears. My friend Ellie had a big fear of death, just like her mother. She was super careful and conservative. She watched the news every day to see where the latest crimes were happening, formulating ways to stay safe. She stayed at home, refusing offers to do adventurous things with her friends. Then one day her mother died, and she realized how much her mother missed out on. Ellie began to think about her own life, wondering how long she had left. She didn't want to have any regrets on her deathbed, so she decided it was time to enjoy life.

"The first thing Ellie did was go skydiving. She used the Opposite Day method. Her thinking switched from *I don't want to die skydiving* to *I don't want to die* without *skydiving.* That one little word made a big difference. Ellie had so much fun skydiving that she went bungee jumping the next weekend! That snowballed into her new thinking: *I did that. I can do anything!* Ellie is still smart about staying safe, but she has balanced safety with the need to enjoy and experience life. She feels more empowered, and this has had positive effects on the rest of her life."

"My friend Ashley was petrified of public speaking. She knew that it came from a traumatic experience in elementary school when a bunch of kids laughed at her while she was trying to give a book report. The teacher was not very supportive and only made things worse.

"As an adult, Ashley avoided speaking in meetings at work, and she was always fearful of doing anything that would cause people to make fun of her. She avoided responsibility and preferred to only do what she was told to do. Her fear was also holding her back in her personal life. She didn't date and always just went along with whatever her friends and family wanted to do, even when she wanted to do something different.

"One day Ashley's boss offered to send her to a public speaking course. He said he used to be very shy, too, and had greatly benefited from the course. After putting it off as long as she could, Ashley reluctantly agreed to go.

"The first night was very difficult. She had to stand up at her chair and introduce herself; she had to work in small groups where everyone had to speak; and at the end of the evening, she had to walk to the front of the room with four others and tell over fifty people what she hoped to achieve by taking the class. Luckily, there were other people who went first that were in the same boat. They talked about their fear of public speaking. There were teaching assistants who talked about how they overcame their fear of public speaking by taking the class and what a difference it had made in their lives. And the instructor talked about his personal transformation from being an introvert to being an extrovert.

"The second night was easier but still difficult. This time Ashley had to give a short talk about herself. During each class, she learned new skills on how to speak in public, and she practiced them in a safe, supportive environment. She even learned that the nervous feeling she had before speaking was just her body helping her get ready. The adrenaline was helping her to create more energy, improve her ability to focus on what she was going to say, and better connect with her audience. It was not something to be feared but something to be embraced, accepted, and appreciated.

"After a month, Ashley began to enjoy speaking in front of the class. She also started to speak up in meetings at work and to state her views amongst her friends. After two months, her boss gave her new responsibilities. After three months she received a raise and a promotion. She even gave a toast and told a joke at her best friend's wedding, to everyone's amazement, including her own.

"Ashley decided to become a teaching assistant in the next public speaking class, and she started helping others at work who had the same fear she used to have. She had successfully turned her unhealthy fear into a strength, and her life was greatly improved as a result.

"Elin, the first step in the unconscious mind cleanse is to *turn your unhealthy primary fears into strengths*. Pick an unhealthy primary fear or two, and tell me how you plan to turn them into strengths."

Elin replied, "I am going to convert my fear of being homeless into a strength by using the *FEAR acronym*. I can always live at Carl's house or at a shelter. I'm going to *prepare*. I'm going to start looking for a job and other ways to make money so it won't be an issue. I am going to *ask an expert* by going to the library today and finding a book on managing my finances. This will make me much stronger financially.

"For my fear of death, I am going to use *opposite day*. Instead of thinking that anything I try to do will be a waste of time because I will probably die before it's done, I am going to ask, 'What can I do today to make my life better?' and 'How can I help someone else?' This will motivate and empower me to elevate myself and others. I'm also going to use *fear is my friend*. I've played it so safe for so long and missed out on so much, it's almost like I died a long time ago. I'm finally going to start living.

"For my fear of abandonment, I am going to apply *no meaning*. I've been thinking that I am not lovable and not worthy. But the fact is, no one has ever said that, and no one has ever truly abandoned me. People have either moved on or died.

"Probably my biggest fear comes from the significant event I had at school when I was eight and decided that talking equals death. I am going to apply *time-out* and *forget the tribe* to realize that this is a false fear. With *practice*, I can learn how to have a conversation in any situation. By smiling and moving, I can use *endorphins* to help me reengage with the other person. This will strengthen my confidence and my connection with others."

"Regarding your last fear, you can also *ask an expert* about how to hold a conversation better," Wes added. "As a matter of fact, I can teach you the **Conversation Stack**, which is an easy way to remember what to ask others. It also helps you prepare answers for the common questions people could ask you. As a result, you will be approaching each conversation with a goal of building closer relationships, and having a process will help you learn more about them. Your relationship-building skills will be stronger than if you had never had the fear in the first place."

"That sounds great. Thank you, Wes."

"To summarize, we are powerful creators. Our highest potential is unlimited. Our conscious compass is critical to our success. It consists of our identity, purpose, vision, and a prioritized list of values. It is important to follow the twelve steps of the unconscious mind cleanse in order to get our unconscious compass to align with our conscious compass. When our conscious and unconscious minds are working in concert, they empower us to achieve our purpose and vision. Fears are just doors to opportunities. There are many ways to manage, reduce, or even eliminate our fears and turn them into strengths.

"Excellent job today, Elin. Are you ready for your homework?"

"Yes, sir! What's my homework?" Elin asked.

"Tomorrow, we are going to work on the remaining eleven steps in the Unconscious Mind Cleanse. First, please review your primary fear transformation from today. Do it tonight before going to bed and then as soon as you wake up tomorrow morning. Second, please think about what new beliefs and habits you want to create that will transform your life.

"Third, please write me a **letter from the future.** I want you to imagine yourself living five years from now. You need to travel in time to experience, with all your senses and emotions, what you have created. You need to feel the excitement, love, peace, joy, freedom, and fulfillment you are experiencing five years from now as a result of your efforts and achievements. Write the letter in the present tense five years from now, as if everything has already happened. Also include some advice for your present-day self to provide some hope and direction. Then, pretend to send it to me so I receive it tomorrow. For example, you'll write something like this:"

September 8, 2027

Dear Wes,

I'm so grateful for the wisdom you gave me five years ago in 2022. You won't believe what I've been able to create! I absolutely love my life!!!

I'm financially free. In addition to my Social Security check, I also created a business that does _____.

I'm in vibrant health. I just completed a 10K, I no longer need to take any prescriptions, and _____.

I have amazing relationships with compatible people I can trust. We _____.

Please tell 2022 Elin that everything is going to be all right. She just needs to _____

Love,
Elin

Go to www.WiseLovingBeing.com/handouts
to find a copy of this handout online.

"Let's meet here tomorrow at the usual time. Any questions?"
"No questions. See you tomorrow, Wes!"

Chapter Fourteen

Transforming Beliefs, Habits, and Relationships

When Elin arrived at the Cinnabon the next day, Wes was already there. He greeted her with a big smile and said, "Good morning, Elin! How are you today?"

"Good morning, Wes," Elin replied. "I'm fantastic. How are you?"

"I'm terrific!" Wes replied enthusiastically. "Today is Transformation Day part two! This is so exciting! Today you will complete your transformation blueprint. Let's get started, shall we?"

They began their morning walk around the mall as Wes inquired about yesterday's assignment. "Let's go over your homework. Were you able to review your primary fear transformation last night before you went to bed and first thing this morning? Also, were you able to think about what new beliefs and habits you want to create today?"

"Yes. I was able to complete both assignments."

"Nice job. The last exercise was writing me a **letter from the future**. Your assignment was to travel in time five years from now and let me know how amazing your life is as a result of your hard work and achievements. The letter is written in the present tense as if it has already happened and it should include some advice for your present-day self to provide some hope and direction.

"Elin, please read me your letter from the future."
Elin took out her letter and began to read it.

September 8, 2027

Hi Wes,

I am so grateful for the time you spent with me five years ago in 2022. You won't believe what I've been able to create! I absolutely love my life!

I am financially secure! Along with my life partner, Tom, I now live on a large parcel of land in a rural agricultural area. We tend an expansive organic garden for our own use, as well as for a local farmers' market. We get lots of daily exercise, with fresh air to breathe and clean well water to drink. Our extended family visits often, which brings us great happiness. I've never felt healthier, and I no longer need medications.

We've created an area close to our home where we care for many different types of rescued animals. We received a multi-year foundation grant to sustain a full-service rescue facility, along with volunteer veterinarians and other supportive animal-loving volunteers of all ages. We are blessed!

Most excitedly, I host weekly, life-enriching workshops, both in person and virtually where, for an income-based donation, women of all ages come together to discuss, learn, and participate in the teachings you have given me to achieve Universal Elevation. Likewise, Tom offers the same workshop to men of all ages. Once a month, both groups come together to share their progress along the path to Universal Elevation.

Please tell 2022 Elin that everything is going to be alright. There are some difficult times ahead, and change isn't easy. But once you get through that and reach the other side, everything is going to be so much better. It's important to focus on the positive and realize that your life has just begun.

Wes, I feel such love, peace, joy, freedom, fulfillment, support, and trust like never before! I now wake up each morning with gratitude, energy, wonderment, and anticipation for what the new day will bring. Each night, I give thanks for so many gifts, most especially gratitude for my WLB!

Love,
Elin

"I love that letter, Elin! I think that is a good five-year target for you. Let's continue with the transformation process. As a friendly reminder, the twelve steps in the Unconscious Mind Cleanse are:

1. Turn your unhealthy primary fears into strengths.
2. Turn your secondary fear statements into empowering beliefs.
3. Create a new set of belonging strategies.
4. Turn your limiting tertiary beliefs into empowering beliefs.
5. Turn your general limiting beliefs into empowering beliefs.
6. Create empowering recurring questions.
7. Make a new list of aligned and empowering desired and avoided experiences.
8. Create new empowering habits.
9. Create an environment where you can be authentic.

10. Reprogram your buttons.
11. Find peace through forgiveness and freedom.
12. Set healthy boundaries.

"We completed the first step yesterday. Today we are going to complete the eleven remaining steps. Steps two and three are about transforming your secondary fears and belonging strategies."

Wes gave Elin a handout titled *Secondary Fear Transformation* and went over it with her.

Secondary Fear Transformation

Convert Secondary Fear Statements

To convert your secondary fear statements into new empowering beliefs, you simply need to reverse them. Here are some examples:

- *I'm not lovable* becomes *I am lovable.*
- *I'm not worthy* becomes *I am worthy.*
- *I'm not good enough* becomes *I am more than good enough.*

Belief Validation

It is important to validate your new beliefs so they transform from just words into something that has been proven to be true. You don't need to be perfect, so just focus on the bare **minimum validation** needed to prove your belief is true. **Objective proof** is based on facts and things that can be validated with our senses. **Subjective proof** is based on opinions and feelings. **External validation** is done by others while **internal validation** is done by you. The **challenge** happens when we try to validate a new belief by using external validation that uses subjective proof. We may have different standards and objectives for achieving it that are not shared by others. Since we can't control what others think, feel, say, and do, we can sometimes open ourselves up to the problem where something is actually true for us, yet we are told by others that it is false. Choose your validation criteria wisely. Internal objective proof is often best.

Change Belonging Strategies

Review your belonging strategies and then create a new list that is better aligned with your new, transformed self.

- **Value Strategies:** Your value strategies typically need some additional powerful items in order to help you be more effective. Add those strategies in and remove the less powerful ones that no longer serve you. You might also need to add strategies that balance you out more. For example if you are an analyst focused on things, you might want to add strategies to create stronger relationships with others like harmonious, helpful, loyal, relationship builder, supportive, or trusted.

- **Coping Strategies:** You will probably need to eliminate some or all of your coping strategies since they are not aligned with your authentic self. You have accepted the fact that you are perfectly imperfect, and everyone else is too. You don't need to hide your faults anymore. You belong and do not need to worry about dying if you get kicked out of the group.

- **Anti-Belonging Strategies:** Review any anti-belonging strategies you have to see if you still want to be a rebel, or if you would like to find more ways to get along. Knowing that you are valuable just the way you are and realizing that you will not be rejected because of your faults may open you up to receiving some of the many benefits of being part of the group.

- **Independent Strategies:** Your independent strategies may need to be strengthened so you can be free to pursue your vision and not be held back by peer pressure or any other limiting factors from a particular group.

Go to www.WiseLovingBeing.com/handouts
to find a copy of this handout online.

"I have an example for you. My friend Charlie discovered the validation challenge when he created the new empowering belief *I am worthy*. He was feeling pretty good about himself until he ran into Joe, an old friend from college who he hadn't spoken with in over twenty-five years. Joe talked about how great his life was: His career was going extremely well. His wife was so amazing and beautiful. His kids were smart and talented and had gone to the best schools to become doctors and lawyers. He owned a house on the beach and had paid off the mortgage. He recently paid cash for a new luxury automobile. And to top it off, he was about to take an incredible two-week European vacation.

"Afterward, Charlie felt depressed and hopeless. He hadn't achieved any of these things and, because of his age, there were things he could never do. He realized that no matter what he did, there was no way he could ever prove his worth to Joe. Even if Charlie could exceed Joe's financial accomplishments, he would never be seen as worthy in Joe's eyes. After all, Joe did it twenty years ago! The other problem was that how Joe measured success was much different than how Charlie did. There was no way he could win this game of proving he was worthy if he had to get Joe to agree.

"I spoke with Charlie about the importance of self-worth and how it builds confidence and self-love through independent belonging strategies. I reminded him that Joe wasn't in charge of deciding if others were worthy. Only Charlie could decide if he was worthy in his own eyes. Charlie created external and internal validation that included a combination of objective and subjective criteria. Everything was aligned with his values and was within his control. He was now playing a game he could win, and he continues to feel worthy every day.

"Let's apply this to your life, Elin. The second step in the Unconscious Mind Cleanse is to *turn your secondary fear statements into empowering beliefs.* Based on your old secondary fear statements, what are the new empowering beliefs you will replace them with?"

Elin replied, "My new empowering beliefs that replace my old secondary fear statements are:

- I am lovable.
- I am good enough.
- I am smart enough.
- I am worthy.
- I belong and fit in."

"Perfect. Now we are going to look at how to validate these new beliefs. Let's take *I am worthy* as an example. How will you validate this new empowering belief? What is the minimum validation needed to prove you are worthy on a daily basis?"

Elin smiled. "I can definitely relate to your story about Charlie. I have three high school friends I haven't spoken with since graduation who are all doing so much better than me in so many ways. There would never be a scenario where they would think I was 'worthy.' I'm definitely going down a different path in life. I can prove to myself that I *am worthy* by making progress toward the items on my magic wand list. Objectively, I can track if I have enough money to pay my bills, and I can look at my savings account balance to see if it is growing. I can track my progress in eating better food, exercising, meeting new people, getting a job, and reading books on personal finances. Subjectively, I can monitor how I feel about myself, and I can have my niece let me know if she thinks I'm being more positive. These are all things I can work toward and that are in my control. Self-worth, here we come!"

"Great job, Elin. Please do this same validation exercise on your other new beliefs. You'll be surprised at how attainable they become. Having control and being able to win has a profound effect on your overall mental well-being. It is incredibly liberating and helps you achieve your fundamental needs."

"I will," Elin replied. "It is so amazing how a small change in perspective can have such a huge benefit!"

"The third step is to *create a new set of belonging strategies.* You will need to revise your list of value, coping, anti-belonging, and independent strategies so they empower you. What will your new set of belonging strategies be?"

Elin replied, "Regarding my value strategies, I will replace *follower* with *leader.* I will also add *successful.* So my new list will be: *funny, good, hard worker, harmonious, helpful, leader, nice, smart, successful,* and *supportive.* I will remove all of my coping strategies: *conceal, escape, helpless, hopeless, invisible, perfectionist, pleaser, punish,* and *sacrifice.* I don't have any anti-belonging strategies, and I will leave my independent strategies alone for now."

"The fourth step is to *turn your limiting tertiary beliefs into empowering beliefs.* What are your new empowering tertiary beliefs?"

Elin replied, "My new empowering tertiary beliefs are:
- We are all human beings.
- We all want the same basic things: have a good job and provide for ourselves and our loved ones.
- We are much more alike than we are different.
- I enjoy speaking with others in order to understand them better and to learn from them.
- Diversity of opinions is good.
- We all have a right to make our own choices, create our beliefs, and formulate our own opinions.
- Everyone deserves to be heard.
- We all want to protect our fundamental human rights."

"The fifth step is to *turn all of your general limiting beliefs into empowering beliefs.* What are your new empowering beliefs?"

Elin replied, "My new empowering beliefs are:

- There are many things I can do to improve my life.
- My best days are in front of me.
- I deserve to live a great life.
- There is more than enough money for everyone.
- There are lots of people who would like to help me if I ask them.
- People can make money at any age.
- I can get a great job.
- I am a hard worker.
- There are lots of ways I can make money.
- I can create my own business.
- I can make as much money as I choose.
- The more money I make, the more I can help myself and others.
- I am a math person.
- I can take action to improve all areas of my life.
- I am an action-oriented person.
- I am an organized person.
- I have a lot to contribute to this world.
- I am just getting started.
- I like being challenged.
- I always do my best.
- I am perfectly human.
- I can make new friends who have common interests.
- I am equal with others and should be treated that way.
- I make valuable contributions to others.
- Some people desperately need my help and leadership.
- I am successful."

"The sixth step is to *create empowering recurring questions*. What new recurring questions do you want to create?"

Elin replied, "My new empowering recurring questions are:
- What great things are going to happen to me today?
- How can I improve the quality of my life today?
- What great things can I create today?
- How can I use my unique gifts to add value and impact to a person or animal today?"

"The seventh step is to *make a new list of aligned and empowering desired and avoided experiences.* Here is a handout to help you with this process."

Wes gave Elin a handout titled *Create Empowering Experiences* and went over it with her.

Create Empowering Experiences

Empowering Desired Experiences

Our empowering desired experiences are usually related to our values or what we want to experience in life, such as financial security and good health. They need to be positive and easily achievable every day using OR Rules. But instead of rules for achieving each experience, we need to use **empowering actions,** which are simple, small, positive things we can easily think, feel, say, or do. It is important to have a combination of fun, challenging, and rewarding actions on our lists. Precede them with the phrase: *I achieve this desired experience any time I do any of the following things.*

Empowering Avoided Experience

Most of the time, we view avoided experiences in a negative way since they are usually attached to our fears. What we need to do is to look at them from a more balanced, positive, and healthy perspective, which is called an **empowering perspective.** Instead of rules, we use **empowering reasons**, which are reasons why this experience is not really as terrible as we think it is and how it might not actually happen. Prefix these reasons with the phrase: *My empowering perspective of this avoided experience helps me overcome it for the following reasons.*

Aligned Experiences

All of your desired and avoided experiences need to be aligned and going in the same direction. There cannot be any conflicts that would take you in multiple directions at the same time.

Empowering Perspective Examples

Here are some examples of empowering perspectives for the most common avoided experiences.

Failure: My empowering perspective of this avoided experience helps me overcome it for the following reasons:

- A failure is a person who lacks success. I can never be a failure because I am successful.
- Failing is not failure, and failing does not mean I am a failure.
- Failing is feedback. It is simply part of the learning process.
- I am no different than the great inventor, Thomas Edison, who is associated with the quote, "I have not failed. I've just found 10,000 ways that won't work."
- Trying and failing is much better than never trying at all.
- Failing is the same thing as trying but getting a different result than what was intended.
- Sometimes the unintended results of my effort are actually more valuable than what I intended.
- Failure is required to learn something new.
- Failure is a sign of life.
- I am a perfect human who is wonderfully imperfect.
- I succeed anytime I learn from my failures and do my best.
- I act like a baby who fails the exact number of times it takes to learn how to walk.

Rejection: My empowering perspective of this avoided experience helps me overcome it for the following reasons:

- Rejection has a negative connotation, when all it really means is that someone said *no*.
- Rejection does not mean I am a bad person or that there is something wrong with me.

- Their reaction is about them and has nothing to do with me.
- They are simply telling me that the request is not a match for their needs right now.
- Rejection only reflects their view. Their view is not a fact. Everyone has a different view.
- Rejection is just feedback, which I can learn from.
- I remove any meaning associated with the actual event.
- I am the only person who determines how I feel.
- I will find someone who says *yes*.
- The person who says *no* today may say *yes* in the future.

Regret, guilt, shame, and embarrassment: My empowering perspective of this avoided experience helps me overcome it for the following reasons:

- I did my best given my knowledge and abilities at the time.
- I had good intentions.
- I am a perfect human who is perfectly imperfect.
- Everyone makes mistakes and experiences failure at some point in their life.
- This experience does not make me a bad person.
- I am defined by my entire life, not by my worse moments.
- Experiencing this and learning from this will help me be a better person.
- I can use this information to do better next time.
- I can always apologize and move forward.
- I forgive myself.
- I can always find a tribe to belong to.

Go to www.WiseLovingBeing.com/handouts
to find a copy of this handout online.

"Elin, what are your new empowering desired experiences and actions?"

"Financial Security," Elin said. "I achieve this desired experience anytime I do any of the following things:

- I live within my means.
- I avoid buying something I do not need.
- I avoid spending any money today.
- I eat food prepared at home.
- I add money to my checking, savings, or investment accounts.
- I reduce my debt.
- I increase my income.
- I increase my net worth.
- I do not pay for something that someone else should be buying.
- I think about ways to make more money.
- I take smart action toward creating a new income stream.

"Success. I achieve this desired experience any time I do any of the following things:

- I learn something new.
- I use my knowledge.
- I use the knowledge that Wes gave me.
- I take smart action toward achieving one of my goals.
- I do something I used to be uncomfortable doing.
- I set or enforce a healthy boundary.
- I create a situation where the other person and I both win.
- I limit or avoid engaging in an escape activity.
- I acknowledge the progress I am making.
- I do my best.

- I focus on doing the most important thing at that moment in time.
- I help someone or an animal in need.
- I catch myself before I say something negative.
- I think or say a positive thing.
- I accept help from someone.
- I express gratitude.
- I show courage.
- I take ownership and act like an adult.
- I acknowledge that I am a perfectly imperfect human."

"Great job, Elin. Please create an empowering perspective for your avoided experience of abandonment."

"Abandonment. My empowering perspective of this avoided experience helps me overcome it for the following reasons:

- Abandonment has a negative connotation, when it only means that someone chose to go somewhere else.
- A person's choice to leave is about them.
- I have mistakenly used the word abandon whenever someone has gone somewhere else.
- People don't abandon me when they go somewhere else.
- My dad never abandoned me. He died; it wasn't his choice to leave me.
- No one has ever abandoned me. They have just chosen to do something else that was more aligned with their needs at that time.
- In the past, I have sometimes motivated people to leave and then labeled it abandonment.
- No one has ever said to me, 'I am abandoning you.'
- I will not use the word abandon to describe what happens when someone moves on.

- I will not use the word abandon when describing the relinquishment of my baby. I made the best choice for both him and me at the time.
- I have never abandoned anyone or anything.
- I may view my decisions of the past differently in hindsight, but I need to remember that I did the best I could, given the information I had at the time, and what I thought was best for everyone involved.
- I can use this experience as feedback and learn from it.
- I forgive myself. I am perfectly human.
- I have always done my best.
- I am a good person.
- I can find people who want to be around me.
- My niece and everyone else in my life today want to be around me."

"Nicely done, Elin! Looking at your new empowering experiences, are they all aligned?"

"Yes. I think they are all aligned and will help me do much better in life."

"Agreed. The eighth step is to *create new empowering habits*. What empowering activities will make up your day going forward?"

Elin replied, "The activities in my typical day will be:
- Get ready to go (2 hours)
- Work on my goals (8 hours)
- Learn something new (2 hours)
- Connect with others (2 hours)
- Lunch (1 hour)
- Dinner (1 hour)
- Watch TV or play a computer game as a reward (1 hour)
- Sleep (7 hours)"

"Elin, I want to make a quick comment. I appreciate your enthusiasm and desire to improve, but I am concerned about you wanting to spend eight hours per day working on your goals, two hours per day learning something new, and two hours per day connecting with others when you aren't doing much today. I think it's commendable, but in my experience, setting a goal this high will eventually lead to problems that result in you giving up on this goal altogether and replacing it with escape activities. I want you to be successful here. Tomorrow, I will introduce you to a method called Ridiculously Easy Goals. I think you'll find it quite empowering.

"Let's talk about your new thought habits. One of my favorite quotes from Louise Hay is, 'The thoughts we choose to think are the tools we use to paint the canvas of our lives.' Our thoughts and words change how we view ourselves and our world, and no two people have the exact same view of the world.

"The **Sunglasses Analogy** illustrates this quite well. Sunglass lenses come in a variety of colors: amber, blue, brown, gray, green, pink, purple, red, and yellow. Each color makes the world look different than it really is. And rose-colored glasses always make the world look perfectly wonderful even when it's not. The thoughts we think and words we use on a daily basis are like the lenses of the sunglasses. If we think people are bad, then that is what we will see. If we think we are going to have a bad day, then that is what happens. It is important to think and express ourselves using words and images that are balanced, empowering, and realistic. We become what we think. What we think and the words we use are the first steps in the creation process.

"Elin, what empowering words and images will you use when you think and express yourself?"

"I will start my day with a positive thought before I even get out of bed. I will recite my new recurring questions, and I will think about how lucky I am to work on my goals and help others. I will end my day by thinking about all the great things that happened during the day.

"I'll be very careful about the words I use. I will try to use positive and empowering words, and when I catch myself being negative, I'll correct myself. For example, I've come to realize that I often blame the weather for not feeling positive about my life. But this is usually intellectual justification and a misdirect from the real problem. The weather is innocent. Going forward, when I catch myself incorrectly blaming the weather for how I feel, I will correct myself, say, 'I love the weather,' and then focus on the real issue and what I need to do to feel better."

"The ninth step is to *create an environment where you can be authentic*. Here is a handout to help you with this process."

Wes gave Elin a handout titled *Create an Authentic Environment* and went over it with her.

Create an Authentic Environment

Our environment consists of both what is happening inside us and what is happening outside us. Both environments are important. We need to do our best to make them both genuinely positive and authentic.

Our Internal Environment

In a genuinely positive internal environment you have a balanced view of yourself. You think about what you are doing well and where you can improve. You remind yourself that you are a perfectly imperfect human and that mistakes are normal and a sign of life. You do your best and are grateful for the blessings in your life.

It is extremely important to be honest with yourself. Set up a time and place where you can reflect on where you are not being authentic with yourself. Awareness is critical, and the truth will set you free. One way to do this is to track what you actually do against what you think or say you are doing. You can review the results to see what reality looks like. You can then adjust your thoughts and actions so they are authentically aligned. We can think that things are worse than they really are or that things are going better than they really are, so be on the lookout for both.

Our External Environment

It is critical that we create a safe, positive, and supportive environment free from abuse and the criticism of others. It is also important to create an environment where we can be authentic. Authenticity is power. It means being comfortable being ourselves and expressing our views. Our external environment consists of where we work and live, what we are surrounded by, and who we interact with. If you can't be yourself at home or at work, then you might need to make some changes. You may be able to create healthy relationships with some of your current coworkers, friends, and family members, or you might need to find new people with whom you can completely be yourself. You may need to set aside time outside of home and work where you can be more authentic.

Go to www.WiseLovingBeing.com/handouts
to find a copy of this handout online.

"Elin, what are you going to do to be more authentic?"

"I am going to interact with my niece more. I am going to make my home a better environment. I am going to avoid negative people, and I am going to find new friends with similar interests. I am also going to stop buying chips and soda at the grocery store and keeping them in my house. If I absolutely have to have those items, then I'll need to go get them. This involves braving the hot weather and other things I try to avoid. In other words, I'm going to make the cost of eating this comfort food much higher in terms of money and time."

"Perfect! The tenth step is to *reprogram your buttons*. Here is a handout to help you with this process."

Wes gave Elin a handout titled *Button Reprogramming* and went over it with her.

Button Reprogramming

Buttons can provide automated responses that exist on a spectrum between healthy and unhealthy. It is possible to change the button response, and this process is called button reprogramming.

Automated Response Summary

To quickly summarize what we talked about before, the Survival Response System (SRS) automatically makes chemical and physiological changes to our body and generates an emotion in response to both our thoughts and to what is happening around us. All emotions are good; they are simply messages being sent to our unconscious mind. Our unconscious mind receives the emotion and sensory data, and it maps it to a button. The button response consists of the feelings and the intensity of those feelings and the automatic behaviors, including thoughts, words, and actions. The goal of button reprogramming is to change some or all of the button response. The button still remains. Friendly reminder that we are actually pressing our own buttons. As much as we would like to blame others for our unhealthy automated response, they are innocent, and we are totally responsible for it.

Vending Machine Analogy

A vending machine can help us to better understand how button reprogramming works. On this particular vending machine, if you want a Snickers bar, you press button A1. What we want to do here is change the vending machine so that pressing button A1 provides a healthy granola bar instead. In other words, we press the same button but get different results.

Here is where the analogy diverges from real life. In the vending machine, the button A1 can only connect with one location. In order to change what the button provides, we have to fill that location with a new snack. In the mind, however, we can't just replace the button's old response. It will always be there. What we have to do is create a new response, which our mind will store in a different location. The mind can actually access both responses for the same button.

Even though we reprogram the button to give us the new response, our mind always has access to the old response. Most of the time after we have reprogrammed the button, our mind gives us the new response. But every once in a while, it gives us the old response. If this happens, then simply ask for the new response.

Reprogramming Process
The objective is to replace the unhealthy, negative, fear-based thoughts, feelings, words, and actions the button automatically creates today with an **invitation** to use a healthy, positive, love-based response that actually serves us and is aligned with our conscious compass. The key is to retrain the button to select the new positive response instead of the old negative response.

The steps to reprogram a specific button are:

1. Write down the specific circumstances that activate the button today.
2. Write down the thoughts, feelings, words, and actions that are automatically generated.
3. What primary and secondary fears are associated with the button? Where did they come from?
4. What will the new response for the button create instead?
5. Write down what you want the new thoughts, feelings, words, and actions to be.
6. How will you invite the button to choose the new response instead of the old one?
7. Practice the new button response in a safe environment.
8. Practice the new button response in the real world until it becomes automatic.

**Go to www.WiseLovingBeing.com/handouts
to find a copy of this handout online.**

"I have an example for you. My friend Henry used to get upset almost every time he went for a drive. The other drivers could upset him when they drove too slow or too fast, didn't know where they were going, did something stupid, were poor drivers, were inconsiderate, or were rude. His button caused the following automatic behaviors: he got angry, yelled, flipped people off, and gave an angry look. He became a completely different person, who I nicknamed Hank. The button response was extremely strong and difficult to control. It came from several significant events that taught him that bad drivers are bad people who are inconsiderate, rude, and stupid. This, of course, was really about him, his significant events, and his primal fear of not belonging. His fears were very intense and created a similar level of anger that he unconsciously used to defend himself.

"Henry decided that Hank had to stop driving. He decided that the button would now be an invitation that told him he was a good person and belonged. The new invitation was for Henry to immediately say, 'Thank you so much for telling me that I am a good, smart, conscientious person who belongs. I really appreciate that.' For his new response, his actions were to smile and wave. His new thoughts were to be patient, understanding, and accepting of the other driver. He told himself not to engage with the other driver and that they were just doing their best. His new feelings were ones of love, peace, joy, freedom, and fulfillment. Henry practiced this new button response in his car every day. He enjoyed receiving 'compliments' that confirmed he was good, smart, conscientious, and belonged. He liked the positive feelings that were generated. He liked having the freedom to choose how he would respond. He liked being in control of himself. It didn't happen overnight, but Hank eventually stopped driving with Henry, and now he needs to get his own ride.

"My friend Stuart had a button for the word *mail*. When his mother would ask him to come over and take a look at her mail, he would get very angry. It was causing a lot of problems in their relationship and to his emotional well-being. Digging a little deeper, I discovered that he added meaning to the word *mail* when his mother said it because of all the criticism and abuse he suffered as a child. When she said *mail* he heard that he was a failure, worthless, unlovable, and a bad person.

"When I used the word *mail* with him, there was no reaction. Likewise, when I said he was purple, there was no reaction. I asked him why he didn't react, and he said it was because it was obviously not the case. I pointed out that it was also not the case that he was a failure, worthless, unlovable, and a bad person. But he somehow still felt the need to defend himself against something that wasn't true.

"I took Stuart through the transformation process and helped him see that his intense reaction was tied to his primal fears of survival and not belonging, which resulted from a very traumatic childhood and adult life. This intense fear that he was going to die produced a strong negative reaction. He became very angry as a way of protecting himself. And his fast, hair-trigger reaction was also an indication of how intense his fears were. But since there was no longer a real threat to his life, his reaction was only causing harm.

"Stuart was finally able to get clarity around this issue. His fear of death wasn't true. The meaning he had associated with the word *mail* wasn't true. His mom wasn't saying anything negative to him; he was the one pressing his own button. He was responsible for how he felt and the challenges he was having with his mom.

"Stuart decided to create a new button response that created a loving and supportive family. He would say to himself, *Thank you, Mom, for telling me that I am successful, worthy, lovable, and a good person.* He would then give her a compliment and offer to take care of something she needed help with. The invitation for the new response was for him to say the silly phrase, *I am purple!* It was so effective that he has never experienced an angry outburst with her since.

"Let's try it, Elin. Pick a button and go through the first six steps to reprogram it."

Elin replied, "I have a rejection button. It happens when I sense that someone doesn't respect me and thinks they're better than me. I feel angry. I reject them first by judging them and labeling them as a bad person. I focus on what is wrong with them. My body posture is geared toward a fight, and my senses are on high alert. I speak to them in a critical tone of voice. I try to avoid them if I can. This is my fear of rejection, which is related to my secondary fear statement, *I'm not good enough.* This button is very strong and is definitely out of my control, probably originating from my experience at school with the ruler.

"I am reprogramming this button into an invitation that reinforces the beliefs that *I belong, I am good enough, I am lovable,* and *I am equal.* For the invitation, I will smile, take a deep breath, and say the word *awesome.* This will remind me to think about my new empowering perspective of rejection. I'll say to myself, *Thank you for reminding me that I am a great person and that I belong.* I will label them as perfectly human. I will think about their WLB, treat them with respect, and seek to understand them better. I will stay centered in feelings of love, peace, and joy."

"The eleventh step is to *find peace through forgiveness and freedom,*" Wes said. "You'll need to complete the freedom and forgiveness exercises we talked about for both yourself and others. It does take some time, so keep working on this. You'll know you've done a good job when you are at peace with those relationships and when you can look in the mirror and say, 'I love you' without experiencing any negative feelings. When forgiving yourself, your ideal goal is to eliminate all unhealthy regret, guilt, and shame. Have you completed this process yet?"

"No. Not yet, Wes. To be honest, I haven't really started on this, but I do see how important it is."

"Okay. Please complete this process. You can't transform without doing it. The twelfth step is to *set healthy boundaries*. Where in your life do you need to set and enforce healthy boundaries?"

Elin replied, "I need to set a boundary with a person named Richard. I need to find a win/win solution that allows me to do what's important for me without causing problems in the relationship. I am going to set a harmonious boundary that accomplishes what I really want, which is to not interact with him so much. I am going to block off two mornings and say I have something I need to do. I can then help out in the afternoons. He'll easily support and justify this because he thinks I have a lot of problems. He'll probably assume that I'm going to a therapist or something similar."

"That sounds like a good first step, Elin. I'd like to wrap up today by telling you the **Lightbulb Analogy**. A lightbulb provides a valuable service to others. But it only works when it is activated by a light switch that creates a closed electrical circuit. We are all like a lightbulb. It's important to become better through continuous improvement so our bulb burns brighter. We must maintain a healthy circuit so we can function properly. We are made to give value and service to others and to receive value from others. But the only way this can work is if we have a closed circuit: we have to give *and* receive, and we have to give *to* receive.

"This means that we can't do things for others for free when they should be paying us. Not everything is about money, of course, but we should definitely also benefit in some way that is roughly equivalent in value. We can't do things for others that they need to do for themselves. It also means that sometimes, we need to first give to those in need before we receive good things. When we follow these principles, the more value we give, the more value we receive. With an equivalent give and take, the circular flow stays healthy, and everyone can benefit for many years to come. Does that help you better understand that a healthy life needs a bit of give and take?"

"Yes it does," Elin replied. "It definitely helps me understand that a sacrifice that isn't for the greater good is not a healthy one."

"Great work today, Elin! You've taken the first big step in the transformation process by creating the blueprint for Elin 2.0. There's a lot more work to do, but you're on your way. I recommend you keep reviewing this information twice a day until it becomes a part of you. First thing in the morning and right before going to bed are the best times for you to absorb this.

"Change isn't easy. It takes time and energy. The **Cargo Ship Analogy** should help make this clearer. Imagine a fully loaded cargo ship going maximum speed in the open ocean. It weighs so much that it has an incredible amount of momentum. It takes a lot of time and energy to change its course or stop. The same is true for you. You've built up a lot of momentum living your life the way it is today for so many years. Making any significant change is going to take a certain amount of time and energy.

"The **Cake Analogy** will help you better understand the process. If it normally takes thirty minutes to bake a cake at 350 degrees, you can't rush the process by baking the cake for fifteen minutes at 700 degrees. It will be burnt on the outside with raw batter on the inside. You're going to need to be patient. Just as a caterpillar doesn't become a butterfly overnight, you are not going to transform overnight either. Change is very subtle at first. Don't compare yourself to others. You might not think you're making any progress, but it will be much more evident to others who know you well. Keep taking those baby steps. You are making progress, and you'll get there at your own pace.

"There are some more words of caution I need to give you. I hope I can make it clear to you by using the **Hurricane Analogy**. It's very calm in the eye of a hurricane. Everything seems to be okay. From an emotional state, this could be described as being numb, hopeless, or depressed. But in order to leave the hurricane and find real safety and healing, you are going to have to go through some bad stuff. Moving from numb to happy usually causes us to go through anger and rage. You might act out. You might need to let your emotions out safely in your car with the windows closed in an empty parking lot or let them out on a punching bag at the gym. You might need to spend time alone and have a good cry or two. Remember that all emotions are good.

"There are physical changes too. You'll probably notice that you feel tired or even feel a little bit under the weather. You might have more extreme physical reactions, depending on how much negative emotion you have stored in your body. Several of my friends had a severe episode of throwing up. This is normal and healthy. Your body is trying to purge itself of all the negative energy. You'll eventually start to feel noticeably better. My friends report that they have fewer migraines, their skin clears up, and they experience fewer symptoms from their chronic illnesses.

"There could be other damage that occurs from a hurricane that is external to you. You'll need to clean some things up and do some repairs. For example, you might need to clean up your house and throw away things that are no longer healthy for you to keep. Remember that you only need to focus on cleaning up your own mess. Let others clean up their mess.

"The emotional, physical, and other changes are a normal part of the transformation process; it's a sign that you're doing something right. Be kind to yourself. Get enough sleep and exercise. Eat nutritious foods and drink lots of water. Just remember that this is actually progress. Tremendous progress in fact. Hang in there because things will get better once the hurricane has completely passed.

"To summarize, our unconscious mind is incredibly powerful, and we need to clean it up and align it with our conscious mind.

Transformation isn't easy, but the rewards are great. It takes time and patience. We need to be kind to ourselves. We sometimes have to get what we think is worse in order to get better. It's important to keep taking baby steps and to remember that life is so much better when we have transformed ourselves.

"Are you ready for your homework?"

"Yes, sir! What's my homework?" Elin asked.

"Tomorrow we're going to start working on the How Process I introduced you to when we talked about the 5W'S Complete Goal-Setting Framework. It's the plan for how you will achieve your new goals and create your new life. Please write down your plan for achieving your highest priority goal of financial security. Do the same for your goal around your purpose and vision. Let's meet here again tomorrow at the same time. Any questions?"

"No questions. See you tomorrow, Wes!"

Part Five:

Taking Action

Chapter Fifteen

The Plan

When Elin arrived at the Cinnabon the next day, Wes was already there. He greeted her with a big smile and said, "Good morning, Elin! How are you today?"

"Good morning, Wes," Elin replied. "I feel super excited! How are you doing?"

"I'm magnificent!" Wes replied enthusiastically. "Let's get started, shall we?"

They began their morning walk around the mall as Wes inquired about yesterday's assignment. "Let's go over your homework first. What is your plan to achieve financial security?"

Elin replied, "The important tasks for me right now are the following:

- Get a job. With the job market the way it is right now, I'm sure I can find something quickly.
- Get books on managing money. I can check them out from the library.
- Meet with my pro bono legal and financial advisor regarding what I can do to improve my credit score and finances.
- Brainstorm ideas on businesses I can start without much money.
- Speak with my niece regarding money-making ideas."

"Good job, Elin. I like that you're focusing on the most important items first." Wes paused for a moment and then asked, "What is your plan for achieving your goal around your purpose and vision?"

"Once I have taken care of my basic needs and financial security, then I can focus on my purpose and vision. I will start the process of creating my shelter by doing the following things:

- Research how to create a charitable organization.
- Research the requirements for starting a shelter that cares for both animals and people.
- Research the requirements for opening a small restaurant at the shelter. This will give people at the shelter a place to work and eat, and it will provide income for the shelter.
- Research grants that can provide initial and ongoing funding.
- Speak with the city about funding and location options.
- Speak with other animal shelters in the area about operating costs and what they charge for pet adoption fees.
- Speak with my pro bono legal and financial advisor about providing free services.
- Speak with veterinarians in the area about providing free services.
- Determine how best to get the word out to find donations and employees.
- Determine the best way to let people know about the restaurant and animal care center."

"Nicely done. And you're right. You can't focus on non-survival tasks until your survival needs are met. That's normal for everyone. And this is a great start on your shelter.

"What you have provided is a list of major tasks that need to be done. Today, I will teach you how to convert these task lists into a plan. I am going to start by talking about planning for big projects before talking about changing and building habits. The information for big projects can and should be applied, in varying degrees, to smaller projects, goals, and habits, so please don't discount it.

"If you remember back to your first lesson, I briefly mentioned the How Process during our discussion of the 5W'S Complete Goal-Setting Framework. Let's explore it in more detail now."

Wes gave Elin a handout titled the *How Process* and went over it with her.

How Process

The How Process is a separate process from goal-setting and usually takes much longer to complete. It is also known as the **planning process**. It is important to do a good job planning so you can improve your chances of achieving your goal on your first try. If your plan doesn't work, then you will have to start the How Process all over again and keep doing this until you succeed. Note that your goal stays the same.

The How Process will be more effective when you include all the **stakeholders**. They are all the people who have an interest or are involved in completing the goal. You want to find people who have a variety of different perspectives, including people outside the usual mainstream groups. If there are too many stakeholders, you can ask for a representative from each group to be appointed for the process.

Process Steps
The How Process is composed of five main steps:
1. **Research:** Learn as much as you can about your goal.
2. **Brainstorming**: Think of all the ways you can accomplish it.
3. **Evaluation:** Evaluate each possible solution.
4. **Selection:** Choose the solutions you think will work best.
5. **Plan Creation:** Create a detailed implementation plan.

Research
Learn as much as you can about your goal. Do research, read books, search for information on the internet. Review what other people have done. Find and interview experts who have done this or something similar before.

Brainstorming

There are lots of ways to get things done. Unfortunately, people usually go with the first thing they think of. Brainstorming happens when several people with different backgrounds and expertise try to think of as many ways as possible to accomplish the goal. This exercise involves creative thinking in the right brain. All ideas are allowed without judgment. The key here is the **quantity of ideas.** Holding multiple brainstorming sessions over multiple days will help you come up with as many solutions as possible. It is important to let things percolate in your brain. Many times, you will generate your best ideas when you are not even trying. Come up with at least five ways to accomplish your goal.

Evaluation

An **evaluation session** is held to determine the **quality of the ideas** for potential solutions. This exercise involves critical thinking in the left brain. Assemble the complete list of options you came up with during brainstorming. For each option, perform the **idea rating** process by doing the following:

- **Value:** Determine how valuable the solution is to you, your organization, and your customers. Assign it a **value rating** using a simple three-point scale: low, medium, high.
- **Effort:** Determine the level of effort required to implement the solution. Assign it an **effort rating** using a five-point scale from 1 to 5, with 5 being the highest amount of effort.
- **Cost:** Determine the cost to implement the solution. Assign it a **cost rating** using a five-point scale from 1 to 5, with 5 being the highest cost.
- **Time:** Determine the amount of time it will take to complete the solution. Assign it a **time rating** using a five-point scale from 1 to 5, with 5 being the highest amount of time.

- **Total:** Add the effort, cost, and time ratings together to get a **total rating.** It will be a value between 3 and 15.

Here is what an example table would look like after the idea rating process has been completed.

OPTIONS	VALUE RATING	EFFORT RATING	COST RATING	TIME RATING	TOTAL RATING	SELECTED
A	High	5	5	5	15	
B	Low	1	2	2	5	
C	Medium	3	1	2	6	
D	High	2	1	1	4	
E	Medium	2	3	4	9	
F	Medium	4	3	3	10	
G	Low	5	3	4	12	
H	Low	3	3	5	11	
I	Medium	4	5	4	13	
J	High	3	3	2	8	
K	Low	1	1	1	3	
L	Low	3	4	3	10	

Idea Selection

Sort the options in ascending order by total rating, then by value rating from highest to lowest. The best options will have the lowest total rating and the highest value rating. Select all the options you want to move forward with that you think will give you the best chance of achieving your goal. Note that if none of the options look good, then you will need to start over and do more research.

Here is what the table would look like after idea selection has been completed.

OPTIONS	VALUE RATING	EFFORT RATING	COST RATING	TIME RATING	TOTAL RATING	SELECTED
K	Low	1	1	1	3	No
D	High	2	1	1	4	Yes
B	Low	1	2	2	5	No
C	Medium	3	1	2	6	Yes
J	High	3	3	2	8	Yes
E	Medium	2	3	4	9	Yes
F	Medium	4	3	3	10	Yes
L	Low	3	4	3	10	No
H	Low	3	3	5	11	No
G	Low	5	3	4	12	No
I	Medium	4	5	4	13	No
A	High	5	5	5	15	No

Plan Creation

You can now create a detailed implementation plan for achieving your goal. This will be covered in a separate handout.

Go to www.WiseLovingBeing.com/handouts
to find a copy of this handout online.

"Elin, let's talk about the importance of planning. The planning process will give you a better idea of how to approach your bigger and more complicated projects, such as your shelter. It will be overkill for your smaller personal goals, like your financial security goal, but many aspects of it can be directly applied in order to increase your chances of success.

"To demonstrate the planning process, let's use an example of the imaginary goal to visit the planet Neptune and return safely to Earth within the next ten years. So are you going to come up with a Neptune plan all by yourself willy-nilly? Probably not. Why? Because your life is at risk! There can't be any mistakes. You have to get it right on the first try. Let's take a look at how to make a proper plan.

"First, you'll need to break down your goal into **phases**, or major logical steps. For example, you might use the following six phases for the Neptune goal: unmanned and manned trips to the moon, unmanned and manned trips to Mars, and unmanned and manned trips to Neptune. You can then work on each phase in order. This will allow you to try things out on smaller efforts first to reduce risk and increase the likelihood of success. At the end of each phase, you will reevaluate what to do next. That way you remain flexible and can easily adapt based on your experiences, new knowledge, the latest technology, and changing conditions.

"Second, you'll need to break down each phase into projects. Projects allow a team to focus its efforts. For example, for the first phase you might create five separate projects for the launch pad, launch vehicle, spacecraft, retrieval pad, and control center.

"Let's now take a more detailed look at what a project is and how to manage it."

Wes gave Elin a handout titled *Projects* and went over it with her.

Projects

A **project** creates something for a customer, who could be you. The **project goal** is to deliver what they want, when they want it, for a price they are willing to pay. A **project plan** is created to determine how to best achieve the project goal. It is like a map that takes you from your point of origin to your destination. For it to be viable, a project usually needs to cost less than what the customer will pay in order to allow for a reasonable amount of profit.

A project plan includes both *what* is needed and *how* it will get done. It contains the following ten **project elements:**

1. **Budget:** The total amount of money needed to complete the project.
2. **Inputs:** The resources needed to create the outputs and run the project.
3. **Outputs:** The products, knowledge, or other valuable outcomes the project will create.
4. **People:** The people needed to do the project work.
5. **Project Management:** The people and process that ensures the project team delivers the outputs on schedule and on budget.
6. **Requirements:** The scope of work and the detailed specifications for the outputs.
7. **Risks:** Anything that can potentially cause a problem.
8. **Schedule:** The major milestones, and the start and end times for all the work.
9. **Scorecard:** A visual representation of project health.
10. **Work:** The tasks to be done, including the skills needed by the people doing the work.

In terms of the project elements, the project goal is for *project management* to deliver the *outputs* that meet the customer's *requirements* on the agreed-upon *schedule* and *budget*. How the project will meet its objectives is determined by finding answers to the following questions for each task that needs to be done:

- What *work* needs to be done for this task?
- What work needs to be done before this task?
- What objective measurements will determine if this task is complete?
- Who (*people*) will do the work?
- What *inputs* are needed?
- What are the *risks*?
- How long will it take to do this task?
- How much will it cost?
- What will be included on the *scorecard* to let us know if we are on track?

Project Management

A **project manager** can be valuable when they have experience with similar projects, have a track record of success, are committed to it, maintain a high-level view, and can objectively see how it is going. Unfortunately, the workers sometimes get so focused on their tasks that they lose sight of the big picture. As the saying goes, "A jar can't read its own label."

Requirements

It is important to clearly define the project outputs using a **requirements document**. The **scope of work** defines what work will be done and what work won't be done. Projects often suffer from a problem called **scope creep**, where more work keeps getting added to the project while the budget and schedule remain the same. This can happen externally when the customer requests changes or additions, or internally when your team chooses to do more work than what was asked for. If something gets changed or added, then something else of equivalent size has to be removed in order to meet the original schedule and budget. Otherwise, the schedule and budget must be increased, and the customer needs to agree to this in writing.

Outputs

The outputs are the products, knowledge, or other valuable outcomes the project will create. These outputs could be inputs to other projects, or they could be the final product the customer asked for. The requirements document provides the exact specifications, quality, and capabilities the outputs must meet. The project often delivers a complete final product at the end. The customer needs to verify and approve that the product meets the agreed upon requirements. If the customer is a company, then usually one representative from the company is given approval authority.

Inputs

Inputs are the resources needed to create the outputs and run the project. Create detailed requirements for each input. You will need to find companies that can supply you with the inputs. For each input, get quotes from at least three possible suppliers. Choose the best supplier and negotiate a contract. Always verify that each input you receive meets your requirements before accepting it.

Work

This is the work that needs to be done in order to convert the inputs into the outputs. The following is determined for each task: what is to be done, when it is due, the skills needed to do it, the estimated time to complete it, and a list of **predecessor tasks** that need to be done before this task can start. Each task is then broken up into smaller subtasks. It is recommended that no subtask takes longer than three days. This allows you to quickly discover any issues. Use an objective measurement of completion: a task is either done or not done. Relying on subjective percentages of completion only causes problems. Prioritize the work so the most important things get done first.

People

Working with the right people is critical. Assemble a list of the skills needed to do the work. Create a list of roles, job descriptions, training requirements, and costs for each person needed. It will definitely help you to find people who are experts, have the right skills and experience, and who have preferably done this type of work before. Everyone has different knowledge, experiences, attitudes, and views, so interview at least three people for each position to determine who will be the best fit for the project. Hire them or bring them on as contractors, then train them as needed.

Schedule

The schedule shows the start and end times for all the work. It includes **milestones**, which are when significant accomplishments have been achieved, including the project **start date** and the **completion date**. The schedule is the aggregate of the time estimates for every task. Each task has a start date, duration, finish date, and list of predecessor tasks. Some work must follow previous work in a sequential fashion, while others can be done at the same time in parallel. The **critical path** is the sequence of tasks that can cause a delay to the project if they are not completed on time. It is important to keep a close eye on these tasks so you can deliver your project on time.

Risks

Risks are anything that can potentially cause a problem for the project. A risk can affect multiple project elements, including budget and schedule. There are some risks you can identify up front, but there are other risks you don't know about yet. Both need to be accounted for. Start by identifying as many risks as you can. Then, for each one, do the following:

- Estimate how likely the risk is to occur. This is usually represented as a probability.
- Estimate how the risk could impact the project in terms of cost and schedule.
- Create a list of possible **mitigation solutions** or ways to respond to this risk in order to resolve it.
- For each mitigation solution, determine its cost, how effective it will be, and the project impact.
- Select the best mitigation solutions.
- Assign an overall **risk rating** of high, medium, or low, which is based on the pervious steps.
- Determine how to objectively measure the risk, the acceptable range of values, and at what point these measurements indicate there is an issue.
- Create plans for implementing the chosen mitigation solutions.
- Assign a person to each risk. They are in charge of monitoring and managing it.

Budget

The budget is the total amount of money needed to complete the project. It includes the cost of the equipment, office space, people, supplies, and inputs needed to create the project outputs. The budget needs to include funds to handle both the known and unknown risks. Don't forget to include the cost of incentives and the end-of-project celebration.

Scorecard

A scorecard is a quick visual representation of the overall health of the project, like a sports **scoreboard**. It includes the important **metrics** that indicate if the project is on track, their current value, expected value, and a color-coded health indication. For example, *budget metrics* track the actual cost compared to the estimated costs. *Schedule metrics* show you if you are on time, ahead, or behind schedule. It is important to update the scorecard daily and display it where everyone can see it. If any key metrics are outside their acceptable range, then you will need to make adjustments to the project to get things back on track.

Go to www.WiseLovingBeing.com/handouts
to find a copy of this handout online.

"Elin, as you can see, there is a lot of work to create an effective project plan for a bigger project, but your effort will pay off when the project is completed on time and under budget. When you are ready, please convert your task list for your shelter into a project plan and include all the important elements. Do you have any questions about how to do this?"

"Not at this time, Wes. I'd like to create a draft of my plan and run it by you when it's ready."

"I'm looking forward to that."

Wes could tell that Elin seemed a bit overwhelmed by the project material, and he was concerned she didn't see its full value. He paused for a moment to think about what he was going to say next.

"Elin, the information on projects may seem overly complicated for most things you do in life, but surprisingly, a lot of it can be used in your simpler goals and tasks to help you be more successful. For example, when you are faced with a goal that seems overwhelming, you can break it down into much smaller tasks that can each be done easily in five minutes or less. For tasks that you have a challenge following through on, you can do a simple risk assessment and create a list of ways to avoid getting sidetracked. Whenever you need to hire a vendor, like movers, make sure you get three estimates. I'll occasionally reference some of the project concepts later today as we talk about habits, so keep that information handy, please.

"Now let's take a look at how to create a plan for simpler goals, like losing ten pounds, running a 5K, and achieving financial security."

Wes gave Elin two handouts titled *Changing Habits* and *Ridiculously Easy Goals* and went over them with her.

Changing Habits

Habits are what you do consistently every day. Doing the right things is critical to achieving your goal. It is what you do every day that matters because it leads you down your default path to your default future, which hopefully is the same as your desired future.

In order to make a change in behavior, you will need to identify the following **types of habit changes:**

- **Change:** Change some things you are doing now so they better serve you.
- **Continue:** Continue doing those things that still serve you.
- **Start:** Start doing new things that will serve you.
- **Stop:** Stop doing things that no longer serve you.

Habit Impact

Determine the overall impact of each habit. **High impact habits** inspire us to do other good habits, while **low impact habits** have little effect. Some habits are so impactful they are called **key habits.** They unlock the doors to many other desired habits that we have difficulty starting or doing consistently. They also lock the doors to bad habits we want to avoid. **Complementary habits** help us to be more successful with our most important habits. For example, a salesman might have his key habit be making two hundred calls a week, and his complementary habits—the ones that will help him be successful—are exercising for an hour every weekday, spending time with his family on the weekend, and eating healthy, nutritious meals at least five days per week.

Go to www.WiseLovingBeing.com/handouts
to find a copy of this handout online.

Ridiculously Easy Goals

Changing behavior requires a different type of goal-setting strategy called Ridiculously Easy Goals. The key here is to avoid trying to be perfect and just do what is ridiculously easy. Instead of meeting your ideal vision of what the new habit looks like, focus on what level of activity you can easily do each time, and how many times you can easily do it over the course of a week. The genius lies in taking small actions on a consistent basis, thereby creating momentum.

You will need to do three things to create a new habit: start out small, build on it, and don't mess it up. Here are the recommendations for creating a new behavior:

- **Set a minimum goal:** This is something you know you can easily do, even on your worst day and week, without any problems or excuses. It is so ridiculously easy that there is no possible way you can give a legitimate excuse for not doing it. This is the ridiculously easy part. The minimum value never, ever changes. Lots of problems happen if it increases.
- **Set a target goal:** This is what you think you can reasonably do each time and how many times you can do it each week. This will start out small and then get bigger as time goes on.
- **Set a maximum goal:** This is the maximum you are allowing yourself to do at any one time, and the maximum number of times you will do it per week. This keeps you from causing problems for yourself, which could lead you to abandon your goal. Note that as time goes on, you may need to increase your maximum.
- **Set a specific time:** Set a specific time each day when you will do the activity. Schedule it in your calendar and block the time. Try to tie it to another activity you already do consistently.

- **Avoid Interruptions:** Pick a location and time where you won't be bothered. If you must do this at home, then do your activity late at night after everyone has gone to bed or wake up before everyone else does.
- **Track your goal:** Track the actual values of your efforts each day on a blank calendar or scorecard that is only used for tracking purposes. Post it on your refrigerator or a similar place you see every day.
- **Hold yourself accountable**: Make sure you accomplish your minimum goal each week. Go over your results on a weekly basis with your coach or **accountability partner**, who is someone you can be honest with and would never want to disappoint.
- **Make it fun:** Have fun doing the activity and reward yourself afterward. Remind yourself of the benefits, why this is important to you, and why it is important for others.

Go to www.WiseLovingBeing.com/handouts
to find a copy of this handout online.

"Elin, let me give you a few examples so you can better understand the concepts.

"You've probably heard the famous quote from Lao Tzu: 'A journey of a thousand miles begins with a single step.' If you think about this in the context of walking from Phoenix to Tucson, you realize that if you don't take at least one step in the right direction each day, then you'll probably never get there. But somehow, our unconscious mind tricks us into not taking a step, and our conscious mind can intellectually justify this as us doing our best and making progress. Building an empowering habit helps us take steps every day that will eventually lead us to our goal. In this way, Ridiculously Easy Goals help us take action on the important things we need to do daily and weekly. These goals also help us stay focused in the present moment on the important things that will take us to our goal and vision. It helps us live life one day at a time and one week at a time.

"My friend Thomas uses exercise as a key habit. When he exercises consistently, everything else improves: he eats healthy foods, he gets enough sleep, he feels better about himself, he is more confident, he is more productive at work, his relationships are better, and he avoids time-consuming escape activities. He told me that without exercise, nothing good gets done.

"My friend Lizzie wanted to run a local 10K event in six months, but she wasn't currently exercising. She wanted to run for one hour, five days per week, but she never ran at all. I introduced her to Ridiculously Easy Goals. She set a minimum goal to run for five minutes, three days per week. Her target goal was ten minutes, three days per week, and her maximum goal was fifteen minutes, three days per week. She added one more restriction that she couldn't run on two consecutive days. She felt this would help her avoid getting injured, which would derail her attempt at the 10K. She asked one of her running friends to be her accountability partner.

"Lizzie consistently ran three days per week, and most of the time she met her target goal. Some days she didn't feel like running at all, but when she started a run focused on just achieving the minimum, she found that she felt better after a few minutes and usually decided to keep running longer. After two months, she increased her target goal to fifteen minutes and her maximum goal to twenty minutes. She then increased these values by ten minutes each month after that. She never modified the number of days she ran per week or her minimum goal. Lizzie completed her 10K, enjoyed the race, and wasn't even sore the next day.

"My friend Sarah was complaining that she didn't read self-improvement books anymore. She believed that the only acceptable amount of time to read was for one hour every day, but she never read at all. She set a minimum goal to read for five minutes, three days per week; a target goal of twenty minutes, three days per week; and a maximum goal of thirty minutes, five days per week. I was her accountability partner. She scheduled her reading time for right after she put her daughter to bed. Sarah rarely just met her minimum goal. She almost always hit her target goal, and she began to consistently read five days per week. After two months, she set her target goal to thirty minutes during the week and sixty minutes on the weekends. There were rare instances when she only met her minimum goal, but that was still regarded as a win.

"Here's an example of someone who encountered a challenge in changing their habit. My friend Catherine wanted to write a novel, but she wasn't writing at all. She decided to try using Ridiculously Easy Goals to see if it would make a difference. She set a minimum goal of writing for five minutes, three days per week; a target of writing for one hour, five days per week; and she decided not to set a maximum goal. After two weeks she was consistently exceeding her target goal, usually writing for more than three hours per day.

She then set her minimum goal to what her target goal was, writing one hour per day, five days per week. Things went well for about a month until she burned herself out and stopped writing altogether. She didn't write for the next six months.

"I worked with Catherine to help her see where she went wrong: she went from thinking the minimum goal was a win to thinking she had to be perfect. She decided to keep her original minimum goal. She changed her target goal to one hour, three days per week and added a maximum goal of three hours, five days per week. She also committed to not increasing her minimum. As a result of these adjustments, she was consistently able to meet her writing goals and completed her book after one year. Catherine found out the hard way that you need to follow the process: focus on small wins, build momentum, and keep perfectionism from stopping all progress. She clearly understands now that it's what you do every day that truly matters. She said focusing on small wins one day at a time made a huge difference for her.

"Elin, yesterday when you were talking about your new activities in a typical day, you mentioned you wanted to work on your goals eight hours per day, learn something new two hours per day, and connect with others two hours per day. I told you I thought this would lead to problems. I'd like you to set a Ridiculously Easy Goal for each one now."

"I understand your concern better now," Elin replied. "For working on my goals, my minimum goal will be five minutes per day, three days per week; my target goal will be thirty minutes per day, three days per week; and my maximum goal will be one hour per day, five days per week. For learning something new, my minimum goal will be five minutes, three days per week; my target goal will be fifteen minutes, three days per week; and my maximum goal will be one hour, three days per week. For connecting with others, my three goals will be five minutes, three days per week; twenty minutes, three days per week; and thirty minutes, three days per week. After a month, I can reevaluate my target and maximum goals."

"Nicely done, Elin. Now let's look at ways that can help you build a new habit."

Wes gave Elin a handout titled *Building New Habits* and went over it with her.

Building New Habits

Building a new habit can be challenging. Here are some suggestions to help you with your mindset and your environment. Some of these will work better for you than others. Selecting more items from the list generally increases your chances of success.

1. Associate bad things with doing the old habit.
2. For the new habit, associate good things with doing it and bad things with not doing it.
3. Tie the new habit to an existing activity. For example, tie exercise to leaving work.
4. *Schedule* the new activity for the same time each day.
5. Block the time on your calendar and set a reminder.
6. Choose a place and time where you will not be interrupted.
7. Track your progress using a *scorecard* so you can see the improvements you are making over time.
8. Ask those around you to support you in your new habit.
9. Use the buddy system and find someone who will do the activity with you.
10. Get an accountability partner you can be honest with and who will be honest with you. Pick someone you won't want to disappoint.
11. Add peer pressure by posting your goal in writing, posting your scorecard, and by telling your friends and family.
12. Make it a game by finding someone you can compete with.
13. Put skin in the game by having monetary penalties or other consequences if you don't reach your goal.
14. Select a reward you will receive each time you do the new activity.
15. Choose a valuable reward for when you complete your goal.
16. Put pictures of what achieving your goal looks like on your refrigerator.
17. Talk to an expert, learn new things, and acquire new skills that will help you achieve your goal.

18. Create a list of *risks* or obstacles that might keep you from doing your new activity.

19. For each risk, create a list of things you can do to mitigate the risk and get yourself back on track. For example, if you are craving something, then give yourself a buffer of thirty minutes and go do something productive like walking around the block. Most of the time the craving will go away.

20. Create an environment that promotes success. For example, if your biggest weakness is watching sports on your couch, then disconnect the TV and remove the couch cushions.

21. Increase the cost and effort to do the old habit. For example, if you like eating junk food, don't allow any of it in your house. When you really want candy, you'll have to go to the store and buy just one item, which is more expensive than buying a pack.

22. Be kind to yourself. If you make a mistake, just acknowledge it and get back on track. It is not easy to change, and you are not a robot.

23. Be patient. If you want to climb onto the roof, you have to climb the ladder one wrung at a time. Rome was not built overnight; your changes will probably not happen immediately.

24. Live one day at a time. Focus on what you need to do and not do today and in the present moment.

Go to www.WiseLovingBeing.com/handouts
to find a copy of this handout online.

"Elin, here's an example. My friend Kenneth decided to quit eating his favorite food, cheeseburgers. He was addicted to them and would have them at least four times a week. He loved the taste and the perfect satiated feeling he got from eating them. They reminded him of the good times he had when he was a kid.

"But Kenneth was getting older, and he was concerned about having a heart attack from his many years of eating unhealthy food. He went to his doctor, who confirmed his high cholesterol levels and gave him advice on how to lower it. He watched videos showing open heart surgery and blocked arteries. He talked to a friend who had survived a heart attack, and he spoke with the family of a friend who didn't.

"There's nothing wrong with having a good cheeseburger once in a while, and although reducing his intake of cheeseburgers was a reasonable option for improving his health, Kenneth saw them as an enabler that led him to eating unhealthy foods. He decided that the key to avoiding unhealthy food altogether was to give up cheeseburgers. He then associated death with eating unhealthy food. He associated wonderful things with eating healthy food, like being active in his old age, enjoying life, and seeing his grandkids grow up.

"Kenneth researched healthy diets and came up with a weekly menu. He got rid of all the unhealthy food in his house and replaced it with healthy food. He told his family and friends what he was doing so they would support his activities. Then, he stopped eating cheeseburgers cold turkey, pun intended. He met his cholesterol goal, he feels great, and he no longer craves cheeseburgers and unhealthy foods. He sometimes chooses to eat unhealthy food on special occasions, but this is rare and completely under his control. And because his tastebuds have changed, the unhealthy foods don't taste as good as they used to.

"Elin, do you have any questions about how to build new habits?" Wes asked.

"Not at this time. It's clear to me now that my habits have made me who I am today, and I need to make a lot of changes. I don't want to do too much at once, so I think for right now, I'll stick with the main two changes of getting exercise at the mall and working on my goals."

"Sounds good, Elin.

"To summarize, planning is critical for your success. It's important to create a project plan that will help you achieve your bigger goals on the first try. The concepts in project planning can be applied to your smaller goals to help you increase your chances of success. Ridiculously Easy Goals can help you create new habits. There are lots of things you can do to be more successful at building new habits. Your daily habits determine your default path and your default future, so make sure you're doing the most important things every day so you can reach your desired future.

"Are you ready for your homework?"

"Yes, sir! What's my homework?" Elin asked.

"Tomorrow, we're going to work on what actions you'll need to take in order to achieve your new goals and create your new life. There are two parts to the homework. First, please write down any challenges or obstacles you think might get in the way of achieving your goals. Second, write down where in your life you need to make a commitment. Let's meet here tomorrow at the same time. Any questions?"

"No questions. See you tomorrow, Wes!"

Chapter Sixteen

Action

When Elin arrived at the Cinnabon the next day, Wes was already there. He greeted her with a big smile and said, "Good morning, Elin! How are you today?"

"Good morning, Wes," Elin replied. "I'm absolutely fantastic. How are you doing?"

"I've never been better!" Wes replied enthusiastically. "Let's get started, shall we?"

They began their morning walk around the mall as Wes inquired about yesterday's assignment. "Let's start with the homework. What challenges or obstacles are in the way of you achieving your goals?"

"I think the biggest challenge I have is seeing myself as a leader," Elin replied. "I'm not. I'm more of a support person. So creating a foundation and leading an organization isn't something I think I can do, although I would love to help someone else do it."

"Everyone can be a leader, Elin. The simplest definition of a **leader** is someone who sees possibilities to make things better, takes the initiative to make it a reality, and inspires others to help. Robert K. Greenleaf took this further when he developed the concept of **servant leadership**, which says that the leader's next job is to support and serve his team so they are able to effectively create the vision in the fastest way possible.

"You've already done the first part: you see a group of people who need help. The second step is to create the foundation. You can do that by speaking with an attorney. You can then create the mission, vision, and values for the organization. The third step is to find experienced people to help you. You'll need to find people who can help you lead the foundation, which is called a board of directors. Then you can hire people to manage the main parts of the organization, like running the restaurant, running the animal shelter, and reaching out to the community. Finally, you can then support and serve the team to help them make your vision a reality.

"Everyone can be a leader no matter their role. For example, you are a leader by creating the foundation. Then you hire Stacy to run the shelter. She's a leader. She hires Emily to care for the animals. She's a leader. Emily hires George to feed the animals. George has no one reporting to him. He is still a leader though. He can look for ways to make things better. He can come up with a plan and can inspire Emily to act on his idea. Everyone is a leader. Do you think this foundation will ever get created if you don't lead this effort?"

"Probably not," Elin replied.

"That's right. If you don't do it, no one will, and all those people and animals won't get the help they desperately need. It's up to you. You're already a leader, so please start acting like one. What other challenges do you see?"

"The other challenges are around changing my habits," Elin added. "I've been doing the same thing for a long time now, and I think one of the reasons is that it's been a reasonably safe and pain-free way to live. There are also challenges around doing new things, like creating my charitable foundation. So I'm basically concerned about escaping the inertia of my past and trying new things that are uncomfortable."

"That's a good observation, and we'll be working on that today. Now for the second question from the homework: Where in your life do you need to make a commitment?"

"I don't think I need to make a commitment to just one area of my life," Elin reasoned. "I need to make a commitment to all of the new me. I need to commit to Elin 2.0."

"Nicely done, Elin. Let's get started with the lessons for today. I'd first like to step back and take a look at the big picture. Here are the ten essentials people need in order to achieve their goals."

Wes gave Elin a handout titled *10 Essentials for Goal Achievement* and asked her to read it.

10 Essentials for Goal Achievement

In order to achieve your goal, you will need the following ten essential items.

1. **Goal:** Create a complete goal with a timeframe. Anything else is just a dream that will never come true, no matter how much wishful thinking you do.

2. **Motivated:** Get extremely motivated to achieve your goal for both yourself and others. This motivation must come from within you and not be imposed upon you by others.

3. **Obstacles:** Free yourself from all the obstacles in your way, both internal and external. Most people are stuck in the past and fearful about the future.

4. **Experts:** Surround yourself with experts who have done this or something similar. They can help you uncover the truth, learn skills completely, and reach your goal much faster than you could on your own. Most people are naïve and think they can just figure it out themselves.

5. **Plan:** Create a detailed written plan for reaching your goal. It should address everything that needs to be done. An accurate, detailed map is essential if you want to reach your destination on time.

6. **Scorecard:** Track critical measurements every day so you know where you have come from, where you are going, and where you are now. Think of it as your GPS that gives you your exact location on the map.

7. **Habits:** Consistently do the right things, for the right amount of time, every day. Most people do unimportant things that take them further from their goal. They become depressed by not making progress and choose to escape from their pain with addictive behaviors.

8. **Belief:** Believe in yourself, believe in the plan, and believe in your ability to achieve this goal. Belief is not hope or wishful thinking. It is an inner knowing that you can do this without a doubt.

9. **Commitment:** Engage with an extremely high level of commitment. You will neither give up nor will you retreat. The only way is to move forward to your objective.

10. **Focus:** Take smart action by doing the most important thing in the present moment. Focus on achieving your goal. Most people focus on their past or the future, providing a plethora of excuses for why they are not winning.

Go to www.WiseLovingBeing.com/handouts
to find a copy of this handout online.

"Elin, we've already worked on the first seven items. Today we're going to work on the last three items: belief, commitment, and focus.

"Let's start with **belief**. In this context, it's about how certain you are that you can achieve your goal. Do you **believe** you can do it? One of my favorite quotes around certainty and belief comes from Henry Ford: 'Whether you think you can or think you can't, you are right.'

"Elin, you've set a goal, you're motivated, you've removed the invisible walls that served as obstacles, you've consulted with experts, you've got a plan, you have a scorecard, and you've created new empowering habits. Based on all of that, is there any reason to believe you can't accomplish your goal of financial security? In other words, what is your certainty level?"

"I absolutely believe I can do it," Elin replied. "There are still some small unknowns, but I'm sure I can figure those out by working with my experts. I'm quite certain I can do this. I'd give it a ninety-five percent certainty level."

"Great. If you didn't believe you could do it, then I'd take you back through the exercises associated with the first seven items. You worked very hard on all of those, and you are now enjoying the benefits of your efforts. Congratulations, by the way. You wouldn't have told me this two weeks ago. You would have told me that it wasn't possible for you, and you didn't have the abilities. You've made a lot of progress, haven't you?"

Elin gave Wes a big smile and nodded her head in agreement.

"Now let's talk about commitment. I have a great story to tell you. But let me preface this by stating that I don't support this kind of behavior, since it is the exact opposite of the principles of Universal Elevation. Nevertheless, I believe this story will help you better understand commitment.

"In 1519, Hernán Cortés, a Spanish conquistador, arrived in what is today, Veracruz, Mexico, with eleven ships and 608 men.

The goal was to beat the army of Montezuma, conquer the Aztec Empire for Spain, and plunder its gold. As you might imagine, not everyone was on board with this plan, and there was a mutiny. Cortés overcame the mutiny and realized his men needed a little extra motivation. Cortés rounded up his men on the beach so they could see all the ships in the harbor. He had ten of his eleven ships set on fire, and they were completely destroyed, cutting off his men's only hope of retreat. There was no other option than to head inland. They had no choice but to achieve their goal. This expedition ultimately led to the fall of the Aztec Empire to the Spanish on August 13, 1521."

Wes gave Elin a handout titled *Commitment* and went over it with her.

Commitment

Burn the boats means making a commitment that forces you to continue with a particular course of action. You must meet whatever challenges head-on. You can only move forward. You cannot go back. You can't retreat. You are all in. All your thoughts and actions are focused on succeeding in your new endeavor. You must be creative and resourceful. You must find a way and get results—no excuses.

Burning bridges sounds conceptually the same, but it has a much different meaning. Obviously burning bridges accomplishes the same goal as burning the boats: retreat is impossible. Here is the difference. Burning the boats is your choice. You can always build more boats or find some other mode of transportation home. And when you arrive home, you will be welcomed and accepted. Burning bridges means that you did something to offend your home. You can't return home because they don't want you there. You don't belong and are most unwelcome. It is their choice, not yours. It is no longer an option for you. It is nice to have more options, but sometimes it is necessary to burn the bridges too. Just don't burn yourself.

Commitment Levels

There are two levels of commitment: low and high. **Low-level commitment** is conditional. You know you are at this level when you say things like, *I'm committed to our relationship until someone better comes along*, or *I'm committed to this course of action until it becomes too difficult*. **High-level commitment** is unconditional. Nothing can change your mind. You know you are at this level when you say things like, *I'd die for you*, or *I'd do anything for my kids*.

Commitment Length

Commitments usually last for a specific period of time. The commitment length can be short, medium, or long-term. **Short-term commitments** usually last less than a year. For example, you might commit to working on a project or playing with a sports team for the season. **Medium-term commitments** last for a longer period of time, usually more than a year but less than ten. For example, you might enlist in the Army for four years, accept an offer of employment, or go to college to get a bachelor's degree. **Long-term commitments** are for a much longer period of time, usually for your entire life. For example, you might marry someone or decide to have children.

Avoiding Commitments

You might avoid making a commitment because you are fearful, you don't have enough information, you can't decide which way to go, you want your freedom, you want to try different things, you aren't ready, or you know that you won't be able to honor it.

Breaking Commitments

It is sometimes okay to change or cancel a commitment. This does not make you a bad person or a person who lacks integrity. It's important to stay true to yourself as you learn, grow, and elevate your life. You might break a commitment for the following reasons:

- It was entered into under false pretenses.
- You were manipulated.
- There is abusive behavior.
- The other party is not honoring their part of the commitment.
- It is not aligned with the principles of Universal Elevation.
- You have evolved in your thinking and needs.
- New information has come to light that invalidates the commitment.
- Keeping the commitment creates problems that can't be resolved.

Commitment Questions

Answering these commitment questions can help you succeed:

- Where in your life do you need to make a commitment to move forward and never return?
- Why do you want to do this?
- What has been holding you back?
- What are the benefits of moving forward?
- What are the costs of not moving forward?
- Who has done this before? Who can you model?
- What are the minimum resources, money, and capabilities you need to succeed?
- What is the earliest date you can burn the boats and move forward?
- What could tempt you to return? What are the risks? How can you mitigate or avoid them?
- Who can help you stay on track and keep your commitment when things get tough?

Go to www.WiseLovingBeing.com/handouts
to find a copy of this handout online.

"Where do you need to make a commitment, Elin?"

"I am committed to achieving financial security, and I am ready to start today, Wes!" Elin replied enthusiastically. "I am also making a commitment to creating my foundation. I have burned my boats."

"Excellent! To keep your commitment in focus initially, please recommit at the beginning of every day, and several times throughout the day. Now let's look at ways you can better focus your energy on the critical items in your life."

Wes gave Elin a handout titled *Focus* and went over it with her.

Focus

Focus has two parts: immersion and presence. When you are immersed in your goal and focused on the present, you are able to identify the most important thing to do, get it done quicker, and adapt in the moment to doing the next most important thing. Things you used to rely on, such as extensive to-do lists and fancy time management tools, are no longer needed.

Immersion

Immersion means being completely surrounded by something. For example, if you completely submerge an egg into a bowl of pink dye, then you are immersing it. The longer you immerse it, the pinker the egg becomes. **Goal immersion** means making sure you are completely submerged in it at all times: your thoughts, feelings, words, actions, and your senses. Most importantly, you think about how this goal benefits others. There are two times each day where your mind is extra absorptive: when you first wake up and just before going to sleep. These are the perfect times to remind yourself of what is important to you and why.

Immersion means doing as many of the following as you can around your goal.

- Dream about your goal.
- Think about what you need to do next, how you can improve, and what the final state will be.
- Think about how things will go today, what challenges could occur, and imagine what you can do to ensure success.
- Stay in touch with your current feelings, and imagine how you will feel when you achieve your goal.
- Use true, positive, and empowering words about yourself and your goal.

- Review your conscious compass and your transformation blueprint containing what you want to experience each day and the simple actions you can take to achieve each experience.
- Take action and ensure that everything you do is getting you closer to your goal in the quickest way possible.
- Imagine yourself achieving your goal.
- Place pictures of your goal at your desk, on the refrigerator, on the bathroom mirror, and everywhere else you look.
- Listen to music and watch movies that inspire you.
- Get a theme song and listen to it daily.
- Smell success and taste victory.
- Feel strong emotions attached to your fundamental needs of love, peace, joy, freedom, and fulfillment.
- Imagine someone else thanking you because their life is better from your efforts.

Presence

The second part of focus is about presence The only thing you have control over is what you think, feel, say, and do in the present moment. If you are focused on *now*, then you no longer carry baggage from the past, and you aren't restrained by fears of the future. The present moment focuses you on your current path and the journey you are on.

You can only do one thing at a time, and you can't do everything on your list. Only the most important things can get done, which means some things never will, and that is okay and perfectly normal. The best you can ever do at any point in time is to do that one thing that is of the highest importance.

Maximum Value in the Present Moment

As you are headed toward your vision, you have to focus on your mission in the present moment, on your current path. You can create maximum value in the present moment by asking yourself the following question:

- What action can I take
- in the present moment,
- doing my best,
- maximizing my resourcefulness to
- add the most value,
- while being consistent with my identity and my vision?

It may seem overwhelming to you when you think about doing this all day, every day, forever. Do not worry about that. Only focus on the current moment and make the most of it. You really only need to worry about one moment at a time.

Go to www.WiseLovingBeing.com/handouts
to find a copy of this handout online.

"Elin, let me bring this concept to life with an example from boxing. Former world heavyweight champion Mike Tyson said, 'Everyone has a plan until they get punched in the mouth.' Yes, it is necessary to properly prepare and have a plan, but once things start, we need to live in the present moment, go with the flow, use our intuition, adapt to the changes, and do our best. We may have to take a brief detour, but if we keep heading in the right direction, we'll eventually get there. By remaining flexible, we might actually end up in a better place than we could have imagined from the start.

"My friend Tracy is a novelist. Before she starts writing, she generally has a concept, a basic storyline, and the main characters. She also has a plan: start at chapter one and then go to the next chapter, continuing sequentially until she completes the final chapter. She sets a schedule, with a goal to finish one chapter each week, and has metrics she wants to track about her writing each day, like the total number of words, the number of hours spent writing each day, and her level of excitement about the story.

"Tracy sometimes goes off plan and works on chapters out of order. She often works on multiple chapters at the same time. Sometimes the storyline changes to make it more impactful. New characters may be introduced, and some of the existing characters may need to change. She tracks her metrics closely and reviews them at the end of every day. She can see that, even though she hasn't followed her original plan to the letter, she is headed in the right direction and is making good progress.

"My friend Judy loved to-do lists. She had taken several time-management classes and applied almost everything she had learned. She had a document on her computer with goals and to-do lists for all parts of her life that was over one hundred pages long. She even had the goals she wanted to accomplish laid out for the next thirty-five years. It overwhelmed her instead of empowering her. It also constrained her because it limited her ability to be flexible in the moment.

"I helped Judy create a very high-level, concise statement of her identity, purpose, vision, and values. She no longer looks at her big goals document. Instead, she enjoys making decisions in the moment based on her intuition and instinct, going with the flow, and being pulled toward her vision. She has been able to accomplish the truly important things in her life much sooner than she would have before, and the results are far beyond what she imagined she could do. She finds that creating maximum value in the present moment is exciting and inspires her to do more.

"My friend Joyce wanted to be a compassionate leader. She thought that meant she had to go do something like join a charitable organization or take a class. I told her that it isn't about going and doing something. It's not about something in the future; it's about what you do in the present moment. It's how you consistently show up every day. It's about *being* a compassionate leader in the moment, and she can do that anywhere with anyone.

"I gave Joyce some examples so she could better understand. When she is talking to her husband, she could be a compassionate leader by not interrupting him when he is speaking. She could come from a place of love and choose to do something nice for him that he values. At work, she could take more of an interest in each of her team members. She could ask for their input and recommendations, look for ways to help them elevate their careers, and look at the human side of her decisions and actions. Joyce learned that these seemingly small ways of being in every moment added up quickly to define who she was, and she could do them regardless of her circumstances.

"Here is an example from software development that can be applied to any area of your life where you are trying to create something new. There is a method called **Agile**, which is the fastest way to create a new system that will actually be used. In the traditional method called **Waterfall**, the complete system is built before the customer gets to use it. It could take over a year for the users to receive the system. When asked if the final system meets their needs, the users usually say one of two things: 'It did meet our needs a year ago, but things have changed, and it no longer does,' or 'This is what we asked for, but not what we need.'

"The Agile method solves this problem by getting the system into the hands of the users as soon as possible. A set of high-level requirements is determined. The team then defines the **minimum viable product** (MVP), which is the minimum functionality needed by the users. The team builds the system in small chunks, similar to how you build something with Legos. Every two weeks the users are presented with a working system. Their feedback is incorporated into the next release. This goes on until the users get what they actually need: a system that usually looks quite different from the one they requested.

"My friend Susan is a project manager for an e-commerce company. She told me about a time when the chief marketing officer (CMO) came to her with the requirements for a new marketing website. He wanted an extensive administration page that would let the marketing department tweak everything that appeared on the website. And he wanted it in two weeks to meet the company's strategic needs. Susan told the CMO that his request was impossible. In order to meet the timeframe, she'd have to create a site that used default values that couldn't be changed on the fly. The CMO agreed, and Susan's team delivered the website on time. After it had been in production for a month, Susan asked the CMO if he wanted to proceed with the admin page. The CMO said no. The website was performing better than expected, and they now had higher priorities.

"One of the key takeaways here is that it's usually much better to get something out there and get feedback than to try to create that perfect thing. As Winston Churchill said, '*Perfection is the enemy of progress.*' When in doubt, take action. If you don't know where to start, just pick something you think you can do. Everything is connected.

"And remember that very few things need to be perfect. In most cases, it just needs to exist. In other cases, it simply needs to meet the minimum requirements. Sometimes it just needs to meet a certain level of achievement. So ask yourself, *How good is good enough?*

"My friend Debbie used this strategy when she went back to school for her master's degree. She was working full time and had lots of responsibilities at home with her family. She was a perfectionist and was concerned that her competitive nature would end up causing problems throughout her life. She looked at her options. She could do just the minimum to graduate and get Cs. She could be average and get Bs. She could be great by working just hard enough to get As. Or she could be her normal perfectionist self, be the best, and get the highest grade in the class. She decided that a reasonable compromise was to do just enough to get a solid A in each class. She didn't need to be the best in school because it didn't match her needs. It would cause her to make compromises in other areas of her life that she wasn't interested in making."

"Elin, do you have any questions about focus?"

"I don't, but I can certainly relate to not getting things done because of being a perfectionist. I think I'll try the Agile method on my shelter."

"Great idea. Now I'd like to speak with you about a very important topic that will help you succeed."

Wes gave Elin a handout titled *Persistence* and went over it with her.

Persistence

Persistence means you keep going even when things are difficult and don't go as planned. The key here is to not give up. You find ways to make things better next time. You find ways to win. Persistence creates a positive feedback loop and builds momentum from each of your successes. The more often you can overcome a situation, the better able you will be to overcome future challenges. You are building a muscle that gets stronger each time it is used.

Persistence rests on a solid foundation of belief, commitment, and focus. You start with an inner knowing that there is a way to solve the problem. You believe you can find a way. You commit to making it happen, and there is no turning back. You focus on finding viable solutions. Two things can help you be more persistent: ask powerful questions and use your unlimited resourcefulness.

Powerful Questions

Ask powerful questions, discover the answers, and take action to improve your situation. As you can easily see, the following question is definitely unproductive: "Why does this always happen to me?" Better questions would be: "Who has done this before?" or "What can I do to make this work?" or "What is working and what is not working?"

Unlimited Resourcefulness

Your creativity and resourcefulness are unlimited. When you exhaust yours, you can simply tap into the creativity and resourcefulness of others. Just believe there is a way to solve your challenge and then go find it. Do not give up; keep going. See the truth and learn from your mistakes. Find a way. It's interesting to note that when an important deadline is approaching, and your fear and worry are increasing, your creativity and resourcefulness also tend to increase.

Competition

If you are in a competitive situation and keep getting rejected for a position, you might ask yourself the following questions. Then you will create a plan and take action to make yourself better, increasing your chances of success on your next attempt.

- What do the people who are chosen have that I don't?
- What will the people chosen in the future need to have?
- What does the selecting organization need that they currently don't have?
- How can I best differentiate myself from my competitors?
- What are the best things I can do to improve myself to increase the likelihood of being chosen next time?
- Who can I hire to train me to be my best?

Go to www.WiseLovingBeing.com/handouts
to find a copy of this handout online.

"Elin, where do you need to be more persistent?"

"Wow. Pretty much everywhere. It's been a long time since I've been persistent about anything. Definitely my financial security. I need to be persistent and fix my awful financial situation."

"Agreed. Now let's take a look at what you can do every day to improve your life."

Wes gave Elin a handout titled *Critical Daily Activities* and went over it with her.

Critical Daily Activities

Peter F. Drucker, one of the thought leaders on modern management theory, said, "It's more important to do the right thing than to do things right." Taking that quote one step further, it is even more important to do the right things *and* to do them right—every day.

A day is the basic measuring block for tracking your success. It's what you do every day that counts. The following critical daily activities, when done right, will have a tremendous impact on your life:

- **Act:** Taking smart action is the single most important thing you can do on a daily basis. Do the highest priority thing first. Focus on progress, and do not wait for perfection. Learn by doing.
- **Connect:** Make meaningful connections with others. Surround yourself with like-minded, experienced people who can help you achieve your goals. Anything great requires a team.
- **Energy:** Create and maintain your positive physical energy. Smile, sit up straight, reach up for the sky, or go for a walk around the block.
- **Goals:** Review your goals and your plan for achieving them. Visualize your success.
- **Gratitude:** Think about all the things you are grateful for. Express gratitude to others.
- **Lead:** Take ownership. Be proactive. Go first. Lead by example. Inspire others.
- **Metrics:** Record and review your metrics on a scorecard throughout the day to make sure you stay on track.

- **Perspective:** Always look at things from multiple perspectives. Reframing what you see from a new perspective can help you add more value, solve problems more effectively, and stay more positive. Get additional perspectives by asking others with different backgrounds. Use the new perspectives provided by the Wise Loving Being, Universal Elevation, and The Play Exercise.

- **Positive:** Stay positive, especially in this negative world. Focus on your capabilities, not just your liabilities. Look for the positive in people and in situations. Be careful though. The last thing you need is **toxic positivity** where you ignore the negative or create positive where none exists. That could harm you and lead to delusion. A balanced view is best.

- **Prepare:** Prepare for the day. Think about what you will need to do in order to succeed.

- **Self-Care:** Take good care of your body. Everything is connected. Exercise produces endorphins that make you feel better. The increased blood flow helps you think better.

- **Transformation:** Review your transformation. Remind yourself of who you really are. Review your conscious compass: your identity, mission, vision, and values. Continue to reprogram your unconscious mind with all the new information it should contain. Make sure it knows what you need from it now.

Go to www.WiseLovingBeing.com/handouts
to find a copy of this handout online.

"Elin, the first activity on the list is Act. Nothing will ever change in your life unless you act. There are a lot of people who know a lot of things yet don't apply what they've learned. Knowledge by itself is of no real value except when playing Trivial Pursuit or Jeopardy! As a matter of fact, it's much worse if you know something and never act on it than if you didn't know it in the first place.

"Taking action is so critical. One of my favorite quotes from Ralph Waldo Emerson rings true here: 'Your actions speak so loudly, I cannot hear what you are saying.' The opposite is also true: your lack of actions speak so loudly; I can't hear what you are saying. You must take action every day; do what you say you will do.

"You also need to be smart about what actions you take. It's easy to do something that 'just feels right' or blindly listen to others and follow their advice. It's critical that you protect yourself by following the due diligence processes we talked about yesterday in the planning process. Focus on becoming an expert and listen to a diverse set of viewpoints before making an informed decision.

"My friend Patti was evaluating her investment options in 2021. She was given a lot of different advice. The mainstream advice from her stockbroker, financial advisors, and wealth management firm was to buy and hold the S&P 500 index, FAANG stocks, and Tesla. There was also a lot of talk about the meme stocks like GameStop. But she saw that the Federal Reserve was about to raise interest rates and taper its asset purchases that were stimulating the economy, and she was concerned about the impact this would have. During a chance conversation at work with someone she rarely spoke with, she received advice about moving all her investments to cash. This was the first time anyone had ever said this, but the more she researched it the more she liked it. She decided to move the investments in all of her accounts and her 401(k) to cash, and she successfully avoided the market crash that started in January of the following year. When the markets dropped twenty percent, she reinvested her cash into a variety of investments and enjoyed the subsequent market rise.

"When making decisions about people, it is also important to not extend trust blindly. It's easy to extend blind trust, especially if you always see the best in others, believe that people are inherently good and represent themselves authentically, and if you think you can tell who is good or bad by just a few short conversations. Unfortunately, there are many people who use standard thinking and believe they win when you lose. These people are experts at hiding their true intentions.

"It's important to have others prove themselves to you by extending smart trust to them, not blind trust. As Stephen M. R. Covey said, 'The job of a leader is to go first, to extend trust first. Not a blind trust without expectations and accountability, but rather a 'smart trust' with clear expectations and strong accountability built into the process.'

"Elin, do you have any questions about taking smart, informed actions and extending smart trust?"

"No, I don't. But this is obviously a critical daily activity that I need to focus on. I can see why it's first on the list."

"Excellent. The second activity on the list is Connect. We all win when we work together, and we all work together better when we have strong relationships. Let me teach you the **Conversation Stack**, which is critical in the process of building positive relationships. It uses a memory stacking technique to help you remember what to talk about in a conversation. This includes what you ask others, and what questions you should be prepared to answer.

"Stacking involves creating a sequence of images that are somehow connected to each other. The sillier and more exaggerated things are, the more likely you are to remember them. You are free to modify this to make it better for you. Also, you can use this memory technique for a variety of applications, including public speaking and remembering your shopping list.

"Here are the images. Imagine a yellow happy face that is jumping up and down with excitement. On its head is a large Abraham Lincoln hat with your name flashing on it. Then a giant red *X* made of ribbon falls down on top of the hat and the smiley face. Next, the Empire State Building comes crashing down and squashes everything. Adding to the chaos, your childhood home falls from the sky and lands on top of the Empire State Building, skewered by the spire at the top. You see a giant tree is growing out from where the chimney on your home used to be. Suddenly, a giant cruise ship falls from the sky, lands on top of the tree, and rests in its branches. A whistle sounds from the ship, and you notice something coming out of its three smokestacks. The smokestacks are actually rolled-up school diplomas, and what's coming out of them are thousands of graduation caps and gowns in every color imaginable. Then a giant butterfly net comes down to capture everything, all the way to the ground. Holding the butterfly net is Oscar from the Academy Awards.

"Let's go through what the pictures mean. What is the first picture, Elin?"

"A yellow happy face jumping up and down with excitement."

"That's to remind you to smile and have fun. People like to be around others who are genuinely positive and enthusiastic. It will also help you generate those positive endorphins that will give you more confidence and keep you from entering the fear state. What is the next picture?"

"A large Abraham Lincoln hat with my name flashing on it."

"That's to remind you to tell them your name and to get theirs. Normally, we forget someone's name immediately after they tell it to us. You want to focus on remembering their name. Use it immediately when speaking with them and multiple times during your conversation. You might ask them to spell it. You'll want to write it down as soon as you can so you won't forget it. Think of a way to remember their name—the more exaggerated the better. For example, my friend Marty Wolf has a thick beard and is very outgoing. I imagined him as a werewolf, partying on top of a roof, howling at the full moon. For me he became Marty the Party Wolf. What is the next picture?"

"A giant red X made of ribbon floats down on top of the hat and the smiley face," Elin replied.

"If you look at the map of this mall, there is a red X that tells you, 'You are here.' This picture reminds you to ask about context. If you're at a social gathering, you might ask how they know the host or the person of the hour, and if they know anyone else here. In other situations, you might ask them if they've been here before or if they come here often. At restaurants, I follow this with asking for recommendations on what's good to eat here. Okay, what is the next picture?"

"The Empire State Building comes crashing down and squashes everything."

"That's to remind you to ask about work: past, present, and future. Some example questions are what do you do for work, what company do you work for, where is it located, how long have you worked there, how did you get started, what do you like about it, what did you do before this, and what would you do for work if you didn't need the money? And for you, Elin, you can ask if they are hiring," Wes said with an exaggerated look to make his point. "What is the next picture?"

"My childhood home falls from the sky and lands on top of the Empire State Building and is skewered by the spire at the top."

"That's to remind you to ask about where they live: past, present, and future. People don't like stalkers, so you want to avoid direct questions such as, 'Where do you live?' and 'What's your address?' Instead, ask what city they live in. Then you can ask questions such as, 'How long have you lived there?' 'What do you like about it?'

'Where did you live before?' 'Where did you grow up?' 'What was your favorite place to live?' and 'Where would you like to live if you could live anywhere?' What is the next picture?"

"A giant tree is growing out from where the chimney on my home used to be," Elin replied.

"This is a family tree, and it is there to remind you to ask about their family. This can be a sensitive topic, so you want to avoid questions such as, 'Are you married?' and 'Do you have any kids?' You also want to avoid stepping on a landmine by asking about their parents and finding out that they recently died. These questions can end the conversation quickly. A better question to ask is, 'Do you have a family?' Then they can tell you whatever they're comfortable talking about. If they say they have a partner, you can ask about how they met and where their partner works. What is the next picture?"

"A giant cruise ship falls from the sky, lands on top of the tree, and rests in its branches," Elin replied.

"That's to remind you to ask about their vacations: past, present, and future. You can ask them questions such as, 'Do you have any vacations planned for this year?' 'What places have you been to?' 'What was the best vacation you ever took?' and 'If you could go on your dream vacation, where would you go?' What is the next picture?"

"A whistle sounds from the ship, and I notice something coming out of its three smokestacks. First of all, the stacks are actually rolled-up school diplomas, and what's coming out of them are thousands of graduation caps and gowns in every color imaginable," Elin replied.

"That's to remind you to ask about where they went to school. This is also a sensitive question, and you don't want to offend someone who didn't graduate from high school by asking them where they went to college. Start off by asking, 'Where did you go to school?' They'll tell you what they want you to know. You can follow up by asking about their major, best memories, favorite teacher, thesis, and extracurricular activities. What is the next picture?"

"A giant butterfly net comes down to capture everything, all the way to the ground," Elin replied.

"That's to remind you to ask about what they do when they're not working, like hobbies, charities, and sports. What is the last picture?"

"Holding the butterfly net is Oscar from the Academy Awards," Elin replied.

"That's to remind you to express gratitude to them. Think about something internal, not external. Instead of saying 'nice shoes,' you might thank them for something they did for you, or something you admire about them. At a minimum, you can tell them you enjoyed speaking with them.

"When you're speaking with someone, you can go through the pictures, asking them questions and listening to their answers. Be considerate and do not interrupt. Ask them follow-up questions to further explore the topics and to understand them better. As Dale Carnegie emphasized in one of his principles in *How to Win Friends and Influence People*, 'Be a good listener. Encourage others to talk about themselves.' Most people like to talk about themselves, but if you encounter someone who is quiet and shy, it will help guide you on what to say. They'll enjoy listening to you. Of course, the ideal situation is for you to speak half the time and listen to them the other half.

"Elin, do you think this will help you feel more comfortable in social situations?"

"Yes! Thank you, Wes!"

"Now let's talk about physical energy, which is the third item on the list. Is there a difference between how you feel before we meet versus right after one of our sessions?"

"Absolutely. Some days I don't want to leave the house. I feel depressed and negative. I complain about the weather. But after one of our sessions, I feel fantastic. I'm positive and excited."

"Elin, let me tell you a story about my friend Luis. He used to work a day job and then taught classes for three and a half hours at night, from six thirty until ten o'clock p.m. One day, he was really sick and had no energy. He just wanted to go to bed and sleep it off for a couple of days. He would normally have called in sick, but his boss told him that there were only two reasons not to teach: you're dead, or you're in the intensive care ward of a hospital. So he went to work, although he didn't know how he was going to pull it off.

"Luis knew that teaching a class normally required him to exert an extraordinary amount of positive energy so he could lift the low-energy and negative-energy class members, and to prevent them from sucking all the positive energy out of him. So being sick was an additional challenge because he didn't have access to his normal energy reserves. What was interesting is that he was able to find the energy he needed. After teaching for five minutes, he felt good, but after everyone left at ten o'clock, he felt fantastic, more than one hundred percent. He told me that going from such a low energy level to such a high one was an amazing experience that changed his life.

"Luis realized that he had full control over how he felt at all times. In fact, we can all create our own energy even when we think we have none. We all have the power to put ourselves in a positive state. You can energize yourself by being around positive people, doing yoga, and exercising. You can also energize yourself by recalling a pleasant memory, reading a book, listening to music, or watching a video you find inspirational. The knowledge that you have the power to create and maintain your energy by what you think, feel, say, and do is truly one of the most incredible bits of wisdom I can give you.

"Elin, I'd like to take credit for the change in how you feel before and after we meet, but you did that. It's a very common belief that we aren't in control and are subject to what happens around us. That's just not true. Furthermore, your energy level is your responsibility, and maintaining high energy is very important."

"Very interesting, Wes. I didn't realize I was responsible for my own energy levels," Elin remarked.

"The fifth critical daily activity on the list is Gratitude. Expressing gratitude can have a very beneficial effect on both ourselves and others. It can calm us down and put us in a peaceful, joyous state. My friends, who have a practice of saying what they're grateful for before going to bed, tell me that they sleep better and wake up feeling more refreshed.

"If I asked you to write down everything you are grateful for, how many things do you think you could come up with?"

"I think I could write down about a dozen or so items," Elin replied.

"That's sounds about right based on my experience working with others. But I'm pretty sure you could come up with a lot more. Think about all the great things you've experienced and all the great people you've met. Think about all the things you take for granted today that would be difficult to live without.

"My friend Barney never recovered from losing his left pinkie toe and was dead within two years. When was the last time you told your left pinkie toe how much you appreciated it? What do you have today that you complain about, that people in other parts of the world desperately want? There are thousands of people who would change places with you in an instant and would be thrilled to live with things you don't like because their life is so bad. I'd like to challenge you to write down at least one hundred items. That really shouldn't be too difficult for you to do. In fact, let's go with two hundred items. Do you accept my request?"

"Uh . . . that seems like an awful lot. Do I have to write them down?" Elin remarked. "Can't I just think of them? I mean, I have

written and typed so much in my life. That's how I made a living."
Seeing that Wes wasn't budging, Elin reluctantly said, "Okay. I mean
yes. I accept."

"Great! Then I have another challenge for you," Wes said,
seeming to enjoy the look of shock and irritation on Elin's face.

Wes gave Elin a handout titled *PILES of Compliments* and went
over it with her.

PILES of Compliments

Giving a Compliment

A compliment is a true statement about something you admire in the other person. It benefits the person receiving the compliment and is a selfless act by the person giving it. Use the **PILES** acronym to remind you to give piles and piles of compliments every day. You know you have done it correctly when both of you feel the emotion behind the compliment. Here is the meaning of PILES:

- **Positive:** Be positive. Don't talk about how bad they were before. Only speak about their current abilities.
- **Inner:** Focus on their inner qualities or abilities. These are more important and meaningful to the other person than external qualities.
- **Look:** If you give the compliment in person, look into their eyes as you speak. If you want to give them something they can look at in the future, send them a letter or email.
- **Evidence:** Provide evidence to back up your compliment.
- **Sincere:** Be honest and sincere. Use your emotions.

Receiving a Compliment

When you receive a compliment, it is important to thank the person. Let them know you appreciate them taking the time to deliver the compliment to you. If you would like, you can also tell them why their compliment means a lot to you at this time.

Don't deny or negate their compliment in any way. It harms you because you are denying the truth about yourself. You don't allow yourself to be seen in a positive light, and you continue to fuel your false fears and negativity. It can also be a negative experience for the other person and may deter them from trying to compliment you again. From an extreme perspective, you are basically telling them that they are either stupid or a liar. If you don't understand their compliment, then you can always ask them to explain it to you.

Go to www.WiseLovingBeing.com/handouts
to find a copy of this handout online.

"Let's try this, Elin. I'm going to give you a compliment, and you are going to say *thank you*."

He looked into her eyes, smiled, and said, "Elin, one of the things I admire most about you is your courage. It's very difficult for people to face the truth about themselves and to become aware of all the unpleasant things that are hiding in their unconscious mind. It is also difficult for people to make real changes in how they think, feel, speak, and behave. Most people won't do what you have done. And there are a lot of people who haven't been able to accomplish in a lifetime what you've accomplished in such a short period of time. I appreciate your hard work, your open mind, and your incredible amounts of courage."

Elin wanted to deny what Wes had said, just like she normally did with her niece and everyone else in her life. It was such a familiar habit. But she stopped herself and simply said, "Thank you, Wes. I really appreciate you saying that." It was difficult for Elin to say those words. But it was amazing how they affected her. She completely absorbed the compliment this time, and it felt really good for a change. She could feel the sincere emotion, and her eyes welled up with tears.

"You're very welcome, Elin. Nicely done." Wes smiled and paused briefly before he continued. "I'd like to close today by reading a quote from one of my favorite US presidents, Teddy Roosevelt. He definitely lived his best life."

Wes read the handout and then gave it to her.

The Man in the Arena

By Teddy Roosevelt

"It is not the critic who counts; not the man who points out how the strong man stumbles, or where the doer of deeds could have done them better. The credit belongs to the man who is actually in the arena, whose face is marred by dust and sweat and blood; who strives valiantly; who errs, who comes up short again and again, because there is no effort without error and shortcoming; but who does actually strive to do the deeds; who knows great enthusiasms, the great devotions; who spends himself in a worthy cause; who at the best knows in the end the triumph of high achievement, and who at the worst, if he fails, at least fails while daring greatly, so that his place shall never be with those cold and timid souls who neither know victory nor defeat."

Go to www.WiseLovingBeing.com/handouts
to find a copy of this handout online.

"Elin, today especially, with the advent of social media, we are bombarded with negative messages. There seems to be no shortage of people who think their valuable life's purpose is criticizing others. You will even have people you respect tell you that you are bad and wrong and going to fail. You will encounter plenty of these misguided folks. They are spectators sitting in the stands, and they don't matter. The only people who count are the players on the field or in the arena. In order to live a life you love, you must spend all of your time on the field. Do not let yourself become distracted and wander into the stands to become a spectator.

"Listening to spectators can be okay in small doses because sometimes they will tell you something valuable you can use to make yourself better. But most of what they say is pure garbage. They are like your fellow crab you thought was your friend who keeps you from crawling out of the pot of boiling water. Misery loves company, and no one wants to be left behind in shabby town.

"Nicholas Sparks said something poignant and fitting to this theme: 'Just because you're right doesn't mean I'm wrong, you just haven't seen life from my side.' You'll encounter lots of people who will tell you that you are wrong or tell you that you can't do something. Be true to yourself. History is full of courageous people who have proved their critics wrong and done things that were thought to be impossible. So can you.

"You are very different today than when we first met, Elin. You have learned some valuable wisdom, and are now about to be unleashed on the world, in the arena. You are only competing against yourself, and you are the only one who can judge how you are doing. Please, don't forget that."

"I won't forget that. I promise," Elin replied solemnly.

"To summarize, everyone is a leader. If you don't believe you can do something, then you need to figure out why and get the answers you need to succeed. Commitment is critical, but only commit to what you truly believe in. Burn the boats and move forward. Focusing on your goal requires immersion and presence. It's important to take smart action and build your dreams using the Agile method. Overcome obstacles by being persistent, accessing your unlimited creativity and resourcefulness, asking powerful questions, and doing the critical daily activities. Be grateful. Give and receive compliments. Stay in the arena, be true to yourself, and be open to receiving new ways to make yourself better.

"And with that, we're all done. Great job!"

"What's my homework, Wes?" Elin asked.

Wes smiled. "There's no more homework, Elin. I've taught you everything I wanted to teach you. Now it's time for you to apply it in the real world. It's time to take action."

"Well, can we still get together at the Cinnabon every morning? I mean, I could really use your coaching and your company."

"Unfortunately, I can't right now. I need to go check on my family in Hawaii. I've enjoyed working with you, but I'm sorry to tell you that the *Intermission* is over. It's time for the *Second Act*. Make me proud. Or should I say, 'Break a leg'?"

He gave her a big hug and said, "I'm not abandoning you. I'll always be around. I love you very much. Don't worry, Elin. Everything is going to be okay. You've got this!" Wes looked at her one last time and said, "I can't wait to see what you'll do." He then walked away and disappeared into the crowd.

Chapter Seventeen

The Final Piece

It was 10:00 a.m. on Wednesday, November 30, 2022. Elin was sitting in front of the Cinnabon. She hadn't been back here since her last day with Wes in September, and hadn't seen or heard from him since then either. She didn't have an appointment with Wes today, but she felt stuck and needed to be in the place that had been so inspirational for her.

Things had been going well until she entered the "bad months." November was when she gave up her son for adoption, and December was when her father died. These were the months for family get-togethers, which painfully reminded her that she had none. These were also the two months when she had to deal with Richard the most. She had set a boundary with him that made things a lot better, but she still had to deal with him almost every day.

The bad months were depressing. She focused on her regrets, guilt, shame, and loss. She was negative and thought about what she didn't have. If several good things happened, she would ignore those and focus on the one that went wrong. Nothing seemed to go right, as always, during this timeframe.

The bigger problem was that now she knew better. Wes had given her some valuable tools and information. She thought for sure she could overcome her challenges and turn the bad months into good months. She had failed. Again. This made her feel even worse.

But she wasn't giving up this time. She had reviewed all the handouts Wes had given her and had replayed their conversations over and over in her head.

Maybe some powerful questions could help, she thought. "What am I missing? How can I overcome the bad months? What can I do to overcome these challenges? How can I be more creative and resourceful?"

"How do you turn that frown upside down?" came a familiar voice. It was Wes.

Elin sprang to her feet and hugged Wes. There was a mixture of tears and joy on Elin's face. She stepped back and tried to compose herself as she wiped her tears with the handkerchief Wes had given her months before.

Wes smiled and said, "It's great to see you, too, Elin! I've missed you."

"I'm so glad to see you, Wes!" Elin replied as relief filled her voice. "I feel like I've failed you. I'm so sorry. I'm stuck and I could really use your help."

"I know. That's why I'm here," Wes said. "Let's go over to that table and sit down for a little bit. There's something important I need to tell you."

Elin and Wes sat at a table that was the farthest away from the bustling holiday shoppers.

"How long have you been punishing yourself, Elin?" Wes inquired. "It's been over sixty years. I know of cold-blooded killers who've been punished a lot less. And what did you do actually? You gave up a child for adoption. That's not a crime. You did what you were told to do, and what you thought was best for everyone involved. Knowing what you know now, you obviously would have done things differently. But knowing what you did then, you did the best you could. You can't go back in time, and you can't stay stuck in time either. You can see that, right?"

"Yes, I can see that, but it's one thing to understand it rationally and quite another thing to actually overcome it."

"Agreed. It's not easy to change a behavior that's been going on for so long, especially when there's so much pain and fear associated with it. It's really an existential fear for you. I've given you the tools you need to succeed; unfortunately, you've encountered a massive obstacle keeping you from using the tools and making productive changes."

Elin nodded in agreement.

"Did you ever do the exercise of writing a letter of apology to your son and asking for his forgiveness? Did you ever follow the process to forgive yourself?"

"No. I'm sorry but I never got around to that," Elin admitted. "I guess I feel I don't really deserve to be forgiven. I'm still struggling with feeling like a bad person for letting him go."

"Let me see if I understand. You believe you are a bad person because you got pregnant, gave birth to a healthy son, and gave him up for adoption so he could have a better chance at having a good life. You should be punished for this forever. And you think you need to keep this a secret because if anyone finds out about it, they'll either treat you badly or kick you out of the tribe, and you will die. In other words, *disclosure is death*. Is that correct?"

"Yes."

"How many people do you think actually knew your secret back then, and how many know it today?"

"Very few people knew my secret back then. Today, I think just two people know it. But I've had some weird conversations with my cousins where they've asked me if I've ever used websites like Ancestry.com. I just wrote the conversations off at the time. They've always been nice to me and treated me well, so they obviously don't know."

"Well, let me put this question to bed once and for all. Everyone knows! All of your cousins know because they learned it from their parents, who were told by your mother. Everyone in your high school knows because any girl who left their family behind for a year was obviously pregnant. And your high school friends all talked. I'm just confirming what you already know, aren't I?"

Elin was in shock and fell silent. She looked at Wes in disbelief before nodding her head slowly.

Wes continued, "Your conscious mind knew the truth, but your unconscious mind stepped in to protect you. It hid the truth from you because it knew you couldn't handle it. All these years you've been keeping a secret that was never a secret. Your powerful fear of not belonging was connected to a belief that if people knew your secret, then they would treat you badly and kick you out of the tribe.

"But the facts are that everyone knew your secret, yet they all treated you kindly and went out of their way to make you feel part of the tribe. You still belong to your tribe. They even supported you by keeping your secret to themselves and never bringing it up. They knew you wanted it to remain a secret. As a matter of fact, they have a lot of respect for you. You went through a terrible experience where society labeled you a bad person. You survived that and became the kind and caring person they love.

"Views about teen pregnancy have changed dramatically since you were seventeen. Today, most people regard teen pregnancy as something that just happens sometimes. They don't view women getting pregnant outside of marriage as bad. There are a lot of support systems in place to help, and it's even discussed and celebrated in movies and television shows like *16 and Pregnant*.

"You have a fear about something that doesn't even exist, and you have a false belief about being kicked out of your tribe. You need to create a new belief, such as, *Everyone knows my secret, accepts me, loves me, and is kind to me. They have all gone out of their way to keep me in the tribe.* And you can turn your fear into a strength by adding this belief: *I can have an enormous impact on others when I accept myself, when I am vulnerable, when I tell them my story, and when I am the real me."*

Wes looked closely to see how she was doing. "Elin, you have a more peaceful yet puzzled look on your face. How do you feel?"

"Wow. That is such an amazing revelation. I think it's going to take me some time to process it all. A part of me is thinking about all the time I've wasted living my life the way I have. I was never able to be authentic since I was pretending to be someone I wasn't. I can see that by hiding my real self, it led to a lot of my problems. It also kept me from doing important things for myself and others. But yes, I feel relieved, and I do feel more at peace with myself."

"Excellent. Don't forget to do the Human Resolution Process with your son. You'll be quite surprised that he will forgive you and will understand why you made the decision. And he will agree that you did the best you could at the time. Once that is complete, do the self-forgiveness process. It will enable you to accept yourself, love yourself, and feel the confidence and power that comes from that. You won't successfully transform until you do both exercises. Do I have your commitment that you'll do those two exercises today?"

"Yes, I agree. I'll do them later today. Thank you, Wes. I really needed that."

"You're very welcome. There's one more tool I can give you that will make a big difference for you. That's what we're going to do for the rest of our time today. Are you ready?"

"Yes, sir! I'm so ready!"

"Elin, if you were to compare us, what would be different besides our genders? In other words, what do you think about me, and what do you think about yourself?"

"That's easy, Wes. You are smart and successful and capable and happy. You are everything I'm not."

Wes smiled. "Thank you for the compliment, Elin. It's true. I am all of those things, and so much more. And so are you. As a matter of fact, we have a lot more in common than you might think. For starters, we're both very kind, loving, generous, and conscientious."

Wes pointed to Elin's phone. "Elin, what apps on your phone do you use the most?"

"I use the address book, camera, text messenger, the browser, a local news app, and an app for my favorite store."

"Nice. All of those apps take turns running on your phone, which is basically a computer. Let's make things simple and say that your phone can only run one app at a time. You select an app, and then you observe the phone doing things, like displaying information or playing videos.

"Your brain is just like your phone. It is physical and allows five apps to run on it. The apps aren't visible or physical. They take turns running on your brain, swapping in and out as needed. Here are the four commonly used **brain apps**:

- **Conscious Mind App:** This is your ego, or rational mind. It is who you think you are.
- **Sensory App:** This monitors all the sensory data coming in from your body.
- **Survival Mind App:** This is your Survival Response System that manages your 4F Response.
- **Unconscious Mind App:** This app runs by default. It serves as your autopilot.

"Elin, I'm going to demonstrate to you how each app works with the **Mind App Exercise**. I want you to load the sensory app into your brain and focus on all the sensory data that comes in. Now tell me what happens."

Elin replied, "I can see you, the shoppers, the holiday decorations, the stores, merchandise, and the sale signs. I can smell the coffee and the fresh cinnamon rolls from Cinnabon, as well as the perfume and scented candles. I can hear people talking, people walking, music, and laughter. I can feel the cold air on my skin from the air conditioning. My body is warm. I can feel my phone and the bench I'm sitting on. I can still taste the leftover pumpkin pie and coffee I had for breakfast."

"Excellent. I want you to become aware of something. The sensory app is telling you what is happening based on the information it's getting from your body. You aren't your sensory app, and you aren't your body. You are something separate from it and simply observing it. You observe your brain and the sensory app in a very similar way that you observe your phone and the camera app. The only difference is that it is happening inside you. Are you aware that this is happening right now?"

Elin nodded. "Yes. I am aware that I'm observing my brain running the sensory app. I am separate from my senses and separate from my body."

"Great. Let's separate you from your body even more. Think of your body like it's a onesie you are wearing. Imagine that you take it off and put it on an imaginary shelf next to you.

"Now I want you to close your eyes and load your conscious mind app into your brain. Observe your thoughts similar to how you would watch leaves float down a stream. You are relaxed, sitting on the bank of the stream, and feel the warmth of the sun. Only one leaf appears at a time. You observe each leaf appear for a short period of time and then watch it disappear, followed by a new leaf that appears. Each leaf is a thought. Acknowledge each thought, accept it, and let it go without dwelling on it or trying to solve anything. Don't judge it or assign any meaning to it. Each thought is neither good nor bad; it just is. Tell me what thoughts you are observing."

"I'm observing a thought that says I'm a bad person," Elin replied. "I'm observing a thought of shame over getting pregnant out of wedlock. I'm observing a thought of guilt about giving up my son for adoption. I am concerned that he might have had bad parents. I'm observing a thought of sadness over losing my dad when I was so young. I'm observing a thought of depression during a time of year that's supposed to be so much fun. I'm observing a thought of being stressed about spending time with Richard. I'm observing a thought of me being a failure. I'm observing a thought of appreciation for you being here, Wes."

"Well done, Elin. Notice that these thoughts and feelings only exist in the app. They aren't anywhere else. You can't touch them. No one else can see them or is even aware of them. Also notice that they are temporary. They come and go. There is a steady flow of thoughts.

"Now I want you to become aware of something. You are observing your thoughts coming through the conscious mind app. You are observing your mind thinking. You are separate from it. You aren't your thoughts, or your conscious mind, or your brain or your body. Are you aware of that?"

"Yes. I am aware that I am separate from my thoughts and my conscious mind," Elin replied. "I am also separate from my body and my brain."

"Great. Note that both your unconscious mind app and your survival mind app behave in a similar manner as the conscious mind app. Now let's separate you from your mind even more. Think of your mind as a hat you have on. Take it off and put it on the imaginary shelf next to you.

"Now, just sit with yourself. You are not your body or your senses. And you are not your conscious, unconscious, or survival mind. If you happen to receive sensory data or thoughts, just acknowledge them and let them go. Just be with yourself.

"Let's talk about what app is left. Who is observing the sensory data and the thoughts? This is another part of you. This is the fifth app. It is your **Wise Loving Being App**. It is always there, but it rarely gets used. Unfortunately, most people don't even know it exists. I want you to allow this app to run. When this app runs in your brain and you focus on it, then you are acting as a Wise Loving Being.

"I am now going to take you through a very important exercise."

Wes took out a handout titled *Wise Loving Being Reflection Exercise* and read it to her.

Wise Loving Being Reflection Exercise

The **WLB Reflection Exercise** will help you get more familiar with a very powerful part of you. Think about what a Wise Loving Being is and what it means to actually be one. If the sensory app, conscious mind app, unconscious mind app, or survival mind app loads, just acknowledge it, let it go, and then reload the WLB App. If you think a negative, intrusive thought, then just say to yourself, "Delete, delete, delete," and move on.

Close your eyes so you can concentrate. Take slow, deep breaths. Think about what each of these phrases really means. Think about how each affects the relationship with yourself and others. Repeat after me:

- I am a Wise Loving Being.
- I am very wise.
- I am very loving and good.
- I am a powerful creator.
- I am selfless and focus on helping others in need.
- I know everything about myself.
- I am okay with who I am, and I am okay with how others are.
- I know I am a perfectly imperfect human just like everyone else.
- I have unconditional and unlimited love, patience, respect, understanding, acceptance, appreciation, kindness, and forgiveness for myself and others.
- I am genuinely positive.
- I am generous with myself and others.
- I see the highest potential in myself and others.
- I celebrate my successes and reward myself for doing my best. I do the same for others.
- I learn from my failures and comfort myself. I do the same for others.

- I don't criticize, condemn, complain, or judge myself or others.
- I have no secondary fears of not belonging. I am more than good enough. I am smart enough. I am lovable. And I belong. I also help others feel like they belong.
- I give myself and others what is needed, but not necessarily what is wanted.
- I have my best interests at heart. I do the same for others.
- I want everyone to win.
- I love myself very much. I love others very much.

**Go to www.WiseLovingBeing.com/handouts
to find a copy of this handout online.**

"I want you to feel the positive energy that is being created inside you. Feel the love. Feel the joy. Note that love, peace, joy, freedom, and fulfillment only come from within. They don't come from outside you. Let this positive, loving energy expand out past your body so it creates a bubble of golden light around you. The more you practice this, the better you'll get at creating this bubble. Eventually, you'll be able to keep negativity out. It's like a tortoise shell. You can stay inside it and be safe.

"The bubble can be created before going into a difficult environment, or it can be used when you encounter negativity. You aren't running away from anything. You're just creating an environment where you don't allow anyone or anything to bother you. Nothing will be able to get inside unless you allow it. You'll be able to respond calmly to the external world from a place of love and power.

"Notice that in this state, you are good enough and you belong. You don't have any negative feelings. There is no anger, depression, regret, guilt, shame, or grief. You don't feel like you need to be punished. Those feelings and thoughts don't exist in the WLB app. They only exist in the mind apps. However, you can always download updated versions of the mind apps that don't have these negative features. I have taught you how to do that with the Unconscious Mind Cleanse and my other teachings.

"The WLB app puts you in control of your life. You are no longer being controlled by your circumstances or by others. You are no longer reacting to the world; you are acting on it. You choose how you want to think, feel, speak, and act. This is where your true power comes from.

"As a WLB, you have the ability to do whatever you need to do in each moment that is consistent with where you want to go in the future. You have the ability to make a big difference. The world is excited that you are here. It desperately needs your help. It's time to stop letting your mind punish you and move forward. It's time to let your nine-year-old self go play and let your powerful adult-self emerge. It's time to live a life you truly love. It's time to live as a powerful WLB. November and December aren't the 'bad' months. These months, and every month for that matter, are the *great* months.

"Elin, when you're ready, I'd like you to slowly count to five, open your eyes, and return to our conversation."

When her eyes opened, Wes asked, "How do you feel?"

After taking a deep breath, Elin replied, "I feel great, Wes. I don't feel helpless or hopeless anymore. I feel quite powerful and peaceful."

"I'm glad to hear that. I want you to practice this WLB Reflection Exercise a couple of times each day, especially when you feel stressed or overwhelmed. Just sit in a comfortable space, load your WLB app, and think about the WLB concepts and what they truly mean to you and to others. Feel the positive energy of love, peace, joy, freedom, and fulfillment inside you. Do this for as long as you need to. There is no right or wrong way to do this. Create an audio recording of the handout so you can better focus on the concepts when listening to it.

"You can also take this exercise one step further. You can radiate positive, loving energy out into the world and help others feel better. I do this with you every time we get together, and by the end of each session you feel noticeably more calm, positive, and loving, don't you?"

"Yes, I do."

"Let me tell you how to use the WLB app in your real life. When you are a WLB and you encounter Richard, you won't be affected by him in any way. He can say or do what he will, and you will see that it has nothing to do with you. You'll be aware of his WLB, and you'll have unconditional love for his human. Richard is the perfect human who knows how to push all of your human buttons. Richard, along with all the other people from whom you feel so much guilt and shame, have brought you to this moment in time. You're on a new path thanks to them. They were all critical in motivating you to seek answers and elevate yourself. You might even want to thank them.

"Load your WLB app and put up your bubble before your next interaction with Richard. You'll create a new relationship with him with healthy boundaries. Instead of being angry, you'll stay positive. Instead of criticizing him, you'll be kind, loving, and accepting. This doesn't mean being weak or letting him get away with his bad behavior. You are very strong. You won't let him take advantage of you. And by radiating positive, loving energy, you'll help him and further improve your relationship. Any questions?"

"No questions, Wes."

"Elin, your WLB app is a very powerful part of you. You, essentially, are a WLB with a body and a mind. Using the Universal Elevation principles to describe you, *all* three parts are *equally* important and *required*. They are *connected*, and there needs to be *balance*. They need to *collaborate* and work together as a team in order to achieve *excellence* so you and everyone can *win*. When you embrace the *truth* about all that you are and load the WLB app into your brain, then your life will be completely different and the world will never be the same. I hope you have clarity around that now."

"Yes. I do now, Wes."

"Let me further demonstrate this with the **Flying Analogy**. With your current unconscious mind app loaded in your brain, it's like being in an airplane on the tarmac in Denver. It's a cold, dark winter day. Snow is everywhere, and there's ice on the wings. You can barely see outside your window. You worry that you'll have to go back to the terminal or that you might crash on takeoff. You think about all the plane crashes you've ever heard about. When you find the courage to load the WLB app, it's like you take off and punch through the clouds. Now the air is smooth and there's nothing but sunshine and clear blue sky. Your unhealthy feelings of fear, guilt, regret, and shame are gone. There is nothing but love, peace, joy, freedom, and fulfillment. This is what it's like when the WLB app is running in your brain.

"To make a slightly different point, here is one last story. My friend Sally had a son who didn't like her. When he graduated from sixth grade, she asked him what he thought about Santa Claus, the Easter Bunny, and the Tooth Fairy. He said he believed in them, and he really liked them. They always brought him what he wanted. They were always very kind and generous. Sally then asked her son what he thought about her. He said he didn't like her and thought she was a jerk. Sally smiled and told him that there weren't four different people. They are all part of the same being who loves him very much and who only wants what's best for him.

"Elin, I started this conversation today by asking you what the difference is between us. You said we are opposites, but that couldn't be further from the truth. Here is the final piece to the puzzle. I *am* your Wise Loving Being. I am not separate from you. I am part of you, and you are part of me. I had to create this external Wesley L. Bean persona because you couldn't hear me from the inside. You wouldn't load your WLB app. You wouldn't remember who you really are. You are everything I am, and you can do everything I can do. You are smart, successful, and capable—and so much more."

Elin was speechless. She wanted to deny everything Wes said. The WLB was just a concept from his teachings. So was The Play Exercise. How could it be real? Surely, he was just messing with her.

But Elin knew deep down that what Wes was saying was true. He always felt so familiar, and he knew too much about her from the very beginning—from her favorite Pepperidge Farm cookies to her darkest memories from when she was seventeen. Even today, he knew that she needed to talk with him, and he knew that everyone knew her secret. She had gone along without questioning things much, somehow rationalizing that everything was just a coincidence.

Wes saw that Elin understood and so he continued. "I love you very much, Elin. I believe in you, and I believe in us. Let's get going. We have a lot of important things to do. The world desperately needs us. There are many people who have been patiently waiting for us to show up and lead the way. You must embrace all that you are and take smart action now to achieve your Big Strong Why. It's time for you to believe in yourself and to believe in us. It's time to start being a hungry wolf and go hunting for success. Can you do that?"

Her doubt crept back in again. How could she, an old lady with nothing to show for herself after all these years, really make a difference? How could anyone need her?

But Wes was her Wise Loving Being. He obviously knew things way beyond what she did. He had her best interests at heart, and he would never lie to her.

Elin found her words and spoke with a level of surety that surprised even her. "Yes, Wes. I can do that. I really get it now."

"Great. I think this quote from Winston Churchill will help you keep things in perspective: 'Success is not final, failure is not fatal. It is the courage to continue that counts.' It is now time for you to dig deep and show tremendous courage in transforming yourself and those around you. I wish you nothing but the best.

"Now that you know I exist it's important for you to pay attention. Make time to focus inwards. I will periodically try to communicate with you and help guide you toward your highest potential. It's important for you to listen. Sometimes, I communicate in words. More often it will be like a lightbulb flash of inspiration, realization, or an inner knowing. I can also communicate through others or circumstances. It takes some practice but you'll eventually get good at hearing me. You'll know when I have something important to say to you. You can also communicate with me. Just quiet yourself, load the WLB app, ask me a question, and listen for my response. The answer might not come immediately but it will come. Does that make sense?"

Elin nodded her head indicating she understood.

"My final gift to you today is this."

Wes gave Elin a flyer titled *Free Seminar* and asked her to read it.

Free Seminar

You deserve to live a life filled with love, peace, joy, freedom, and fulfillment.

You are important. Your life matters. You can make a difference.

You have a purpose in life that is very important. There are things you can do that no one else can do or will do. There are those who desperately need you to show up and help them. This includes people, animals, plants, and the planet.

What more needs to happen to you before you wake up and start to listen? Do you really want to relive this life?

It is time to stop playing small and start living into your full potential. It is time to become the leader you were meant to be. It is time to live a meaningful life you love.

Everything is better when you transform your life. Your best days are ahead of you. There is no time to waste.

Don't know how to transform? No problem! We will show you how. Held back by fear? We will help you turn your fears into strengths!

Please join us in front of the Desert Sky Mall Cinnabon on Saturday mornings at 11:00 a.m.

Go to www.WiseLovingBeing.com/handouts
to find a copy of this handout online.

"Wes, what's this for exactly?"

"It's for your second objective in life. When you encounter someone who needs help, you can give them a flyer. And by the way, you'll need to make some copies on your way home today. One thousand should do it. All of your WLB friends will be sending humans your way. You'll also need to make some copies of all the handouts I gave you. You'll need them for your students."

"My students?! But Wes, I'm not ready!"

"Elin, sometimes life calls on us to do things we don't think we can do. I can assure you that it is never the case. We are always more prepared than we think. We aren't given something we can't handle. Sometimes we just need a little push to get us going. Consider yourself officially pushed."

Elin looked a little bit perturbed, but before she could say anything, Wes continued.

"There are two kinds of humans on this planet. There are those who fit in and embrace the limiting beliefs handed down to them throughout the generations. They are good at following directions without questioning them. They use standard thinking and want to fit in with the herd. They are the followers, although some of them pretend to be leaders. They are referred to as a **leader in name only** (LINO). Followers are driven by fear. Leadership by the followers is a recipe for disaster.

"And then there are those who don't feel like they belong in today's society. Their hearts beat to a different drum. They think for themselves and make choices that aren't always aligned with societal dictates. They are stronger than the followers and can better handle the challenges of life. They focus on internal, meaningful pursuits and helping others. It's not about what they own, who they know, and what they've done, it's about who they've become as a person. They are the **true leaders.** They see life as it could be. They see the change and inspire others to help make it a reality. They use Universal

Thinking and are driven by love. True leaders can lead from anywhere, regardless of their position or title.

"But sometimes these true leaders let the followers get to them, and they start to think that the followers are right and there is something wrong with who they are. True leaders are greatly outnumbered by the followers. As a result, they sometimes give up, settle, and let the followers win.

"True leaders just need to be reminded of how powerful they are and what important things they are here to do. They need to take ownership and fulfill their responsibilities; fully embrace their purpose and lead those who desperately need their help; remember that they are important, their life matters, and they can make a significant difference; and wake up and remember who they really are.

"Elin, it's time for you to wake up, remember who you are, and lead. It's time for you to find the other true leaders and help them wake up. The world needs all of them right now. The followers are hopelessly lost. They need the true leaders to guide them to a better way of life.

"You've got a very important job ahead of you, Elin. There's no time to waste. Now, get busy! If you need anything, you know where to find me. I can't wait to see what you'll do!"

With a blink of her eyes, Wes was gone. Elin looked around to see if anyone had witnessed his disappearance, but no one seemed to notice.

She was trying to figure out what had just happened when she became aware of changes slowly occurring within her. She could feel a positive, loving energy that was getting stronger. For the first time, she was aware that Wes was a part of her. He had been with her all along and would always be with her. She knew now that no matter what, she wouldn't be alone anymore, and they would face the world together.

All the weight fell off her shoulders; she felt centered and strong. Elin realized, from this new perspective, that all the negativity, the unhealthy guilt, shame, regret, and fear she had felt most of her life was just a bunch of *silly nonsense*. She now understood why she didn't fit in: she was a true leader.

Things were going to be a lot different now. There was no going back to how things used to be. She knew she was on the right path now and headed in the right direction toward a much better future. There was a new fire burning inside her and a powerful force calling her to move forward. She couldn't ignore it.

Elin smiled and looked around at all the holiday decorations lighting up the mall. She felt better than she had in a very long time. That sense of magic, hope, and wonder had returned—something she had lost shortly after the Christmas when she was nine. After all these years, she was finally ready to enjoy the holidays again. But there were so many ways she could celebrate, so many activities she could participate in.

Can I celebrate them all? she wondered. Then she shook her head and laughed. *Of course, I can. I can do whatever the hell I want!*

Final Thoughts

Our rapidly changing world has been optimized to invoke our primal fears and to do so with greater frequency and with higher levels of intensity. Our "smart" phones are loaded with various apps that can deliver fear-based information to us instantly. Individuals and organizations of all kinds can amplify problems and discord for their own benefit. They sometimes use false and misleading information and create problems that don't actually exist. Instead of resolving issues, they prefer to fan the flames of discontent.

They know how we will behave: we are motivated by fear and are hardwired to react to danger. They also know that we primarily run on autopilot and that we will believe what we are told by authoritative sources because that's what good tribe members have been taught to do for thousands of years. We join their tribe for protection but we are actually being manipulated and exploited by them.

Their gain is our loss. We are more stressed and worried than ever before. We are more frustrated, depressed, and angry too. We have higher levels of fear and hate. We are less tolerant and patient of others. The news is full of stories that confirm this. Some people are doing terrible things we rarely heard about thirty years ago. Our world is suffering from an increase in homelessness, substance abuse, addiction, overdose, suicide, discord, prejudice, intolerance, hate, divorce, environmental destruction, crime, violence, murder, mass shootings, terrorism, and war.

I meet people every day who are struggling, looking for better ways to cope with the problems and pain in their lives. They are seeking ways to better manage their frustration, anger, anxiety, depression, and other negative emotions. They are looking for ways to improve their relationships and better connect with others. They feel lost and are looking for direction.

They are reacting to this crazy world by looking for ways to change themselves so they can live better lives. They want to evolve and experience more love, peace, joy, freedom, and fulfillment. These people are the true leaders. They know there is a better way, and they are actively looking for solutions. They begin by working on their first objective in life, which is to elevate themselves.

And it doesn't stop there. They also want to live fulfilling and meaningful lives, which can only be found by helping others. They leverage their backgrounds to determine how they can provide the maximum possible value and have the greatest impact on this planet. That's their second objective in life.

I presented the Forest Fire Analogy in this book to describe how a new world can emerge from seemingly complete destruction. Something similar is currently happening with the human experience. Look around at all the threats to humanity over the past five years alone. Almost all of them were caused directly or indirectly by other humans. We are our own worst enemy. Our current set of leaders are completely lost, and they represent the *fire* in the analogy. Instead of looking for ways to elevate the human experience, they are more interested in destroying things and harming others. They don't understand Universal Thinking and the basic principle of *connected:* what they do to others they do to themselves. Harming others only causes self-harm.

Just like the seeds from the pinecones, the world needs its true leaders to wake up, grow their abilities, and create a new, thriving world that is based on love, not fear and hate. Now more than ever, we need our true leaders to step forward, to create a world that works, and to save humanity from causing more problems and destruction. It's not an easy job, but there is nothing more rewarding and fulfilling than to help others who desperately need your help.

I hope this book can help you with this critically important transformation process. My goal is to help one million true leaders who each help a thousand more. That creates one billion transformed leaders who can make a significant impact on a world that so desperately needs our help.

I hope this book has awakened the true leader in you. Welcome to the team. This is where you belong. Now hurry up and get busy. We've got a lot of work to do!

Acknowledgments

I would like to acknowledge the key people who helped make this book a reality. First, of course, is my Wise Loving Being, who helped me discover a much higher purpose for myself of helping others make meaningful transformations that add a tremendous amount of value and impact to this world. Thank you for your love, guidance, and support. Thank you for always pushing me. Thank you for your persistence and for never giving up on me. I am forever grateful. I look forward to our continuing partnership and collaboration to achieve my full potential, and to add as much value and impact as possible to this world.

I would like to thank all the amazing people who have done this work. I appreciate their courage to see the truth, their commitment to make the critical changes, and their determination to transform their lives. Their stories are truly inspiring. I am looking forward to seeing where their transformational journey takes them and what important contributions they will make to this world.

I would especially like to thank the real Elin who served as the inspiration for this book. Every interaction with her was an opportunity for me to improve and for me to learn so much. I appreciate her incredible courage, openness, and trust that made it possible for us to have such a tremendous impact on each other. She is such an amazing and perfect human. I can't wait to see what she does next.

I'd like to thank my son, Alex Miller, my daughter, Katarina Miller, and my aunt, Linda Miller, for the countless hours they spent reading the many versions of the manuscript, teaching me grammar and spelling, and coming up with so many ideas on how to make this book better. I especially appreciate their patience and understanding as I sometimes struggled to fully grasp the genius of their comments. It only took five weeks for me to write the initial manuscript, but it took several months for them to help me get it into a form that could actually be sent to a publisher.

I'd like to thank my parents. My mom, Eleanor Miller, demonstrated what unconditional and unlimited love is, not only with how she raised me, but with every interaction she had with her family, friends, and middle school students. She was an incredible cook, and I am truly blessed to have had her as my mother. My dad, Frank Miller, demonstrated how to work well with others, how to be dependable, and how it is possible to transform your life at any age. He had an incredible sense of humor, and I definitely miss the many times we laughed so hard that we ended up in tears.

I'd like to thank my grandparents. My grandfather, Frank D. Miller, was always an underlying force in my life. Although we never met, the *Barney Baxter* comics he wrote, and his portrait and paintings that I saw on the walls at different family gatherings, have had a profound effect on me. He was someone who showed me what courage, creativity, and resourcefulness can accomplish. I'd like to thank my grandmother, Frantzes Miller, for teaching me that when life gives you lemons you make lemonade, for always providing me with unconditional love, and for always looking for ways to cultivate my creativity.

I'd like to thank three other relatives who have had a profound impact on my life. My Aunt Pat Rightmire showed me how important it is to be genuinely positive, to work hard, and to always find ways to make the most of any situation. I'd like to thank my Aunt Sally Sakala for showing me that it is possible to be positive, kind, loving, and generous regardless of your circumstances. And I'd like to thank my cousin Deanna Hewitt for always reminding me that I am my mother's son, and for being so wise and loving to so many people.

I'd like to thank my friend Harvey Kilpatrick for showing me that the true measure of a man is the amount of positive value and impact he has on this planet. He always left things better than he found them, and he inspired me to do the same. He was an amazing, kind, and generous person who showed me that leadership is critical, excellence is required, unconditional love is needed, and that there is no way of knowing how seemingly small acts can help inspire others to be their best.

I'd like to thank all the people, experiences, and events, that helped me become who I am today. I understand that I stand on the shoulders of the many great intellectual and spiritual teachers who came before me. They have inspired me and taught me so much. There are also the many people I encountered in this world who saw the best in me and helped me become better.

And there are the many negative people and experiences I encountered too. When they were happening, I didn't enjoy the difficult times and the "bad" people, but I can see now how important they were for my growth and transformation. Some things can only be learned through experience and reflection. Knowing what I know now, I wouldn't trade those experiences for anything. I only wish I had been more perceptive, done a better job of listening, and made important changes sooner. It is clear that they were always on my side. Thank you.

Finally, I'd like to thank the amazing team that helped get this book out into the world. I can't overemphasize how important and valuable they were in helping me fulfill my vision.

I'd like to acknowledge my incredible editor, Jenna Love Schrader. Sometimes in life, the stars align, and the perfect person with the right experience and background shows up to help. Jenna understood the importance of this project from the very beginning and treated the manuscript as if it were her own. She partnered with me to find ways to make the book more relatable, complete, and impactful. She is unique in that she can see the big picture and can also focus on the details. I'm thankful for her many valuable suggestions. I'm especially grateful for her encouraging me to deliver some of the more impactful wisdom I was reluctant to share out of concern that it would alienate some of my readers. Jenna is so easy to work with. She is an amazing person who always finds a way to bring more love and joy into whatever she does. This book is so much better because of her.

I'd like to acknowledge my amazing book designer, Sarah Lahay of C'est Beau Designs. She is clearly an incredibly talented designer, but perhaps her best skill is her ability to listen and see beyond what is being said. We've all heard the expression that *a picture is worth a thousand words.* She does the opposite: she took my few words, that were vague at best, and intuitively created a perfect picture that included things I wanted to say but simply didn't know how. For the interior design, she took my few ideas and delivered creative solutions that made the book more appealing and easier to read, especially for the visually impaired. I had a much bigger challenge providing guidance on the cover. How she took so little input and created such an extraordinary cover design on her first try that I instantly recognized as *perfect,* was nothing short of miraculous. The cover captures the essence of the book and provides the critically important attractive visual elements I wanted but had no ability to communicate. She also did a great job directing me to get the remaining items needed to publish the book on time. Thanks to Sarah, this book was published much sooner and designed much better than I could ever have hoped or imagined.

Index

About the Author

Kim W. Miller is a powerful force for change. He is the founder and Chief Learning Officer at Two Aspirins Corporation. He is on a mission to help people overcome their limitations and reach their full potential by transforming their careers, lives, organizations, and relationships. He works with individuals, couples, families, leaders, managers, teams, and organizations of all sizes.

He founded Two Aspirins to help individuals and organizations eliminate their headaches. Aspirin of course, only alleviates the symptoms of a headache. It temporarily stops the pain but it doesn't prevent them from reoccurring. He goes much further. He developed a unique, holistic approach that helps you identify the root cause of your headache, heal it, and eliminate it, so headaches don't occur in the first place. And as a nice side benefit, you don't need aspirin anymore either.

He has helped individuals overcome their challenges and love their lives; couples save their marriages and create loving, supportive, intimate relationships; families reconnect, build trust, and learn how to better understand, accept, appreciate, love, and support each other;

individuals get a new job or the raise and promotion they deserve; and leaders increase their value, impact, influence, and effectiveness.

He has a consistent, 25-year track record of applying the principles of Universal Elevation to create high performance teams and lead organizational change. He specializes in creating software development and IT organizations that consistently deliver projects on-time, on-budget, on-scope, on-quality, and that meet customers' highest priority needs. He also helps companies improve revenue, processes, quality, morale, productivity, teamwork, employee engagement, and customer loyalty.

He has worked in a variety of industries including automotive, ecommerce, defense, healthcare, restaurant, retail, training, and travel. He has worked in a variety of roles in management, sales, information technology, and software development. He earned a bachelor's degree in computer science and a master's degree in business administration (MBA) from the University of California, Irvine. He is the creator of the Achieve Your Dreams Workshop, the Lose the Fat Forever Workshop, the Confident Leadership and Public Speaking Course, and the Leadership Coaching for Managers program.

About Two Aspirins Corporation

We're on a mission to help people overcome their limitations and reach their full potential by transforming their careers, lives, organizations, and relationships. We provide transformational career, leadership, management, organizational change, family, health, life, public speaking, and relationship coaching, courses, books, and other resources.

Our vision is to impact a million lives, who each go on to impact a thousand more. That's one billion people elevating the world! We're passionate about giving. We donate ten percent of company profits to charities.

Our company values are:

- **Love.** We love ourselves and each other. We see value in our differences and include everyone. We treat each other equally and with dignity. We all win when we work together.
- **Courage.** We have the courage to embrace truth, try new things, and confront our fears. We allow ourselves to be vulnerable. We do what is right and best for all our stakeholders.
- **Humility.** Continuous learning is critical. The more we know the more we become aware of how much there is to know. We can learn from everyone and everything.
- **Service.** We deliver the highest possible value and outcomes to our clients, employees, communities, and stakeholders. Outstanding service starts with understanding and empathy.

- **Joy.** We have fun and choose to be genuinely positive. We enjoy what we have and are grateful for our many blessings.

We believe individuals are a powerful force for change. One person can make a huge difference, and there have been many individuals throughout history who have changed their country and the world, with their impact continuing to be felt long after they are gone. Unfortunately, most people only contribute a small fraction of their full potential. We help individuals see their bigger purpose; conquer their limitations; make positive, permanent, and powerful changes that maximize their value and impact; regain their health, improve their finances, and repair relationships; better manage their emotions and overcome unhealthy feelings of fear, failure, rejection, guilt, shame, anxiety, stress, and worry; and live each day with an elevated sense of love, peace, joy, freedom, and fulfillment. This leads to people living a life they genuinely love!

We believe business owners, entrepreneurs, executives, managers, and organizational leaders at all levels have a big impact on the planet. Their thoughts, words, and actions have a direct and lasting effect on their customers, employees, stakeholders, and communities. Making small improvements to a leader makes a big difference. Unfortunately, many leaders and organizations only contribute a fraction of their full potential. We help leaders play their biggest game, and maximize their effectiveness, influence, value, and impact. We also help leaders elevate their organizations by unlocking the full potential of their employees. This leads to better financial results, customer loyalty, employee engagement, innovation, and impact.

Our clients have achieved amazing results, especially for those who have tried everything else without much progress and who feel frustrated and stuck. We avoid the five fundamental flaws of today's coaching, counseling, therapy, and self-improvement methods. We've developed a unique, holistic approach that addresses the root cause of your limitations, allowing you to make positive, permanent, and powerful changes. We help you overcome obstacles, see new possibilities, build new skills, perform at your best, and achieve your goals much sooner than you could on your own.

For more information about our latest products and services, please go to www.TwoAspirins.com.

www.ingramcontent.com/pod-product-compliance
Lightning Source LLC
Chambersburg PA
CBHW060851120626
46553CB00001B/42

*9 7 9 8 9 9 1 2 9 3 7 2 3 *